Social Care under State Socialism (1945-1989)

Sabine Hering (ed.)

Social Care under State Socialism (1945-1989)
Ambitions, Ambiguities, and Mismanagement

Barbara Budrich Publishers
Opladen & Farmington Hills, MI 2009

All rights reserved. No part of this publication may be reproduced, stored in or introduced into a retrieval system, or transmitted, in any form, or by any means (electronic, mechanical, photocopying, recording or otherwise) without the prior written permission of Barbara Budrich Publishers. Any person who does any unauthorized act in relation to this publication may be liable to criminal prosecution and civil claims for damages.

You must not circulate this book in any other binding or cover and you must impose this same condition on any acquirer.

A CIP catalogue record for this book is available from
Die Deutsche Bibliothek (The German Library)

© 2009 by Barbara Budrich Publishers, Opladen & Farmington Hills, MI
www.barbara-budrich.net

ISBN 978-3-86649-168-7

Das Werk einschließlich aller seiner Teile ist urheberrechtlich geschützt. Jede Verwertung außerhalb der engen Grenzen des Urheberrechtsgesetzes ist ohne Zustimmung des Verlages unzulässig und strafbar. Das gilt insbesondere für Vervielfältigungen, Übersetzungen, Mikroverfilmungen und die Einspeicherung und Verarbeitung in elektronischen Systemen.

Die Deutsche Bibliothek – CIP-Einheitsaufnahme
Ein Titeldatensatz für die Publikation ist bei Der Deutschen Bibliothek erhältlich.

Verlag Barbara Budrich ⓑ Barbara Budrich Publishers
Stauffenbergstr. 7. D-51379 Leverkusen Opladen, Germany

28347 Ridgebrook. Farmington Hills, MI 48334. USA
www.barbara-budrich.net

Jacket illustration by disegno, Wuppertal, Germany – www.disenjo.de
Typeset by Frank Gerke-Böhm
Printed in Europe on acid-free paper by
paper&tinta, Warsaw

Contents

Acknowledgments 9

Sabine Hering
Introduction 11

Bulgaria

Kristina Popova
The Development of Social Care in Bulgaria (1945 - 1989) 25

Ulf Brunnbauer, Anelia Kassabova
Socialism, Sexuality and Marriage – Family Policies in Socialist
Bulgaria (1944 - 1989) 35

Kristina Popova
Under the Scarlet Scarf: The Education of Pioneer Troop Leaders
During Socialism 55

Czechoslovakia

Lenka Kalinová
Conditions and Stages of Change in the Social Security
System in Czechoslovakia (1945 - 1989) 65

GDR

Marcel Boldorf
Social Welfare in East Germany (1945 - 1990) 79

Ingrid Miethe
Substituting Social Pedagogy – the Fight Against Disadvantage
in the Educational System in the GDR 93

Sven Korzilius
The Repressive Side of Social Policy in the GDR:
Penal Laws against 'Asocials' and 'Parasites'... 111

Heike Wolter
Farewell/Well-Fare to the Beach – the GDR's Recreational System 131

Hungary

Dorottya Szikra
Social Policy under State Socialism in Hungary (1949 - 1956) 141

Eszter Varsa
Child Protection, Residential Care and the 'Gypsy-Question' in
Early State Socialist Hungary 149

Poland

Barbara Klich-Kluczewska
Social Policy and Social Practice in the People's Republic of Poland 161

Dobrochna Kałwa
Between Emancipation and Traditionalism – The Situation of
Women and the Gender Order in Poland after 1945 175

Romania

Maria Roth, Raluca Crisan, Livia Popescu, Luminita Dumanescu
The Romanian Social System between 1945 and 1989 189

Maria Roth
Child Protection in Communist Romania (1944 - 1989) 201

Soviet Union

Elena Iarskaia-Smirnova, Pavel Romanov
Multiplicity and Discontinuity in the Soviet Welfare History 213

Yulia Gradskova
Maternity Care under State Socialism (1945 - 1970) 227

Yugoslavia

Vesna Leskošek
Social Policy in Yugoslavia Between Socialism and Capitalism 239

Marina Ajduković, Vanja Branica
Some Reflections on Social Work in Croatia (1945 - 1989) 249

Contributors 265

Acknowledgments

20 years after the end of state socialism it seems to be time to look backward at the occurrences that have taken place in the decades between 1945 and 1989 in connection with the Eastern European welfare concepts and the corresponding social practices.

It would not have been possible to realize a project including all nine countries that were members of the Eastern Bloc and to bring them together in a comparative approach without the 'Network of Historical Studies on Gender and Social Work' that was founded 2001.[1] This 'Network' has generated a fairly long and remarkable intensive process of research cooperation (mainly between Finland, Germany, Ireland, the Netherlands, Switzerland and the Eastern European Countries), and it has opened quite a lot of valuable options that have already led to many interesting conferences, editions and curriculum development projects[2] – and now, finally, to the publication of this book.

I have to thank, representative for many others, Vesna Leskošek (Ljubljana), Dagmar Schulte (Siegen) and Berteke Waaldijk (Utrecht) for founding this Network together with me, and for keeping it alive.

Furthermore I have to thank many persons who participated in the translation work of this book and who offered me precious linguistic advice and proof readings. That is: Alex Atkins, Marion Bloos, Peter Herrmann, Sigrid Krafft and Sanjaya Senadheera.

With his layout skills Frank Böhm has transferred, helpfully and efficiently as usual, the copious non-uniform files into a respectable book. And with his imperative inspirations and his constant exhortations for patience and perseverance Kurt Schilde supported me in making it work.

Last, but not least, the 'Volkswagen Foundation', namely Wolfgang Levermann, delivered the financial basis for the cooperation between the authors and the publication of this book. I am very thankful for that.

Sabine Hering, Siegen, April 2009

---

[1] cf. www.sweep.uni-siegen.de
[2] Beside other activities following achievements should be mentioned: The participation in the Athena and the Tempus Programme (EU), the conferences in Belfast, St. Gallen, Mainz and Olten. The research project 'History of Social Work in Eastern Europe 1900 - 1960' (Volkswagen Foundation 2003 - 2005) as well as two conferences of the Balkan Forum in Blagoevgrad (Bulgaria) and the State University Saratov (Russia).

Sabine Hering

Introduction

The Access

In the discourses on 'Social Care under State Socialism' we find, until today, the prejudice, that this subject has, evidently, not existed. This assessment is derived from the fact that social work as a professional discipline was abolished to a large extent. The insight, that many social risks could be avoided by a comprehensive social system, and that the assistance for people in need was actually transferred to other responsible instances rather than being neglected, seems to go beyond imagination. The second ongoing prejudice is the idea that any kind of evidence (that may eventually refer to the real existence of a social care system) demonstrates that its principles were fundamentally instructed by 'Moscow' and have been performed in a totally standardized way.

The results of the research presented in this book show that these images do generally not reflect the actual welfare structure beyond the 'iron curtain', because they are mistaking normative pronouncements for an accurate description of reality. As a matter of fact, the refusal of the bourgeois welfare traditions and the ban of the term 'social work' did not exclude the fact, that the 'care for the people' has been one of the major topics of socialist policies in all Eastern European countries.

Independent of these irritating ideological and linguistic moments, social care was – looking at the decades between 1945 and 1989 – a rather versatile, shifting and contradictory undertaking. It was part of a social political programme "that was determined by a constant extension of incentives, and the tendency towards a prevalence of social guarantees on the one hand, as well as an increasing state intervention into the private sphere, and the official control of all social domains on the other." (Iarskova-Smirnova/ Romanov, p. 213)

The socialist states constituted themselves not least based on the idea that social progress should hollow out the older order of the bourgeois society together with its welfare system which had permanently drawn a curtain over the origins of poverty and disadvantage. The new agents of welfare policy criticized the fact that under capitalist rules the idea of preventing poverty by combating its causes laid beyond the ideological horizon of the prevalent classes.

Alternatively, the politicians of the Eastern Bloc claimed to solve all social challenges by implementing a model of equality, justice and security. Actually, they were groundbreaking in solving certain problems that had been considered before as 'irresolvable'. Mainly the support of families and children surpassed the standards of many preceding models in bourgeois societies. Also the continuous absence of almost any charges for medical and educational services deserves a lot of respect.

But, these achievements were imbedded in a huge 'social laboratory' which, however, produced a lot of new problems – especially due to mechanisms of classification and standardization: The progressive ideological objectives – such as full employment, gender equality and a comprehensive health system – turned quite often into harsh repressive arrangements in order to discipline the wayward and to deter the non-conformists. But also the groups of the disabled as well as the elderly people in need of support were neglected and excluded rather than reasonably supported. Obviously, the communist party was not willing to reconcile the interests of 'minorities' with those of a greater community. As a matter of fact, the ensuing consequences of these strategies produced an increasing number of social recipients which belonged not only to the marginalized parts of the population. A convincing substitution of 'social work' through a comprehensive concept of social policy could not be realized in general terms.

Also the access to other spheres of the society that might have been able to support the idea of social progress was not sufficient to solve the main social problems: The commitment of mass-organisations as well as some voluntary action at the local level were ultimately ineffective measures to compensate for the lack of professional social work. Even the attempt to oblige teachers, district nurses or works committees to perform an individualized system of social assistance was not the sufficient arrangement that the desperate situation in the Eastern European countries often would have required.

In the late 1970s and 1980s – finally – in some of the socialist countries the return to the traditional sources of social work was initiated by non governmental groups. More or less tolerated by the administration, they established certain organisations in the spectrum between self-management and voluntary work on local level. Some of these approaches were even combined with the re-inclination to professional social work standards and training.

Nevertheless, the agents of the strictly innovation-orientated processes after 1989 did neither appreciate these germs of self-management nor the achievements of socialist social politics. Social work was imported from the West as something totally new without any relation to the national traditions.[1]

The State of the Art

The relevance of the studies regarding social policy and social work in Eastern Europe under state socialism is rather diverse. Especially the copious German publications between 1950 and 1990 are influenced by the atmosphere of the 'cold war' – either strongly affirmative in case of publications made in GDR, or likewise strictly negative from a 'Western' point of view. Most of them can only be used as historical sources.[2]

The contemporary Anglo-American narratives on the structures of social politics and social assistance in Eastern Europe are much more reliable,[3] but the most interesting results are published in the 1990s and later.

The master concept in these publications deals with the change of the social system from a domain of civil society to a part of state administration (Dixon/Macarov 1992; Hübner et.al. 2002; Pestoff 1995; Popova 2007; Tomka 2004). Although the 'administrators' established a system of general support for the majority of the population, they were neither able nor willing to solve as well the social problems of disadvantaged people (Korzilius 2005). The belief that 'the care for the people' was still a basic concern of the party (Popova 2007) has, at the latest, been destroyed as the marginalized groups were systematically excluded as 'parasites' or 'anti-socials' (Korzilius 2005). Even when the state provided sometimes quite extensive comprehensive welfare rights, the population was expected to give up the slightest hope for receiving civil or political rights in return (Szikra/Szelewa 2008).

Another topic of the current research is the domain of family and gender policy, combining three general elements: equal rights for women and men, work organisation adjusted to economic and familial needs and the promotion of 'natalism' (Brunnbauer 2007). After serious declines in the 1960s,

---

[1] cf. Adams 1991
[2] cf. Friedrich 1950; Manz/Winkler 1979; Meja 1987; Reichert 1967; Zimmermann 1964
[3] cf. George/Manning 1980; Kaser 1976; McAuley 1979; Osborn 1970

certain measures like motherhood awards and child day care were implemented to increase birth rates. Even the stigmatisation of unmarried mothers was replaced by the heroization of their merits in the field of biological reproduction (Kassabova 2007). Haney interpreted issues like these as elements of a 'maternalist welfare state' (Haney 2002).

On the whole, the literature shows a checkered picture of the eight Eastern European countries that belonged to the 'Eastern Bloc'. They analyse their specific 'path dependencies' considering their economic, cultural and religious conditions with special attention – notwithstanding the synchronised legislation and ideological allegation of the USSR (Deacon 1992, Pascall/ Manning 2000).

Question Marks

The findings of the project 'History of Social Work in Eastern Europe (1900 - 1960)',[4] that delivered the grounding of the research activities presented in this book, raised a lot of hitherto unsolved questions concerning the ambitions, the ambiguities and the mismanagement of social care under state socialism. The rise of a strong interest in the following topics was one of the results of our studies on the decades 1900 - 1960.

The Gaps in the 'Overall' System of Social Security

It is obvious that the socialist system of social security in the Eastern European countries between 1945 and 1989 did not reduce all kinds of social risks. Poverty and unemployment turned out to be problems that existed not only under capitalist conditions. Furthermore, the differences between the privileges of the industrial worker and the neglect of the peasants seemed to be a serious lack of equality in the 'Eastern' system of social security. Considering these facts, it seemed to be quite interesting to find out, if the responsible political agents were not able to submit equal provision to all people, especially under the given economic conditions, or if they intentionally

---

[4] cf. Hering, Sabine/Waaldijk, Berteke: Guardians of the Poor, Custodians of the Public. History of Eastern European Welfare (1900-1969). Opladen 2006; and: Schilde, Kurt/Schulte, Dagmar (Eds.): Need and Care – Glimpses into the Beginnings of Eastern Europe's Professional Welfare. Opladen/Bloomfield Hills 2005

produced the differences in order to regulate inclusion and exclusion processes.

Work and Working Morale

Socialist ideology is based on the idea that 'work' is the fundamental resource of human beings. Consequently, 'work' became the most relevant goal and instrument of socialist socialisation, and the 'right to work' became one of the fundamental rights of the people. At the same time, it became a basic criterion for determining social eligibility. The 'obligation to work' produced a permanent threat that was always latent in the offer of assistance and education as well. Therefore, it seemed to be worthwhile to scrutinize, what consequences the prevalent working moral had for 'deviant' groups such as 'gypsies', 'parasites', 'anti-socials' or prostitutes – and what effects of deterrence were expected on the majority of the population.

Mass Organisations: Forced Conformity versus General Prevention

The socialist mass organisations have often been criticised as an instrument of suppression (with respect to the freedom of independent organisations) and forced conformity (with respect to the freedom of individuality). On the other hand they could be analysed as a measure of general prevention – offering social stability and providing help to overcome isolation and to solve social problems. This preventive character of the mass organisations made them extremely useful to carry out certain social tasks, and opened for them an important place in substituting of social work in the socialist system.

Transferring Social Work to Other Professions

The Eastern concepts of 'welfare' were based on the conviction that the state was responsible for the general system of social care, and that individual care should be made unnecessary. While this idea was evidenced as illusion, because members of certain target groups were still in need of individualized assistance, this experience led only in Yugoslavia to the insight that also socialist nations needed professional social work. In all other countries social work as a profession and, consequently, also social work training was demolished, and the – unavoidable – social tasks were transferred to other professional groups. In other words: Social work was substituted, but the corresponding substitution processes have hither to not been reasonably analysed.

Women's Emancipation and its Bio-Political Barriers

Women's equality is, since Clara Zetkin and August Bebel, one of the fundamental claims of socialism. The responsibility for a constitution that guarantees equal rights for men and women belonged, therefore, to the most important heritages of the socialist countries. But, nevertheless, all governments of the Eastern European countries decided, sooner or later, to implement additional rights with regard to the female maternity functions, in order to protect bio-political challenges, such as the rise of birth rates and the maintenance of the 'basic cell of society': the family. The contradiction of the idea of women's emancipation on one side, and the close ties to the traditional role-models on the other, have never been totally dissolved under state socialism. Considering the special antecedents, these ambiguities seemed to be worthwhile to be systematically studied, especially with respect to their social political consequences.

Correspondences and Specific Items

20 Experts from former Bulgaria, Czechoslovakia, German Democratic Republic, Hungary, Poland, Romania, USSR and Yugoslavia have worked on these questions as well as on further topics, being equally relevant, such as the medicalisation of motherhood (Gradskova), residential child care (Roth and Varsa), educational disadvantage (Miethe) or socialist recreation systems (Wolters).

Comparing the results of their studies, a large degree of correspondence becomes evident, addressing mainly the following issues:

- Definitions and terms play an important role in almost every contribution, because the meaning of the 'words' as well as the 'items' are mostly rather different from the understanding on the western side of the 'iron curtain'.
- The remarkable changes in politics and mentality through the decades (starting with a certain liberality in the first years, followed by the Stalinist 'great terror', ongoing with an interplay of 'thaw', strong industri-

- alisation, protest movements, further repression and careful trials of 'glasnost' and 'perestroika' is another item continuously turning up.
- The competition of labour politics against family politics – summarized in the discourses on the 'working mother' – is a further issue that covers nearly all narratives of 'private' life under state socialism in this book.
- The fact that, more or less, all kinds of improvements for 'mother and child' were brought forward at the cost of women's emancipation, is a corresponding topic which is quite frequently mentioned.
- The substitution of professional social work by other professions (like teachers or nurses) and through activists of mass organisation and cadre groups belongs to the topics that necessarily had to be discussed, when the question 'who cared for the people instead of professional social workers?' had to be answered.
- Last but not least, the growing distance between the government and the people, combined with an unfortunate loss of trust, hope and solidarity, has to be mentioned as a phenomenon that was crossing all the borders of Eastern Europe.

Referring to its use in the GDR, Boldorf explains the meaning of the term 'social welfare'. His interpretation may, however, be even valid in a more general sense: "In Eastern Germany two concepts of social welfare were predominant after 1945: In a larger sense, the term 'social welfare' has been used synonymously with 'social policy', a term avoided in the official language of the GDR until the 1960s. According to this perception, social welfare included the whole of the social services and financial transfer of the state. In a narrow sense, it refers to welfare as individual financial support and as payments of means and delivery of services to those in need, in case they could not claim support from agencies, such as social security." (Boldorf, p. 79)

As already mentioned, groundbreaking socio-political changes (namely the titles and the tasks of the Ministries and the uncountable number of 'new laws') took place during the decades between 1945 and 1989 in every Eastern European country – generating social reforms as well as the misuse of social political responsibility, also in Czechoslovakia: "The majority of changes in the social security system during the era of state socialism was based on the current state of the economy and the political goals of the ruling party. Various acts (…) violated the principles of social justice and were not based on the guaranteed rights of citizens." (Kalinóva, p. 76)

Popova's description of the main characteristics in Bulgaria summarizes some of the most important circumstances of social welfare under state socialism: "Analysing the Bulgarian development it is necessary to distinguish between socio-political achievements on the one hand and the marginalization of social care on the other hand. The social system as well as the health care system achieved a lot of merits in certain respects. (...) At the same time, however, social control was strengthened, and the right to work became a duty. As activities of private welfare were forbidden, the people's consciousness for their own social responsibility was diminished. The places where discourses on these issues took place were dissolved; local traditions of charity were given up. (...) Certain disadvantaged groups of people vanished from the streets to make their problems invisible." (Popova, p. 31)

And she goes on by stating: "Since the beginning of the 'thaw' a change in politics and mentality led to a modernized management of social problems in Bulgaria: In the 1960s and 1970s the attitude towards social care began to change positively. It was officially admitted that there were situations and problems in private life which people could not solve without getting any support and which consequently had to be treated as an issue of public social welfare. (...) At the beginning of the 1970s professional training programmes for social work were established again, as an extra course combined with the training for nurses." (Popova, p. 31f.)

This combination of 'classical' social work tasks with other professions or, in other words, the transfer of social work into other professional domains has – not only in the GDR – been a challenge for teachers to widen their genuine activities: "As the analysis of the 'Workers and Peasants Faculties' illustrates, the work of an instructor comprised much more than merely the transfer of knowledge. It also involved activities that may be classified as social pedagogic or social work domains – although the instructors had not received any specific training to carry out these tasks." (Miethe, p. 105)

Leskošek describes the translation of the general social political concepts into practical assistance in Yugoslavia: "The welfare system provided two types of services: the network of institutions for different target groups (...) and the Centres of Social Work, which influenced the development of a specific type of social work practice or a specific type of intervention. (...) The professionals, especially in the field of pedagogy, psychology, social work and psychiatry, were primarily concerned with issues like pathology and deviancy. The result of this predominant attitude towards social problems was the fact that a lot of social problems were not recognised as general issues. Violence against women and children, sexual abuse, poverty, homelessness and similar problems were only dealt with for the first time at the end of the 1980s when non-governmental organisations began to be established." (Leskošek, p. 244)

Also in Romania the government neglected problems that did not fit into their political ideas. The quality of care was, however, even worse than in Yugoslavia as it existed only a minimum of professional knowledge: "In Romania, there was a legal base to offer social protection for special needs: for abandoned children and families in need, for people with disabilities, for elderly and some other categories of dependent individuals. The lack of resources (and of professionals) imposed the absence of other services then residential homes. The Communist Party did not 'recognize' the existence of poverty, the discrimination of Roma (named 'gypsies'), of unemployment, alcoholism and HIV/AIDS (…). A large number of residential institutions that were supposed to be care facilities became places of deprivation, famine and abuse." (Roth, et. Al. p. 198)

Another deficit, concerning the topic of labour and work moral, seems to be especially typical for the USSR: "As an ideal model, social protection became the essential right of politically loyal workers and their families, while, at the same time, the principles of distribution depending on labor input have been consistently pushed forward. In turn, social guarantees should not be given to those who could support themselves. They were offered only to citizens whose income was insufficient because of employment peculiarities or sickness, i.e. 'according to needs'." (Iarskova-Smirnova/ Romanov, p. 224)

Full employment of women as well as a sufficient provision of families have both been cornerstones of the Eastern European socialist welfare system. In Hungary (as likewise in Bulgaria or Poland) several laws were induced in order to reconcile the ambiguous relation between these two goals: "The system of (almost) full employment, and within that, the full-time employment of women was the most important bases for state socialist social policy. As welfare rights were mainly linked to full-time employment, social policy became a means to fulfill the political and economic aims of the regime. The renewed social policy of the 1960s was carried out partly through family policy which had long lasting effects on the Hungarian welfare system. An 'optional familialist' system was built up by the middle of the 1980s which provided a possibility for mothers to choose between subsidized care at home or kindergarten care for their children." (Szikra, p. 147)

But as a matter of fact, the other side of the efforts to meet the demands of the 'useful people' was to brand those persons who did no longer fit into the established pattern of the 'system': "Throughout modern history, the approach to social problems has been Janus-faced: a helping, caring face always found its complement in a disciplining, castigating face. This fact was not different in the GDR. Even the provisional arrangements of the military government after the war concerning prostitutes, beggars, homeless and the 'work-shy' showed this duality. The officials tried to organise the food and medical supply, but at the same time demanded that everybody should dedicate his or her strength to reconstruction work." (Korzilius, p. 125)

Ulbricht, '*Staatsratsvorsitzender*' of the GDR, tried to impose a certain liberalisation towards 'minorities', but he had to take the repressive Soviet politics into consideration: "At the end of the 1950s, the USSR enacted 'antiparasite laws', which, due to the coercion within the alliance, had to be introduced in the other states of the Warsaw Pact as well." (ibid., p. 126) The acceptance of these repressive ideas after the end of the Ulbricht era was remarkable. "Together with the quasi-totalitarian paranoia of the Honecker regime, this led to a vicious circle of criminalisation, which GDR citizens could not really escape until the system collapsed." (ibid.)

Klich comments, referring to the Polish example, the procedure of this collapse: "The chance of modernizations of the state was wasted as a result of clumsy planning and the low qualifications of the decision-making authorities. The great crash started in 1976. Aroused expectations of millions of people run into a permanent economic crisis. The economy of shortage affected everyone (...) Social disappointment in contrast to the promised prosperity and social justice led gradually to the formation of the so-called alternative society. Economic and social insufficiency of the state produced a kind of moral opposition to the authoritarian state, whose role in the field of social care was taken over by the voluntary civil initiatives. Economic crisis and growing poverty forced the authorities to tolerate the activity of these independent organizations and the support from the West." (Klich, p. 171)

Conclusion

This rather brief selection of insights from the different national points of view shows that the ambitions, ambiguities and mismanagement were created by processes endogenous to the system itself. In general, the assistance that has been offered was determined less by urgent social problems but by ideological rules and available resources. The traditional welfare structures, remaining from the first half of the 20th century, were substituted by three general elements:

- Comprehensive measures, mainly in the field of labour- and family politics.

- Transfer of tasks, that former belonged to the domain of professional social work, into the responsibility of other occupational groups and mass organisations.
- Incentives, surveillance, control and deterrence to regulate the processes of inclusion and exclusion accordingly to the prevailing political direction.

Considering these three elements, there is no doubt that the systematic deconstruction of the welfare achievements, for instance the qualification of the profession and the improvement of the academic discipline, has produced serious disadvantages for the population – mainly for people with special needs. But, it is also obvious that many elements that belonged to the traditional welfare structures have not been completely abolished under state socialism – and that some parts of it even emerged in a remarkable progressive way. The para-professional social practice, however, that was established to substitute the techniques of the 'forbidden profession' was no efficient alternative to the 'bourgeois' model, but – more or less – a rather helpless attitude of self-deception.

References

Adam, Jan: *Economic Reforms and Welfare Systems in the USSR, Poland, and Hungary - Social Contract in Transformation.* New York 1991

Boldorf, Marcel: *Sozialfürsorge in der SBZ/DDR 1945-1953. Ursachen, Ausmaß und Bewältigung der Nachkriegsarmut.* Stuttgart 1998

Brunnbauer, Ulf: *Die sozialistische Lebensweise. Ideologie, Gesellschaft, Familie und Politik in Bulgarien (1944-1989).* Wien/Köln/Weimar 2007

Deacon, Bob (Ed.): *Social Policy, Social Justice and Citizenship in Eastern Europe.* Avebury/Aldershot 1992

Dixon, John/Macarov, David (Ed.): *Social Welfare in Socialist Countries.* London/ New York 1992

Friedrich, Gerd: *Die freie deutsche Jugend. Stoßtrupp des Kommunismus in Deutschland.* Köln 1950

George, Victor/Manning, Nick: *Socialism, Social Welfare, and the Soviet Union.* London 1980

Haney, Lynne: *Inventing the Needy. Gender and the Politics of Welfare in Hungary.* Berkeley 2002

Hering, Sabine/Waaldijk, Berteke: *Guardians of the Poor - Custodians of the Public. Welfare History in Eastern Europe 1900 - 1960/* Helfer der Armen – Hüter der Öffentlichkeit. Wohlfahrtsgeschichte in Osteuropa 1900-1960. Opladen 2006

Hübner, Peter/Hübner, Christa: *Sozialismus als soziale Frage.* Köln/Weimar/Wien 2008

Kaser, Michael: *Health Care in the Soviet Union and Eastern Europe.* London 1976

Kassabova, Anelia: *Begrenzte Transformation oder Transformation der Begrenztheiten? Politik und uneheliche Geburten im sozialistischen Bulgarien.* In: Brunnbauer, Ulf/Höpken, Wolfgang (Eds.): *Transformationsprobleme Bulgariens im 19. und 20. Jahrhundert. Historische und ethnologische Perspektiven.* München 2007, p. 125-148

Korzilius, Sven: *'Asoziale' und 'Parasiten' im Recht der SBZ/DDR. Randgruppen im Sozialismus zwischen Repression und Ausgrenzung.* Köln/Weimar/Wien 2000

Manz, Günter/Winkler, Gunnar: *Theorie und Praxis der Sozialpolitik in der DDR.* Berlin (DDR) 1979

McAuley, Alastair: *Economic Welfare in the Soviet Union: Poverty, Living Standards, and Inequality.* Madison 1979

Meja, Marita: *Die Entwicklung der Sozialfürsorge auf dem Gebiet der sowjetischen Besatzungszone Deutschlands bzw. DDR während der antifaschistisch-demokratischen Umwälzung und der Schaffung erster Grundlagen des Sozialismus.* Berlin (DDR) 1987

Osborn, Robert J.: *Soviet Social Policies: Welfare, Equality, and Community.* Homewood 1970

Pascall Gillian/Manning Nick: *Gender and Social Policy: Comparing Welfare States in Central and Eastern Europe and the former Soviet Union.* In: Journal of European Social Policy. 10/2000, p. 240-264

Pestoff, Victor A. (Ed.): *Reforming Social Services in Central and Eastern Europe - An Eleven Nation Overview.* Krakow 1995

Popova, Kristina: *Die öffentliche Fürsorge nach dem 9. September 1944: bürokratische Kontinuität, soziale Diskontinuität.* In: Brunnbauer, Ulf/Höpken, Wolfgang (Eds.): *Transformationsprobleme Bulgariens. Historische und gegenwärtige Perspektiven.* München 2007, p. 109-124

Reichert, Heinz: *Sozialfürsorge in der DDR.* Berlin 1967

Schilde, Kurt/Schulte, Dagmar (Eds.): *Need and Care. Glimpses into the Beginnings of Eastern Europe's Professional Welfare.* Opladen/Farmington Hills 2005.

Szikra, Dorottya/Dorota Szelewa: *Passen die mittel- und osteuropäische Länder in das ‚westliche' Bild? Das Beispiel der Familienpolitik in Ungarn und Polen.* In: Christina Klenner/Simone Leiber (Eds.): *Wohlfahrtsstaaten und Geschlechterungleichheit in Mittel- und Osteuropa.* Wiesbaden 2008, p. 88-123

Tomka, Béla: *Welfare in East and West: Hungarian Social Security in an International Comparison, 1918-1990.* Berlin 2004

Zimmermann, Hartmut: *Der FDGB als Massenorganisation und seine Aufgabe bei der Erfüllung der betrieblichen Wirtschaftspläne.* In: Kölner Zeitschrift für Soziologie und Sozialpsychologie, Opladen 1964, p. 115-144

Kristina Popova

The Development of Social Welfare Provision in Bulgaria 1945 - 1989

The 'Ministry for Social Politics' and its Successors

After the Patriotic Front had seized power in Bulgaria on September 1944 a 'Ministry of Social Politics' was established in coordination with the other administrative bodies that were concerned with social affairs.[1] In 1947, the Ministry was renamed to 'Ministry for Labour and Social Welfare Provision' including a 'Department for Recreation and Culture' (formerly: Labour and Joy), which should organize the leisure activities of the working class people.

During the first years (1944 - 1947), when social care was still diversified to a certain extent, the 'Ministry of Social Politics' controlled and coordinated the activities in the field of welfare on the basis of the new 'Law on Public Social Welfare Provision' (1945) that had replaced the law introduced in 1934.

In the beginning the Social Democrat Grigor Tscheschmedzhiev was head of the Ministry.[2] In 1945 however, the Patriotic Front split off, and a large number of the Social Democrats started to support the opposition. After the death of Grigor Tscheschmedzhiev in 1945, Ivan Popov[3] became Minister – and later, for a fairly long time, Zdravko Mitovski.[4] Both of them were

---

1 The Department for Public Social Welfare at the Ministry of Health and Interior Affairs, the Department for Social Insurance, the Ministry of Trade, Industry and Labour and also the Ministry for People's Pensions.
2 Grigor Tscheschmedzhiev (1879 - 1945), social democrat, jurist, editor-in-chief of the paper "Free People" (*Svoboden Narod*) 1945, Minister of Social Politics 1944 - 1945.
3 Georgi Popov (1889 - 1958), social democrat, jurist, Minister of Social Politics 1945-1946, Minister of Forestry 1949 - 1951, member of the Bulgarian Communist Party (resp. its central committee) after the dissolution of the Social Democratic Party in 1948.
4 Zdravko Mitovski (1908 - 1992), social democrat, jurist, Minister of Social Politics 1946 - 1947 and Minister for People's Health and Social Politics 1947 - 1950, vice president of the Patriotic Front 1977

Social Democrats and loyal supporters of the Patriotic Front.[5] But, the social democratic influence on social politics led to the fact that the Communist Party mistrusted the Ministry to a certain extent and induced its integration into the 'Ministry of Health', in 1951. This alliance of social politics and health care generated a process of medicalizing social welfare provision, as practiced in the SU. In addition to that, the Soviet model became increasingly influential in Bulgaria, because Petar Kolarov,[6] who became Minister of Health (1950-1962), was strongly influenced by the experiences during his political exile in the Soviet Union.

In connection with the reforms at the end of the 1960s the ministry was renamed into 'Ministry of Labour and Social Welfare Provision'. In 1976, it became, once again, a 'Department of the Ministry of Health', and since 1991 it was called 'Ministry of Labour and Social Politics'.

These frequent changes of names and responsibilities reflect an increasing tendency not only to replace welfare work by certain socio-political measures, but to transfer the responsibility for this domain into other Ministries (for instance 'Education', 'Labour' or 'Health'), and further on to mass organizations, such as the Patriotic Front or the Young People's Union[7] or to the Trade Unions.

Socio-Political Principles

Generally, in Bulgaria the realm of social care was embedded into a socio-political system, in which individual social assistance used to be an exception. In the beginning, the most important tasks of the Patriotic Front were the provision of the former partisans and their families as well as the organization of child welfare and the support of young married couples. According to the ideas of the Patriotic Front social welfare had to be an administrative issue organized by the state. The oppositional parties shared this opinion,

---

[5] This section of the SDP was disbanded and a large part of the members joined the Communist Party.

[6] Petar Kolarov (1906 - 1966), finished his studies in Moscow (1930 - 1933) with a doctoral degree in medicine, President of the Bulgarian Red Cross (1950 - 1956), Minister of People's Health 1950-1962, member of the central committee of the Bulgarian Communist Party (1956).

[7] since 1959 'Dimitrov's Communist Youth Union'.

although they would have been prepared to permit also non-governmental welfare activities or professional social work.

Taking this background into consideration it becomes clear why there was hardly no discussion about the content of social services.[8] The Patriotic Front and the opposition both favoured the emancipation of women, free health care, the provision of free accommodation and the support of young married couples. Both sides even agreed to 'educate asocial people and idle drifters' by forced labour.

There was also no doubt concerning the necessity to arrange and control people's leisure activities. Since work was regarded as the fundamental characteristic of a new kind of human being, it seemed to be a logical consequence that free time could not be a private or individual matter, but an issue that had to be organized collectively.

Changes in Gender and Media Strategies

Already in the transition period from 1944 to 1948, the significance of social activities – traditionally carried out by women organizations and religious groups – changed.[9] Though women were well represented in the Bulgarian parliament, specific female issues were not discussed in parliamentary debates. As the emancipation of women was guaranteed by law, people generally thought that the gender problems had been solved automatically. After the feminist Women's Union (*Bulgarski Zhenski Sajuz*) was dissolved and replaced by the People's Women Union in 1945, and its journal Women's Voice (*Zhensky Glas*) was not printed any longer, the hidden strategies of gender inequality were no longer discussed in the public.

The Social Academy of Women, which had been founded in 1932 by the Women's Union and had played a important role in the process of professionalizing social work, was also closed down. For a short time the Social Minister, Georgi Popov, promoted the idea of re-establishing the Academy, but his intention was not realized. As a matter of fact, the professionalisation of social work was abolished until the beginning of the 1970s.

---

[8] The protests of the Holy Synod of the Orthodox Church against the restrictions on their welfare activities were met with some approval in the parliament, though only by few representatives.

[9] For more information, cf. Popova 2007

At the same time the image of female actors in the field of social welfare provision changed radically. Women were no longer supposed to carry out welfare activities motivated by charity and compassion. As a consequence the idea of 'social motherliness' as a fundamental element of female social work lost its traditional significance completely.

In 1950, political purges were conducted to 'clean' also the ministries, which meant that the political commitment of all the staff members as well as "their loyalty towards the people's government had to be proved."[10] A Soviet 'advisor' was employed to implement this regulation.[11]

In addition to these measures the role of media and research changed radically: The Institute for Social Research, which had been established in 1945 primarily supporting social-democratic opinions, was closed down. While since 1946 the different ministries had to inform the newspapers and radio stations about their achievements every afternoon,[12] now, it was strictly forbidden for the staff to give any information to journalists. All the data concerning social institutions, the number of kindergartens, recreation homes or nursing homes, the quantities of food needed for these institutions and the number of war-disabled persons were kept secret.[13]

Within the following years the discourse on social welfare was reduced even further. Avoiding the public platform of the media, the ministries published their own bulletin containing their regulations and decrees. Therefore, the discussion among independent experts was replaced by information through the officials of the ministry. Data on the social welfare system had become a state secret.

Priorities in the Field of Social Politics

The first years after the war were characterized by expanding the realm of social politics, reducing social welfare provision and exercising increasingly more social control. In the period between 1948 and 1950 the fundamental principles of Soviet social politics were introduced in Bulgaria, that means, they were subordinated to goals of labour and health politics. Social security,

---

[10] Regulation 296, 1950
[11] Regulation M-836, 1950
[12] Regulation N73, 1946
[13] Regulation 648, 1949

free health care and access to recreation homes were considered to be prior aims.[14]

The measures concerning social welfare provision focussed also on aims that had been set in the interwar period, but had not been achieved yet. These were principally the reduction of child mortality, the improvement of health promotion and of the hygienic conditions in villages. Another significant goal was child and youth welfare, a field in which the efforts focussed on expanding the network of advisory centres, summer colonies, children's homes etc. All these institutions and programmes were expected to exercise their educational authority towards strengthening the children's and young people's loyalty to the ideology of the socialist state.

It was no socio-political objective, however, to deal with individual social problems. Socialist social politics promoted strategies that aimed at emphasizing the marked differences between the socio-political realm in capitalist and in socialist countries. It was the general conviction that no comprehensive system of social politics existed in capitalist states and a scientifically based approach, such as the one that the communist party pursued, would be impossible there.[15] According to this view the social security systems in capitalist countries would only deal with current problems, whereas in the socialist states the realm of social politics was integrated into a system that endeavoured to achieve historical aims.[16] For this reason phenomena like 'suffering', 'poverty', 'inequality', 'prostitution' and 'child labour' were only attributed to the capitalist world. It was admitted that social security for every citizen was also a significant aim of socialist social politics, but its most relevant and ultimate goal was to establish a communist society where differences between social classes would cease to exist.[17]

Classification and Standardization in Social Welfare

Child and youth welfare became emblematic of Bulgarian social politics, whereas the care for disabled and old people was only a field of marginal interest. Old people were the main losers from the economic measures of

---

14 Zimmermann 2001
15 ibid., p. 7
16 ibid., p. 7
17 ibid., p. 8

the government (the conversion of land into collective property, the expropriation of private owners), but also from cultural measures (the restrictions on religion, the introduction of communist ideology, the orthography reform). In 1948 the calculation of pensions was re-checked. This meant, among other things, that lists of war-disabled persons were compiled, and as a result these people lost their entitlement to an invalidity pension for political reasons. In general pensions decreased to a level of 25 to 50% of the minimum income, which was considered to be necessary to cover a person's essential needs.[18]

A decree from 1951 laid down clear-cut restrictions in order to abolish the variety of social welfare activities and organizations. The political message was clear enough: "The organisation of social welfare provision is to be unified and therefore the aim is to rescind the laws of the past, which, merely formally, provided social measures and which were humiliating to the working population."[19]

It was emphasized that everybody had the right to work and was consequently entitled to receive social assistance, especially with reference to war-disabled people and victims of the fight against fascism. All forms of begging were prohibited, and the people's councils (bodies responsible for local administration) were assigned the task of implementing this ban. All welfare organizations and charitable foundations were abolished.[20] Children who were mentally or physically severely handicapped were separated in special homes in remote regions where the institutions for them were also located. The fact that educational institutions for welfare work were closed down and also the clear predominance of classifying people on the basis of administrative and ideological criteria influenced the attitude towards the needy considerably. They were simply divided up according to their ability to work and to the degree of their handicap. In order to "cure and improve the situation of those who were ill", workshops within the social institutions were organized in order to increase their ability to work. But economical reasons also played an important role for taking measures like these. The production also fulfilled economic criteria.[21]

---

[18] cf. Konstantinov 2001
[19] Manev et al. 1957, p. 5/6
[20] ibid.
[21] ibid, p. 163

New Developments

It was only in the 1960s and 1970s that the attitude towards social care changed. It was publicly admitted that there were situations and problems in private life which people could not solve without getting any support[22] and which consequently had to be treated as an issue of public social welfare.

At the beginning of the 1970s a professional training program for social work was established again, as an extra course combined with the training provided for nurses. It was Julietta Koeva, director for social welfare at the People's Health Ministry, who was primarily responsible for initiating the new measures.[23]

The most important socio-political goals which were achieved were the establishment of the free health care system and the enlargement of the network of hospitals and maternity clinics. The income of the working population increased and a five-day working week was introduced. Places in the kindergartens (for 76.5 % of the children between three and seven) were provided.[24] The attitude toward old people's care was changed. The fact that the number of pension recipients was raised, that more old people were taken care of at home and that special clubs for pensioners were introduced show that the provision for the older generation was considered to be more relevant.[25]

Conclusion

Analysing the Bulgarian development under state socialism it is necessary to distinguish between socio-political achievements on the one hand and the marginalization of social welfare provision on the other hand. The social system as well as the health care system achieved a lot of merits in certain respects: It effectively dealt with some modern challenges that had already become recognizable in the decades before. Comprehensive material and professional resources were mobilized to reduce child mortality and to fight

---

[22] Golemanov et al. 1976, p. 3
[23] Koeva et. al. 1969. The former director for public social welfare lives in Israel today.
[24] Golemanov et al. 1976, p. 15-32
[25] ibid., p. 32-34

against diseases, such as tuberculosis. A health care system providing relevant services, information on health and sanitary improvements was successfully implemented, also in rural areas. There were other noticeable achievements within the recreational system, which were organized by collectives at the place of employment.

At the same time, however, social control was strengthened, and the right to work became a duty. As activities of private welfare were forbidden, the people's consciousness for their own social responsibility was diminished. The places where discourses on these issues took place were dissolved, local traditions of charity were given up together with the commitment of voluntary as well as professional social workers. The problems of a civil society were to be solved through administrative measures of the state. Certain disadvantaged groups of people vanished from the streets to make their problems invisible. This contributed to their social and physical isolation, which is a characteristic of our society, even today.

References

Bogdanova, Savka: *Kulturnijat otdih na rabotnizite i sluzhitelite* (The cultural relaxation of the workering people). Sofia 1958
Dochev Ivan/ Rumjana Kraleva: *Sozialna politika, Osnovni problemi* (Social politics. Main problems). Sofia 1988
Golemanov, Christo/Miroslav Popov: *Sozialnaja politika Bolgarii* (Social Politics in Bulgaria). Sofia 1976
Koeva, Julietta: *Sozialni grizhi v NRB* (Social Care in People's Republic of Bulgaria). In: Dvadeset i pet godini sozialistichsko zdraveopazvane, 1969
Konstantinov, Nikola: *Sozialno osigurjavane v Bulgaria 1888-1951* (Social Insurance in Bulgaria 1888 - 1951). Sofia 2001
Manev, Andrej/Ognjan Aleksiev/Nikola Nikolov (Eds.): *Sozialni grizhi v Narodna republika Bulgaria. Sbornik zakoni, ukasi, pravilnizi I dr.* (Social Care in People's Republic of Bulgaria). Sofia 1957
Nacheva,Vera: *Vremeto e v nas. Spomeni i razmisli* (The Time is Inside of us. Memories and Thoughts). Sofia 1984
Popova, Kristina: *Die soziale Fürsorge nach dem 9. September 1944: bürokratische Kontinuität, soziale Diskontinuität* (Social Care after the Ninth September 1944: Administrative Continutity and Social Discontinuity). In: Ulf Brunnbauer/ Wolf-

gang Hoepken (Eds.): *Transformationsprobleme Bulgariens im 19. und 20. Jahrhundert. Historische und ethnologische Perspektiven.* München 2007, p. 109-124

Popova, Kristina: 'Das Nationale Kind'. *Biopolitik und Aufklärungstätigkeit des Bulgarischen Kinderschutzbundes 1925.1944* (The National Child: Biopolitics and Advertising Activities of the Union for Child Protection in Bulgaria 1924-1944. In: Hering, Sabine/Schröer, Wolfgang (Eds,): *Sorge um die Kinder. Beiträge zur Geschichte von Kindheit, Kindergarten und Kinderfürsorge.* Weinheim/München 2008, p. 129-138

Zimmermann, Susan: *Wohlfahrtspolitik und die staatssozialistische Entwicklungsstrategie in der ‚anderen' Hälfte Europas im 20. Jahrhundert.* In: Jäger/Melinz/ Zimmermann (Eds.): *Sozialpolitik in der Peripherie. Entwicklungsmuster und Wandel in Lateinamerika, Afrika, Asien und Osteuropa.* Frankfurt am Main 2001, p. 213-237

Historical sources:

Archive of the Ministry of Social Policy, National Archive Sofia, Fond 49

Anelia Kassabova, Ulf Brunnbauer

Socialism, Sexuality and Marriage – Family Policies in Socialist Bulgaria (1944 - 1989)

Introduction

In 1963, the largest mass-organization of socialist Bulgaria, the Fatherland Front, published the book "Let's Live and Work in a Communist Way", which described the socialist family: "Let us visit family D. Bonev in Sofia. Apart from the parents, there are two students and one pupil. Love and respect, mutual help, good order and personal responsibility of each member render this family a terrific small collective in which everyone strives to live and work in a communist way. The curiosity of the random visitor of this house on boulevard Georgi Dimitrov is attracted by the 'Program of the Family' on the wall. There are some general regulations: all family matters are decided jointly; everyone can solve his personal matters freely on his own, as long as they do not touch the dignity and honour of the family; all decisions of the family are executed only after every member of the family is convinced in their rightfulness and necessity; the family council may discuss at any time personal and general problems on request of any family member. In this family, tidiness and feeding the family are not the demanding monopoly of the mother. All three kids do kitchen service. On Sunday, the father is responsible for the kitchen, and does the shopping as well."[1]

In this paper the family policies of Bulgarian communist party will be discussed. The attempts to create a new society and to solve social problems were an essential part of the new political programmes. Family policies was the major element of these programmes, and altered in dependence on the changing actual guidelines of the government.

We will highlight the major trajectories of family policies in socialist Bulgaria and emphasise two case-studies as particularly revealing policy fields: reproduction policies and policies towards single mothers.[2]

---

[1] Bakiš/Halova 1963, p. 8-9
[2] This paper relies on archival sources, legal documents, statistical data, periodicals, propaganda texts and oral history interviews. It was funded by the Austrian Science Fond (FWF) research grant "Family and Women in Socialist Bulgaria". Results are published in Brunnbauer/Taylor 2004; Brunnbauer 2007; Kassabova-

Creating the 'Socialist Family'

In their discussion of the family in post-revolutionary Cuba, Laura Gotkowitz and Richard Turits pointed out that "rather than offering an alternative to the traditional family, most socialists have claimed instead to be its best defenders."[3] This corresponds also to the Bulgarian comrades who came to power in September 1944. Their ideas about family life was close to the Soviet orthodoxy of that time: Under Stalin, the family had been recognized as the 'basic cell of society', and the state pledged to support family stability and to provide assistance for the fulfilment of their reproductive functions. Consequently, Georgi Dimitrov (1882 - 1949), who in 1946 became the first communist prime-minister of the country, declared that radical ideas about withering of the family in socialism "were not a scientific assessment, not a Marxist position."[4]

The Bulgarian communists wanted to liberate the family from all burdens connected with the bourgeois system, and in turn they expected the family to contribute to socialism. For that purpose, the structure of family life in Bulgaria had to change:[5] In 1944, Bulgaria was a society of peasant smallholders far away from modernization. In the late 1940s, only a quarter of the population lived in urban settlements. So, the communist regime tried to transform family relations based on patriarchal authority and seniority into modern structures including female employment and communist education of youth. The party wanted to see families based on the independence of the spouses from the older generation, economic and legal equality between husband and wife and their dedication to socialism.[6]

These aims required a new legislation: In October 1944 a governmental decree declared men and women equal before the law "in all domains of economic, governmental, cultural and socio-political life."[7] In May 1945 the 'Decree on Marriage' declared only civil marriage as legal obligation, while previously the religious communities had registered marriages.[8] The new marriage decree gave spouses all opportunities to choose their profession and

---

Dintcheva 2003, 2004, 2007. We are grateful to Karin Taylor for her invaluable participation in the research project and her comments on our research.
3 Gotkowitz/Turtis 1988
4 Dimitrov 1955, p. 43
5 Family relations before 1944 vf. Sanders 1949; Dolinski 1930; Močeva 1938
6 Sanders 1976, p. 165.
7 Dăržaven vestnik 227/1944, p. 1
8 Dăržaven vestnik 108/1945, p. 1-5

obliged them to contribute to the family income according to their possibilities. Women were permitted to keep their maiden name after marriage or to add the name to their husband's name. Divorce was liberalized: spouses could divorce either by consent, or if one of the spouses sought to dissolve the marriage on the basis of the new law. In the following years further acts were passed with the intention to remove all legal inequalities between men and women.

One of the main intentions of family policies at this stage was to further the emancipation of women, which was a paramount ideological goal and an economic necessity. For that purpose, families were to be relieved from their 'economic' functions, which were defined as 'unnatural' or 'unspecific', Instead, families should concentrate on their 'natural' functions, defined as biological reproduction and child education.[9] In policy terms this meant to liberate women from the 'house-slavery' by establishing day-care centres for children, public laundries and canteens. The intended side-effect of the extensive establishment of crèches and kindergarten was to bring them under state-influence in early age.

Female employment did, indeed, grow quickly: from 25,8 % of the total workforce in 1952 to 39 % in 1965 and almost the half by the late 1980s. This was not only due to the provision of kindergarten places for most working mothers but also to economic pressures, because in the 1950s and 1960s, families could hardly live on one wage alone. Economic and social policies, thus, undermined the concept of the male breadwinner. In 1969, 85 % of married women declared they would not leave their job even if their husband earned enough money to support the family.[10]

The attempt to modernize family relations was accompanied by intensive propaganda efforts. Raina Peševa, a leading ethnographer during socialism and theorist of the socialist way of life, accused men of harbouring old-fashioned attitudes towards women and neglecting to help in the household.[11] 'Capitalist residues' were also often targeted in the print media, especially in magazines directed at female readers. The most widely circulated women's magazine 'Woman Today' (*Ženata dnes*) advocated female employment as a way of overcoming the bourgeois marriage of convenience, in which women married to have comfort and money and were dependent on men. Another point of criticism was the lack of communist education in the families. In the book on "Communist Morality and the Family", the legal expert Nisim

---

[9] Iliev 2001, p. 93
[10] Ženata v stopanskija, obštestvenija, kulturnija život i v semejstvoto 1972, p. 80.
[11] Peševa 1962a

Mevorjah demanded that parents should not spoil their children, but teach them tidiness, cleanliness and accuracy in work.[12] A primer on the family's role in 'communist education' summarized the tasks of parents to familiarize children with the principles of communist morality, and to encourage a scientific worldview and positive attitude towards labour.[13]

One of the reasons identified by party activists and family theorists for the persistence of 'capitalist remnants' was the proximity to religious thoughts, which were held responsible for a wide range of 'negative phenolmena' in the family, such as drinking, superstition, discrimination of women and family problems.[14] Therefore the party strongly promoted newly made 'civic' rituals to replace religious life-cycle ceremonies.[15]

Reification of the Family

While family policies in the first two decades of communist rule were mainly shaped by the struggle against 'capitalist residues', the government shifted to a more affirmative approach during the 1960s. This change was caused by the emerging new social realities after the 'great socio-economic transformation of the 1950s and 1960s': The party became concerned about social stability and reproduction and, therefore, increased the responsibilities of the family in this area, especially with respect to material welfare and biological reproduction.

While the party's 20-years plan of 1962 still promised to socialise most of the domestic work, by the late 1960s the regime increased the private tasks of the family. The 'Family Act' of 1985, which replaced the Act of 1968, defined the functions of the family in article 4: "The basic functions of the socialist family are:

- Birth, bringing-up and education of children;
- to safeguard the conditions for the opportunities of each member of the family,
- to support the fulfilment of their professional and social obligations;

---

12 Mevoriah 1956, p. 54-55
13 Semeistvoto i komunističeskoto văzpitanie 1968, p. 18-22
14 Peševa 1962b, 1964, p. 29-40
15 Peševa 1963; for an analysis cf. Brunnbauer 2007, p. 558-66

- to realise relations within the family, which are based on respect, affection, amicability, common efforts and mutual responsibility (...);
- to care (...) for the old, sick and incapable members of the family."[16]

Thus, the regime accepted the role of families as a welfare agency and a medium of cultural values. Despite rapid urbanization and industrialization which peaked in the 1960s,[17] the family still kept important functions for the economic wellbeing of its members. Rural households, for example, were allowed to run collective farms for 'personal use', while many urban families did some farming on their countryside cottages or in their native villages to avoid shortages of state-run food supply.

Families also remained the main inter-generation welfare agency, as neither retirement homes nor nurseries for toddlers enjoyed popularity. In the late 1970s, only some 18 % of children under three years were looked after in nurseries, while about 75 % of children aged three to six went to kindergarten.[18] Many families, in fact, relied on one of their grandmothers to care for the babies.[19] This arrangement, which originally had been criticized by family theorists who had considered grandmothers as pre-socialist 'remnants', became positively re-evaluated in the 1970s. The new family code of 1985 recognized the status of grandparents and guaranteed them the right to personal relations with their grandchildren: They could adopt grandchildren, if one parent died or in case of divorce of the parents. In 1986, amendments to the labour code introduced paid leave for employed grandparents who cared for their grandchildren.

Private households continued to do most of the domestic 'duties', because the state failed to provide sufficient services. Various sociological studies in the 1970s showed that on average, adult Bulgarians spent about three hours for the housework every day, and the amount of time dedicated to these tasks even increased with the extension of leisure. Public laundries and canteens were only infrequently used even if available, because families preferred to eat privately prepared food and personal cleaning.[20]

---

16 Semeen kodeks 1985, art. 4
17 Some 1.4 million people moved from villages to towns between 1950 and 1970; by the end of the 1960s more than half of the total population lived in urban areas, cf. Brunnbauer 2007, p. 233-54
18 Encheva 1980, p. 35; Committee for the Unified System for Social Information 1980, p. 45
19 Iliev 2001
20 Dančeva 1971, p. 32; Spasovska 1976, p. 129

The party, preferring to channel investment into heavy industry, accepted these arrangements, although they brook their promises to liberate families from 'unnatural' economic functions. Some activists and family theorists criticized the lack of socialist commitment. The regime, however, was aware of the fact that reproduction even in the socialist society depended on unpaid labour. This had serious implications for women because domestic 'job sharing' became rather unfair. According to a survey in 1976/77 women spent an average of 4 hours and 42 minutes a day on housework, men only 2 hours and 20 minutes. Women were almost exclusively responsible for food preparation, washing, ironing and cleaning, while male homework was limited to repairing, shopping and taking care of heating.[21]

Rather than making a consistent effort to change gender relations in families, the government increased a broad pro-family propaganda. The 'Family Acts' of 1968 and 1985 defined the place of the family in society, influenced family relations and included restrictions on divorce. In 1985, the 'Family Act' managed to cut the number of divorces, which had significantly increased since 1970, although more radical proposals for the restriction of divorce had been prevented by wide-spread opposition. But promises of important welfare benefits, such as access to housing for spouses, facilitated the stability of families. The extensive propaganda in the media since the late 1960s as well as corresponding activities by the Fatherland Front presented marriage as the only normal way of life and called it the precondition of the development of socialist personality.

Demographic Concerns and Pro-Natalisme

The second reason which led the party to focus on family stability and reduce the general emancipation rhetoric was the demographic development of the country. Similar to other European countries, Bulgaria suffered under a sharp decline of birth rates and fertility after the post-war baby boom (Table 1 and Table 2). The one- and two-child family became the dominant model. According to a survey in the 1970s most women wished to have max. two children, and many had even less.

---

[21] Dobrianov et al. 1985, p. 85

Year	Live births	Mortality rate	Natural population growth
	per 1,000 population		
1945	24.0	14.9	9.1
1950	25.2	10.2	15.0
1955	20.1	9.0	11.1
1960	17.8	8.1	9.7
1965	15.3	8.1	7.2
1968	16.9	8.6	8.3
1970	16.3	9.1	7.2
1973	16.2	9.5	6.7
1974	17.2	9.8	7.4
1980	14.5	11.1	3.4
1985	13.3	12.0	1.3
1989	12.5	11.9	0.6

Table 1: Natality, mortality and natural population growth, 1945 - 1989

	Live births per 1,000 married women			
Years Age cohort	1925–8	1945–8	1955–8	1965–6
	Annual average			
15-9	291.4	310.6	251.2	263.9
20-4	331.9	282.6	236.0	228.6
25-9	264.8	200.8	136.8	110.2
30-4	200.8	107.1	61.0	44.7
35-9	142.7	56.2	29.1	15.9
40-4	72.6	17.5	8.9	4.1
45 and older	36.0	4.5	1.7	0.8
Total	198.8	124.3	87.8	70.1

Table 2: Age-specific fertility of married women, 1925 - 1966

The government was worried about these trends for two reasons: first, it feared future shortages of workers, because economic growth depended on rising labour inputs. In December 1967, Penčo Kubadinski, member of the 'Politburo' and leading family theoretician in communist Bulgaria, called population growth "the basic socio-economic factor" and "the guarantee for the establishment of socialism and communism."[22] Second, party leaders were worried about much higher population rates among the Muslim minorities, especially the Turks, who made up 10% of the total population. Party leader Todor Živkov described the political implications of Turkish population growth as follows: "If we speak about the decline in birth rates, we have the Bulgarian population in mind. Among the Turks and gipsies, they are high anyway. These people shall have children, we have nothing against that. The point is: the necessity to increase the genuine Bulgarian element, the birth of the third child."[23]

As a result of this discussion, party and government approved the decision "On the Stimulation of Fertility" in December 1967, which became law in February 1968.[24] As a result of this decree the child allowance, which had been introduced in 1951, was significantly raised for the second and third child, and became independent of income levels. Paid maternity leave for the second and third child was extended and the right to non-paid leave opened. Families with two or three children received certain privileges with respect to employment or access to housing and repayment of housing loans.[25]

These progressive benefits excluded incentives for the 'fourth child', because the abundance of children in the Roma and Turkish families should not be rewarded. The size of the allowances was significant compared to wages: parents with three children received monthly child benefits of 55 Leva, while the average monthly wage was 114 Leva. A negative incentive was an income tax for unmarried people over 21 as well as married couples without children five years after marriage containing 10 % of their income in 1951.[26]

Another measure to increase the birth rates were restrictions on abortion, enacted in February 1968. In 1956, abortion on request had been liberalized and became one of the most important means of birth control due to the absence of modern contraceptives. In 1967, for the first time in Bulgaria more abortions (129,900) were registered than live births (108,500).[27] This motivated the government to impose certain more effective restrictions to support

---

[22] Central State Archive, Sofia [abbreviated as TsDA], f. 1, op. 34, a.e. 89, 37 and 53.
[23] Ibid., 86-88
[24] A similar decree, promulgated by the parliament's presidency in 1955, had remained ineffective.
[25] Postanovlenie no. 61, 1
[26] Ukaz za nasărčavane na raždaemostta, 1. The decree of 1951 cf. TsDA, f. 117, op. 17, a.e. 176, art. 7
[27] Vassilev 1999, p. 72-73

their pro-nativity drive. In 1968, abortion on request in cases not motivated on medical reasons or rape was prohibited for women without children. Women with either one or two children could request an abortion only with consent of a commission, which was instructed to persuade pregnant women to accept the baby.[28] This partial ban was a compromise between those in the communist party, who had argued for a total ban, such as introduced in Romania in 1966, and female communists who had strictly opposed against any ban.[29]

The 'stimulation of fertility' had only short-term effects. Birth rates increased from 15.0 per 1,000 inhabitants in 1967 to 17.0 in 1969, but then started to decline again. On the long run fertility rates raised only among young women (aged between 20 and 24), while the effect among women over 24 years had no continuity. The number of legally induced abortions was reduced in the beginning, but since 1970 it was even higher than before, because the ban was not strictly enforced.

Women with at least on child could still have abortions on request relatively easily, and medical indications were also increasingly granted. Therefore, the Central Committee and the Ministerial Council announced a new decree basing rather on stimulation than on restrictions. In 1975, 1979 and 1984, child allowances and lump sums were adjusted upwards, so that in the 1980s a two-child family received more than twenty percent of the average wage. Mothers had the right to stay at home for up to two years receiving compensation as high as the minimum wage. Furthermore, mothers had the right to return to their jobs, and pregnant women could not be dismissed.[30]

A new attempt to restrict abortions in April 1973 caused an extremely negative response in the public discussion, so the government had to modify the ban in 1974.[31] Women still had to present their intention to abort their foetus to a special commission. However, more than half of all applications were approved, so that the number of abortions was not greatly affected by the restrictions.[32] Instead of rigorously enforcing the ban, the government endeavoured to convince women: "Pregnancy and normal birth are physiological acts which contribute to the development and strengthening of the fe-

---

[28] Instruktsija no. 188 za reda za izkustveno prekăsvane na bremenostta i borbata s kriminalnija abort", Dărźaven vestnik no. 13, 16 February 1968, p. 1-4
[29] The protocol of the discussion is kept in TsDA, f. 1, op. 34, a.e. 89
[30] Vidova et al. 1983, p. 81-2 and 103; Ivanova 1990, p. 121-132
[31] Vassilev 1999, p. 77
[32] By 1980 there were again more registered abortions (156:100) than births (138:200).

male organism, (...) while abortion destroys these unique values and her natural obligations."[33]

These strategies were embedded in the already mentioned 'Family Code', passed in May 1968 and 1985. Both Family Codes – especially the one of 1985 – made divorce more difficult, because it was considered a factor depressing birth rates.[34]

The pro-nativity policy was also embedded in a propaganda campaign to change notions of the role of women. Already in the early 1960s, ideological ideas about 'women' and 'family' began to stress the role of women as mothers. Women were described as functionalised stereotypes, such as 'woman-mother' or 'mother-worker'. In its resolution "Enhancing the Role of Women in the Construction of a Developed Socialist Society" (1973), the Politburo officially declared fertility as the primary function of women: "Motherhood is the social and biological function of woman, and it has the first place in the complex of all her functions because of its vital importance for society. Motherhood is an essential foundation of women's complete happiness."[35]

In order to prepare state effective intervention into family life, the government initiated extensive research on the family. From the late 1960s, sociologists carried out a number of surveys, and legal experts, psychologists and ethnographers also published widely on the issue. The largest research project, "The Bulgarian Family", was conducted in 1974 - 1977 and resulted in several publications.[36] Demographic development also became the object of increased academic scrutiny, when the government encouraged demographers to find ways to reverse the falling trend in the birth rate. Thus, demography became deeply politicised and was ultimately implemented to legitimize the monitoring of the reproductive behaviour of the population, and also justified the intrusion of the state into private life. In 1985 an extensive survey on various aspects of the demographic behaviour of approximately 180,000 persons took place.[37]

The demographers underlined, for example, the link between low fertility and lack of living space. The lack of adequate housing also disturbed the model of the autonomous family life for younger people, because many young couples were forced to live with their parents. Thus, in 1970s' Bulgaria the share of three-generation households was higher than in the 19th

---

[33] Kubadinski 1986, p. 113
[34] Kubadinski 1987, p. 115
[35] 'Politbureau' 1977, p. 23
[36] Dinkova 1976; Kjuranov 1987
[37] Höpken 1986, p. 90

century. Although this was not fitting into the official propaganda, Penčo Kubadinski even went so far as to praise this arrangement as the spirit of collectivism.[38]

'Lonely Mothers' Between Stigmatization and Heroization

"Any married or unmarried woman who has become mother deserves our full attention, care and respect. (...) The child born out of wedlock must not be despised only because of the imprudence and lack of care of the mother."[39] This quote from a survey on extramarital births (1982) illustrates how difficult it was for the party to solve the contradiction between its pro-natalism and the affirmation of marriage. On the one hand, extramarital births contributed to support population growth, on the other hand, they undermined the ideal of family stability. Corresponding to general policy priorities, the attitudes towards extramarital births and single mothers, therefore, were continuously changing.

In May 1945 the new 'Decree on Marriage' proclaimed the equality of children born in and out of wedlock. The constitutions of 1947 and 1971 confirmed this principle. Socialist legislation on this issue used the expression 'non-' or 'extramarital' children, rather than the traditional differentiation between 'legitimate' and 'illegitimate' births.[40] The last remaining legal obstacles concerning the responsibility of fatherhood was eliminated in 1949 by the 'Law on Inheritance' which gave equal rights to marital and extramarital children.

Despite these changes, which were also motivated by the need to follow the Soviet model, the regime tried to keep down births outside marriage. The reason for this divergence has to be sought in the demographic differences: Soviet acceptance of extramarital births was caused by the significant majority of women in the fertile cohorts due to war losses. In Bulgaria the gender balance was only slightly in favour of women.[41] Hence the Bulgarian communist regime felt no pressure to modify its dismissive stance on extramarital

---

[38] Kubadinski 1986, p. 167-8
[39] Kostadinov 1982, p. 35 and 39
[40] The shift had already been made by the Law on Extramarital Children and Adoption in 1940.
[41] In 1946, the total population was made up by 3,497,900 women and 3,479,200 men (Statističeski godišnik *1943 - 1946*, p. 19).

births: "It is possible to think of situations when extramarital births solve important social problems. Looking at the demographic processes in our country, however, there is no need (...) to accept children out of marriage in order to secure biological reproduction."[42]

Another demographic factor was the fact that fertility levels of unmarried women were significantly lower than of married women and, thus, did not correspond with the reproductive ideals of the regime. For these reasons, the government adopted various measures to prevent extramarital births in the first three decades after the Second World War. Especially in the 1950s and 1960s this led to an almost definite taboo of single motherhood and to extensive attempts to regulate sexual life "in the struggle for the socialist family".[43]

Stigmatization of Unmarried Mothers

In socialist Bulgaria unmarried mothers were seen as a bad role model and a constant threat considering the limited norms of sexual morals focussed on married couples with the goal of procreation. In the words of a prominent female family theoretician: "Let's not forget that citizens who already once neglected their social responsibility (...), may tomorrow violate other norms of moral and ethical behaviour. Therefore the efforts to restrict extramarital births are reasonable, although we must not cease the struggle against prejudices towards them."[44]

Unmarried mothers were castigated as immature, careless, irresponsible, imprudent, egoistic, psychologically volatile and ugly. Although legislation used the neutral term 'unmarried woman/mother' and provided equal rights to children born in and out of wedlock, many official documents also used the word 'lonely mother', which provided associations with 'loneliness' and 'non-membership in the community'. The medical literature of that time made a connection between loneliness and psychic instability as well as liability to mental illness and suicide.

The stigma of extramarital birth was not attached only to the mothers but also their family of origin. Although the early socialist state rejected the educative functions of the family, parents were still made responsible for the 'correct' education of their children, especially for daughters: "Young girls

---

[42] Dinkova 1972, p. 6.
[43] Ibid.
[44] Ibid.

are not mature enough to anticipate the consequences of friendship neither to assess their own behaviour."[45] If girls ignored the principles of socialist morality, her parents were stigmatised as well, because they had failed as educators and had obviously set a bad personal example: "If we want to prepare others, we must be prepared ourselves."[46] The extension of the stigma forced parents to control the sexuality of their daughters more rigidly than the attitudes of their sons. As there was nearly no sexual education taught in schools, families had to compensate the lack of sexual education.[47]

Instead of useful information, various mass organisations and schools were called upon to send moral appeals to the young generation. In schools compulsory gynaecological testing was introduced, and pregnant schoolgirls were excluded.[48] If the official rules were not strictly imposed, the 'weak enforcement' was criticised as a source of 'moral nihilism'. The expert for family law, Marija Dinkova, for example called upon not only the Komsomol and schools but also the public prosecutor and the police to strengthen control of unmarried cohabitation and to urge marriage.[49]

'Mother and Child Homes' – and the Heroization of Single Mothers

The so called 'Mother and Child Homes' can be considered as a compromise between the rise of birth rates and the disapproval of unmarried mothers. However, the 'price' for keeping a pregnancy secret was to settle down in mostly isolated places. Hence, unmarried mothers in these homes were objects of a certain ghettoization which did not increase public acceptance and tolerance for them.[50]

Since the late 1960s these changes in reproduction policies led, on the long run, to some progressive official attitudes towards the issue of extramarital birth. One reason for this reorientation was the fact that the population practiced a significant growth of births outside wedlock, despite the official attempts: While in 1946 to 1949 only 2.4 % of children had been

---

[45] Doceva 1965, p. 9-10
[46] Markova/Apostolov 1983, p. 38
[47] Kassabova-Dintcheva 2004, p. 168-9
[48] They had only the chance to finish school via distance learning.
[49] Dinkova 1972, p. 7
[50] Kassabova 2007, p. 138-139

born out of wedlock, their share reached almost 10 % by the late 1960s and 12.4 % in 1989.[51] Considering the fiscal scarcity, the government was not prepared to pay the enormous amount of money for the increasing number of mother-child homes, and decided to allow unmarried mothers to raise their children on their own, instead.

To give unmarried mothers the chance to do so, the government introduced generous material, social and educative measures for them. In the beginning of the 1970s, for example, single mothers received twice as much child allowance as married mothers. If they were not employed, they got a monthly allowance in the amount of the minimum wage until the second birthday of their child (in case of second and third children as well as twins, until the third birthday). Children of single mothers enjoyed priority for placement in crèches and kindergartens which were in short supply.[52] 'Social-legal cabinets' were instructed to support single mothers searching for jobs or housing, but the consultation was not obligatory and often remained on paper only.

Now, single mothers who raised their child were praised in the media as 'saints' and 'heroes'.[53] In 1972, a reader wrote a letter to the editors, responding to a series of articles on single motherhood in the popular women's journal 'Woman Today' (*Ženata dnes*): "I would kiss the hand of the one, who remains mother, who does not give away her child and who realises motherhood as the point of her life. A person like this, I can absolutely respect. But I cannot respect those, who come to the maternity hospital only in order to liberate themselves from the unwanted pregnancy."[54]

So, in the 1970s finally the break of the taboo 'single motherhood' took place. The press published articles about 'lonely mothers' discussing also the problems of fatherhood and family relations:[55] "In case the parents or friends do not give her shelter, the single mother has no place to live (…). She also hardly finds a job."[56] It is interesting to see that critique is now directed against 'public opinion' and, above all, 'family morale' and 'philistine parents' regarding their unmarried daughter as a personal disgrace. Of course,

---

[51] In 2001, it was 42 % (ibid., p. 142).
[52] Sbornik materiali za nasărčavane na raždaemostta 1986
[53] Konstantinov 1978, p. 4
[54] Ilieva 1972, p. 19
[55] E.g. Dinkova 1972; Popova 1972, p. 14–5; Martinova 1978, p. 4; Stamatov 1978, p. 4
[56] Dareva 1978, p. 8

there was no reflection about the fact that these attitudes had been produced by the negative stance of the government towards single mothers.

Now, those mothers were blamed who left their children in mother-child homes. People were particular critical against educated women who deserted their children. Mass media portrayed them as women who were full of egoism and bourgeois behaviour, searching for a comfortable life and adopting 'Western' models. Public discourses continued to condemn unmarried pregnancies, without reflecting the social structures which dominated this kind of fate. Hence, despite the heroic portray of single mothers, the stigmatization of extramarital birth survived.

On the other hand the propaganda for marriage as the only legitimate form of cohabitation continued. Only very few publications discussed the right to divorce and the results of single parenthood. Some authors of sociological studies considered the so called 'incomplete families' as an honourable form of life, with no harm for the children. Plamen Georgiev showed that children who grew up with only one parent were not more likely to become criminals than children of 'normal' families. He concluded that "from the perspective of social progress, families with only one parent are no anomaly".[57] This was, however, a minority position which could not break the mainstream of ideas about family, neither the official, nor the public one.

Conclusion

The discussion on reproduction measures and family policies in socialist Bulgaria shows, that it often had not the intended consequences. Neither families became 'socialist' germ cells, nor was sexuality reduced on fertility. The government even had to support certain social arrangements, such as the welfare role of families or the caring role of grand-parents, which contradicted the initial ideas connected with socialist family policy. The party had to accept the functional responses on the socialist economy of shortage. Considering the stability of these social practises and the limitations on its own capacities, the government was prepared to support the same customs it once had condemned. In socialism, it was important to maintain ideological coherence, e.g. the correspondence of ideological programmes and social practice. In case of doubt, the former had to be made correspondent to the latter.

---

[57] Georgiev 1978, p. 4.

However, this does not mean that family policies in socialist Bulgaria were generally of no consequence. They influenced family relations, reproductive behaviour and life courses, though sometimes not in the way that was intended by the regime. The family policies definitely contributed to maintain the family as the 'basic cell of society', because all kinds of alternatives were not efficient. Family relations were changed with respect to women's interests, but the promises of total emancipation were not fulfilled. The kind of contact between man and woman was at the end of state socialism was similar to the traditional patriarchalism at the beginning. Therefore, a general influence of communist policies on the modernization of family can not be neglected. But the results remained partial because of the undemocratic nature of the regime, the economic problems and the conservative attitudes of many party-leaders. These ambiguities became even more evident during the period of transformation in the 1990s. This is another story, but one in which the family also played a very important role.

References

Bakiš, S./Halova S.: *Da rabotim i živeem po komunističeski* (To work and life in a communist way). Sofia 1963

Belčeva, Marija: *Izvănbračnite raždanija v Bălgarija – ličnostni i sotsialni problemi* (Extramartial Births in Bulgaria – Personal and Social Problems). Sofia 1989

Benovska, Milena: *Tradition as a Means of Survival Under the Conditions of Economic Crisis in Bulgaria.* In: Ethnologia Balkanica 1/1997, p. 113-123

Brunnbauer, Ulf/Taylor, Karin: *Creating a Socialist Way of Life: Family and Reproduction Policies in Socialist Bulgaria (1944-1989).* In: Continuity and Change, 19/2004, p. 283-312

Brunnbauer, Ulf: *Die sozialistische Lebensweise. Ideologie, Gesellschaft, Familie und Politik in Bulgarien (1944-1989).* Wien/Köln/Weimar 2007

Čakărov, Najden (Ed.): *Semejstvoto v sotsialističeskoto obštestvo* (The family in the socialist society]. Sofia 1964

Committee for the Unified System for Social Information: *Women in the People's Republic of Bulgaria. Demographic and Socio-economic Survey.* Sofia 1980

Dančeva, Stanka: *Analiz na bjudžeta na vremeto na trudeštite se ot grad Kazanlăk v uslovijata na petdnevnata rabotna sedmitsa* (Analysis of the Time Budget of the Working People From the Town of Kazanlăk Under the Conditions of the Five-Says-Working Week). In: Sotsiologičeski problemi (Sociological problems), 3/1971, p. 30-40

Dareva, Velislava: *Detsa na ljubovta (Children of love).* In: Komsomolska iskra (Comsomol flame), 4/1978, p. 8

Dimitrov, Georgi: *Săčinenie (Works),* vol. 14. Sofia 1955

Dinkova, Maria: *Labirinti na lekomislieto i bezotgovornostt* (Labyrinths of Carelessness and Irresponsibility). In: Ženata dnes (Woman today), 7/1972, p. 6

Dinkova, Marija: *Săvremennoto bălgarsko semejstvo* (Today's Bulgarian family). Sofia 1976

Dobrianov, Velitchko et al.: *Bulgaria.* In: Bodrova/Anker (Ed.): *Working Women in Socialist Countries: The Fertility Connection.* Genf 1985, 57-91

Doceva, St.: *Majkata i sazrjavaštata devojka* (The Mother and the Adolescent Girl). In: Zdrave (Health), 9/1965, p. 9-10

Dolinski, N.V.: *Količestven săstav na bălgarskoto domakinstvo, osobeno na selskoto* (Quantitative Structure of the Bulgarian Household, Especially the Peasant One). In: Godišnik na Visšeto tărgovsko učilište. (Annual of the Higher Trade School). Varna 1930, p. 3-53

Encheva, Anastassia: *Public Care of the Family and Children.* Sofia 1980

Georgiev, Plamen: *Protivodejstvie na predrasădaka* (Counteraction against the Prejudices). In: Narodna mladež (People's Youth), 17/1978, p. 4

Gotkowitz, Laura/Turtis Richard: *Socialist Morality: Preference, Family, and State Intervention in Cuba.* In: Socialism and Democracy, 6/1988, p. 7-29

Höpken, Wolfgang: *Demographische Entwicklung und Bevölkerungspolitik in Bulgarien.* In: Südosteuropa, 2/ 1986, p. 88-99

Iliev, Ilija: *Familie, Ideologie und Politik: Die Großmutter in der städtischen Familie seit 1945.* In: Brunnbauer, Ulf/Kaser, Karl (Eds.): *Vom Nutzen der Verwandten. Soziale Netzwerke in Bulgarien (19. und 20. Jahrhundert).* Wien/Köln/Weimar 2001, p. 89-114

Ilieva, Nikolina (Ed.): *Ženata v Narodnata Republika Bălgarija. Sotsialno-ikonomičeski pridobivki* (The Woman in People's Republic of Bulgaria. Socio-Economic Gains). Spravočnik (Reference book). Sofia 1989.

Ilieva, Violeta: *Čuždata žena, kojato me e rodila* (The Unknown Woman, who Gave Birth to me) In: Ženata dnes (The Woman Today), 5/1972, p. 19

Ivanova, Slavka: *The social policy of the People's Republic of Bulgaria and the problem of welfare in socialism.* In: Deacon/Szalai (Eds.): *Social Policy in the New Eastern Europe. What Future for Socialist Welfare?* Aldershot 1990, p. 121-32

Kassabova, Anelia: *Begrenzte Transformation oder Transformation der Begrenztheiten? Politik und uneheliche Geburten im sozialistischen Bulgarien.* In: Brunnbauer, Ulf/Höpken, Wolfgang (Eds.): *Transformationsprobleme Bulgariens im 19. und 20. Jahrhundert. Historische und Ethnologische Perspektiven.* München 2007, p. 125-148

Kassabova, Anelia: *Der Diskurs über die Reproduktion im sozialistischen Bulgarien – Eingriff und Realitätsverleugnung.* In: Pasteur/Niederacher/Mesner (Eds.): *Sexualität, Unterschichtenmilieus und ArbeiterInnenbewegung.* Wien 2003, 217-228

Kassabova, Anelia: *Neue alte Normen. Die versuchte Normierung der Sexualität im sozialistischen Bulgarien.* In: Ethnologia Balkanica, 8/2004, p. 155-178

Keremendčieva, Mariana: *Fertilnoto povedenie na bălgarskoto semejstvo* (Fertility Behaviour of the Bulgarian Family). In: Bălgarska akademija na naukite (Ed.): *Semejstvo i sotsialno-demografsko razvitie* (The Family and the Socio-Demographic Development). Sofia 1982, p. 227-236

Kiselinčev, Asen: *Za kapitalističeskite otživelitsi v săznanieto i bita na trudeštite se i preodoljavaneto im* (About the Capitalistic Anachronisms in the Consciousness and Way of Life of the Working People and About their Overcoming). Sofia 1956

Kjuranov, Čavdar (Ed.): *Dnešnoto bălgarsko semejstvo* (Today's Bulgarian Family). Sofia 1987

Konstantinov, Dimitar: *Te zaslužavat uvaženie* (They Deserve Respect). In: Narodna mladež (People's Youth), 17/1978, p. 4

Konstantinov, Yulian: *Nahrung vom Dorf, Beziehungen durch die Stadt. Über den gegenwärtigen Charakter des bulgarischen Land-Stadt-Haushalts.* In: Brunnbauer, Ulf/Kaser, Karl (Eds.): *Vom Nutzen der Verwandten. Soziale Netzwerke in Bulgarien (19. und 20. Jahrhundert).* Wien/Köln/Weimar 2001, p. 43-67

Kostadinov, Dimităr: *Koj e baštata?* (Who is the Father?). Sofia 1982

Kubadinski, Penčo: *Za sotsialističeskoto semejstvo* (About the socialist family). Sofia 1986

Markova, Stanka/Apostolov, Miladin: *Intimen razgovor s mladežta* (Intimate/Personal Conversation with the Youth). Sofia 1983

Martinova, Margarita: *Kukuvitsi jaitsa v gnezdoto na blagočestieto* (Cuckoo's Eggs in the Nest of the Devotion). In: Narodna mladež (People's Youth), 7/1978, p. 4

Mevoriah, Nisim: *Komunističeskiiat moral i semejstvoto* (Communist Morality and the Family). Sofia 1956

Minkov, Minko (Ed.): *Harakteristika na bălgarskoto naselenie. Trudovi văzmožnosti i realizatsija* (The characteristics of the Bulgarian population. Employment Opportunities and their Realization). Sofia 1984

Močeva, Hristina: *Selskoto zemedelsko domakinstvo v Bălgarija prez 1935/36 godina: bjudžet, obstanovka i razhod na trud* (The Farming Peasant Household in Bulgaria in 1935/1936: Budget, Conditions and Labour Costs). Sofia 1938

Peševa, Rajna: *Buržuazni otstatătsi v otnošenijata kăm ženata* (Bourgeois Remnants in the Attitudes Towards Woman). Sofia 1962a

Peševa, Rajna: *Religiozni zabludi* (Religious fallacies). Sofia 1962b

Peševa, Rajna: *Da săzdadem novi bitovi tradicii* (Let's create new everyday traditions). Sofia 1963

Peševa, Rajna: *Cărkovnijat obred pri braka – otživelica ot minaloto* (The church ritual of marriage: a remnant from the past) . In: Semejstvoto v socialističeskoto obštestvo (The Family and the Socialist Society). Sofia 1964, p. 29-40

Politbureau: *Za izdigane roljata na ženata v izgraždaneto na razvitoto sotsialističesko obštestvo. Rešenie na Politbiuro na TsK na BKP ot 6 mart 1973 g.* (For the Raise of the Role of Woman in the Building of the Developed Socialist Society. Decision of the Politburo of the Central Committee of the Bulgarian Communist Party from March 6, 1973). Sofia 1977

Popova, Pavlina: *Stop, 'Žulieti', stop! (Stopp, Juliettes, stopp!)*. In: Ženata Dnes (The Woman Today), 9/1972, p. 14-15

Sanders, Irwin: *Balkan Village*. Westport 1949

Sanders, Irwin: *Factors Influencing the Contemporary Bulgarian Family*. In: Tony Butler (Ed.), *Bulgaria. Past and Present*. Columbus/Ohio 1976, p. 164-170

Semeen kodeks (Family Code). Sofia 1968

Semeen kodeks (Family Code*)*. Sofia 1985

Semejstvo i komunističeskoto văzpitanie (The family and communist education). Sofia 1968

Semejstvoto v sotsialističeskoto obštestvo [The family in the socialist society]. Sofia 1961.

Spasovska, Liljana: *Rabotničeskijat bit. Sotsiologičeski aspekti* (The workers' way of life. Sociological aspects). Sofia 1976

Stamatov, Atanas: *Problemăt za 'baštite'* (The problem of the 'fathers'). In: Narodna mladež (People's Youth), 17/1978, p. 4

Vassilev, Dimiter: *Bulgaria*. In: Henry P. David (Ed.): *From Abortion to Contraception. A Resource to Public Policies and Reproductive Behaviour in Central and Eastern Europe from 1917 to the Present*. Westport, London 1999, p. 69-89

Vidova, Maria et al. (Eds.): *100 Questions and Answers Concerning Bulgarian Women*. Sofia 1983

Ženata v stopanskija, obštestvenija, kulturnija život i v semejstvoto (The woman in economic, public, and cultural life and in the family). Sofia 1972

Archives:

Central State Archive, Sofia (abbreviated as TsDA), State Archive Sofia (abbreviated as DA Sofia)

Periodicals:

Dăržaven vestnik; Statističeski godisnik (ed. by Centralno statističesko upravlenie)

Kristina Popova

Under the Scarlet Scarf: The Education of Pioneer Troop Leaders During Socialism

"The most cherished wealth of the Bulgarian People, which they keep as the apple of their eye, are their children. The song of the children rings in towns and villages, and fills the country of Georgi Dimitrov with cheerfulness and joy. Wherever you go in Bulgaria, you will see happy children with scarlet scarves. They are the Bulgarian Pioneers. They love to go to school, to play in the stadiums, to sing and dance on open-air stages and concert platforms, to visit their country side, museums and places of historical interest, where they learn about the heroic events of the past (...) Joyful groups of Pioneer children cross the co-operative fields to yield the wheat, to mow the meadows, and to pick up herbs and fruits. You can see the Pioneers wherever there is something of interest and amusement to them. The Pioneer organization is entirely voluntary. It is under the direct supervision of the Dimitrov Communist Youth Union, which appoints its best members as Pioneer instructors." (Asen Bosev 1959, p. 4)

The Beginning

The foundation of the Children's Pioneer Organization '*Septemvrijche*' was proclaimed on 23. September 1944 – only two weeks after the takeover of the Fatherlands Front[1] in Bulgaria took place, supported by the Soviet Red Army. Initially the new organization was created as a children's section of the youth organization of the Communist Party – uniting only the children of the so called 'revolution activists'. 1945 '*Septemvrijche*' was attached to the Fatherlands Front to organize all children in the country. In the beginning of 1946, the Ministry of Education declared a new statute which integrated the pioneer organization into the school system. In every school a unit named 'band' (*druzhina*) had to be organized for all children until the age of 14 – and every school class became a group named 'smaller band' (*cheta*). Every pioneer band had its name, usually a hero or a patron, who had taken part in revolutionary struggles in the past. Later on, the bands were also named after socialist heroes or space men.

---

[1] which was led by the Communist Party

Until 1947 '*Septemvrijche*' was only one organization inside the pluralistic political system in Bulgaria. Other political parties (as the agrarian Party and the social-democrats) organized their children's units too. Even the Orthodox Church had its own child organization. There were also hundred local units of the 'Union for Child Protection' in Bulgaria which continued their activities, organizing summer camps or soup kitchens.

After the repression of the political opposition in 1947 and the creation of the unified 'Union of the People's Youth', '*Septemvrijche*' became the only child organization in Bulgaria and existed under these monopolistic political and organizational conditions until 1990.

In the same year, the symbol of the pioneers organization was introduced: It was a red scarf, which also became part of the school uniforms and presented different signs for the leaders. Additionally gestures, slogans and other symbols were implemented. The red scarf made the pioneers visible in the family, in the streets, everywhere. The view of their smart lines and orders, singing songs, was created to support the vision of a well organized social order in the country.

In the end of the 1940s local pioneer homes started to be opened. These centers were the place where the troop leaders offered a lot of activities for the young pioneers – separated from the school system.[2] The purpose of the pioneer homes was to give the young pioneers the opportunity to develop their interests in special circles, to touch the world of science and arts, and to reflect different professional perspectives.[3]

According to the political and educational ideals, a local pioneer home had a meeting room, a room of the socialist heroes (Stalin, Dimitrov, Lenin and others), a celebration room, a fairytale room, a library where also discussions about books took place, and rooms for different scientific, agricultural or technical groups and circles.[4] It was a place where the communist cult as well as leisure activities and needs of everyday life had to be united. These pioneer homes were located at important places in the socialist topography - first of all at the Pioneer Palace in Sofia.[5]

---

[2] Vinagi gotov, Dokumenti i reshenija za dejnostta na DPO "Septemvrijche" 1975, p.158
[3] ibid.
[4] cf. Parvanov 2004
[5] cf. Dzedzeva 1962

Theory and Concepts

'*Septemvrijche*' implemented the Soviet pioneer model, which was established in the late 1920s and 1930s. It became a very important element of the official social policy, supporting the political education of children and families and organizing children's leisure activities. '*Septemvrijche*' also helped to communicate the image of a happy childhood as a sign of the happy future of socialism towards the whole society. Lenin's wife, Nadezhda Krupskaja, was often cited as one of the main authors of the theoretical foundation of the pioneers work. According to her, the pioneers were no organization made 'for the children', but made 'by the children'. The main topic of their concepts was the 'self activity' (*samodejnost*), which had nothing to do with 'anarchy', but with a well organized systematical work, based on the initiative of the children. The competence to do so, was a knowledge that had to be imparted by the troop leaders,[6] who were specially trained "to support the initiative of the pioneers in the most effective way."[7]

Krupskaja focused in her book 'Pioneer Movement and school' (*Pionerdvizhenie i shkola*) not only the most relevant relationship between the pioneer organization and the school, but also the education and training of the pioneer troop leaders. She pointed out that the troop leaders had to avoid any dissociation between the activists pioneer group and other children[8]. As the most important goals of pioneer work she underlined the ideas of education, service for the public and physical training. To understand what exactly this concept meant, the Bulgarian chief leaders of '*Septemvrijche*' visited for the first time the SU in the summer 1945 in order to learn from the Soviet example.

To motivate young people to become a troop leader, different incentives had to be set up. The main incentive was the privilege to be invited to famous holiday accommodations. In 1925 in the place of Artek, at the Black Sea, a former sanatorium became the central place, where the happy childhood of the Soviet Pioneers could be presented. Every year, thousand of the best pioneers were selected to spend their holidays in Artek, as the highest award for their activities. Artek became also a place for training courses of pioneer troop leaders. In the 1930s and 1940s many films about Artek were produced

---

[6] ibid., p. 8.
[7] Karpelceva 1953, p. 2
[8] Krupskaja: Pionerdvizhenie I shkola, p. 213 (cited after Oshanin 1953). cf. also N. Krupskaja 1949.

in order to show both the Soviet and the international public, how happy soviet pioneers did live.

In 1949 the first group of Bulgarian pioneer activists were awarded to be sent to Artek. Since then, each year the best pioneers in Bulgaria spent a few weeks in this place. Thus, Artek became an utopian 'Pioneer realm' where a cloudless childhood as a symbol of the communist future could be seen. It was the most important place of the imagined topography of the socialist childhood which remained a pioneer dream for many generations.

The Pioneer Troop Leader

To organize the schoolchildren as pioneers, thousands of troop leaders were needed. In 1945 a journal called 'New Shift' (*Bodra smjana*) started to be published in order to instruct the increasing number of these young people. In the beginning the leaders were trained only in short courses. Parallel to their political and educational work, they had to solve mainly the practical problems of the postwar period – connected to health and food. Many young people were eager to do this job, because the summer camps helped to survive both, children and troop leaders, giving them enough meals and clothes.

The control over the troop leaders´ work was not very strict, because it included only some basic pedagogical criteria. As the vocational training was rather short, the 'inborn' organizational competences and the ideological devotion seemed to be more important.

The pioneer troop leaders had to create some kind of friendly atmosphere, and to be accepted as a close confidant by the children. They should always be ready to support the self-organization of the children, sitting near to them during the meetings. But they were not only responsible for 'leadership and initiative', but also for 'freedom and discipline'. In the journal '*Bodra smjana*' some authors tried to overturn the antagonism of freedom and discipline. They argued that discipline is necessary, although it has to be developed voluntarily, and not implemented by force: "Today we are free to create our own history by using the laws of history and be obedient to these laws."[9] Another important point of the pioneers´ conception was the work with the so called 'pioneer activists', a group of trustworthy children, who

---

[9] Zaimov 1946

assisted the initiatives of the leaders, and whose authority was accepted by the other children in the unit.[10]

At local and national meetings, the pioneer band leaders discussed their practical work to exchange their experiences and to deliver best practice models to the others. 1952 the band leader Vera Popova was chosen as an excellent example for her elaborations on the topics: "Following the steps of the partisan unit 'Anton Ivanov'", "The April Rebellion" (against the Ottoman Empire in 1976), and: "The socialist architecture in our country". She wrote: "The pioneers went to old veterans, who described the living conditions in the town of Batak in the past. In the preparation of the meeting many pioneers and teachers were engaged. In the units the tasks were divided with the aim to study the Batak local history as well as (...) to ask old men and women to tell about the Batak massacre. The choir prepared old folk songs, the dance group studied local folk dances. The pioneers visited the old church, where an old man told them about the massacre (1876). They saw the bones, which are preserved there and - at the place where Batak citizens were killed - the walls sprinkled with blood. The pioneers became more conscious about what happened there, and they were proud, that their ancestors were so courageous people."[11]

This report of a troop leader shows, that the activities of the organization were not only addressed to the children, but to a wider public. The intention of these kind of statements was to eliminate obsolete ideals:[12] In the first years, it was the influence of priests, church and other religious institutions, as well the influence of the bourgeois relicts. Later on, it was the western capitalistic influence which had to be eliminated. Therefore historical, geographical or sportive topics should always be presented with a political background. Activities, where pioneer units had 'only' taken pictures to prepare a photo album or to collect herbs and plants to prepare a herbarium[13] were increasingly criticized, because they were considered to be not 'political minded' enough.

Nevertheless, the favorite subjects of the pioneer troop leaders' work did not really change. Patriotic, geographical and historical topics still remained on the agenda, like: 'Our country – a flourish garden', or: 'Planting of a

---

[10] Oshanin 1953, p. 43-45
[11] Materials of the national meetings of pioneer troop leaders, cited according to Oshanin, 1953, p. 32-33
[12] Paunova 2003, p. 208-219
[13] Oshanin 1953, p. 36

Pioneer Forest'. But there was also health promotion, like: 'Cleanse, health and beauty', or pure political education, like: 'The Ministry of Inner Affairs through the eyes of a pioneer'.[14]

The pioneer troop leaders' work represented a balance between political truth, organizational enthusiasm and pedagogical professionalism. "We have to give the organization true, well prepared, enthusiastic leaders. Leaders who are able to develop an interesting and rich life in the units, and who will assure the real revolutionary antifascist character of the organization."[15]

Therefore the political devotion was – besides other personal qualities – the most important assumption for pioneer leaders. In order to work against 'the class enemy', '*Bodra smjana*' recommended to avoid troop leaders with 'a wrong class background': "It is not possible that sons and daughters of former industrials, fired military officers, kulaks or members of nationalistic organizations will educate our young Septembrists in a socialist spirit."[16]

On the Way to Professionalization

In the beginning, the most important qualifications of the pioneer troop leaders were described as "enthusiastic, devoted, willing to work". But later on, '*Bodra smjana*' argued that these attributes were not sufficient without pedagogical training.[17]

Therefore, already in 1949 the professionalization of the pioneer work was initialized by the foundation of a school for pioneer troop leaders named 'Anton Makarenko' in Sofia. The education there lasted two years. The curricula included: pioneer work, pedagogy, geography, sport, music, history of the Bulgarian Communist party as well as of the Communist Party in USSR, languages: Russian and Bulgarian). Most of the students were women. All of them were selected by the local authorities of the Youth Organization.[18]

According to the words of Kostadina Spassova, headmistress of the 'Anton Makarenko Institute', the new shift to more professional skills should not eliminate the political grounding of the pioneers. She pointed out that the

---

14 Instruction: V pomosht na druzhinnite rukuvoditeli, no. 17/1978
15 Bodra smjana, no. 1/1945
16 Koen 1948
17 cf. ibid., p.1-3
18 Trenev 1987, p. 40

main purpose of the pioneer troop leaders was to create 'the new child', 'the builder of the socialist society'. On the occasion of the first examination in 1950, she said: "Comrades, young pioneer group leaders, graduates of the 'Institute Makarenko', there are unlimited horizons in front of you. The new shift is waiting for you!"[19]

In the 1960s and 1970s the pioneer troop leaders´ work became an academic discipline as well as a scientific research topic. Students in pedagogy studied this discipline and were allowed to choose it as their specialization and future profession. Until 1976, 12 PhD dissertations in this scientific area were written.[20] Social psychologists started to study the structure of the pioneer groups and the shaping of the public opinion processes in the collective.[21]

In 1969 (after the radical protests of the western youth and after the Prague Spring 1968) an 'Institute for Youth Research' at the 'Dimitrov Communist Youth Union' was opened. One of the main subjects of research was the role of the pioneer troop leaders in the school system: "The pioneer troop leaders are (...) personally responsible for the continuous development and the effectiveness of the public activities of the pupils"[22] – in cooperation with the school director as well as with the communist party secretary.

In fact, the normal place of the troop leaders in school was located between the teachers and the children, which made their work often invisible for both sides. The idea to stress the 'self-activity' of the children, to 'help' and to 'support' their initiatives, made their own work more or less 'anonymous'.[23]

Also the official agenda complicated the situation of the troop leaders. One of the studies about the pioneers' work presented the following weekly agenda:

"3-4 hours for meetings with the school board; 10-12 hours for individual work with single pioneers, teachers and public persons; 6-7 hours for visiting the units; 3-4 hours for the discussion of special problems together with other troop leaders; 10-11 hours for preparation of forthcoming activities; 4-5 hours for meetings with the school director and Com-

---

[19] Album na purvija vipusk na Institute 'Makarenko', 1949/50, p. 3
[20] Stanoev 1977, p. 9
[21] Markova 1975
[22] Stanoev 1977, p. 298
[23] I asked more than 40 people to tell me the names of their pioneer troop leaders at school. Nobody remembered the name, but everybody remembered their outlook.

munist Party Secretary; 6-7 hours for other technical, social and school activities. Totally: 42 to 50 working hours a week."[24]

The results of the research projects showed not only the bureaucratization of the profession. Analyzing the changes of the pioneer work after Stalin's death in 1953, the Bulgarian sociologist Svetlana Paunova wrote in her article "Forming the future socialist citizen" that in the 1960s the pioneer troop leaders had no more the mission 'to form' the pioneers, but to work with the real existing pioneers.[25] The troop leaders' work was considered as a process of communication, not as a 'leadership'.[26] And the pioneers themselves were recognized more than 'children' than as 'small communists'.[27]

The gender bias of the pioneer troop leaders' existence became obvious too: The studies underlined that 'troop leading' remained more a temporary job than a lifelong profession. Therefore it became a 'typical job' for women. Although since the beginning the pioneer organization was open for both, men and women, in the end of the 1940s most of the pioneer leaders were women. In the next decades the tendency for men to avoid these activities increased - and finally it become an entirely female position.

Nevertheless, the troop leaders work was not considered as an easy job, because it included too many challenges and responsibilities. But it was not enough appreciated neither by the political nor by the school authorities. The female troop leaders invested an enormous amount of hours in the preparation of celebrations, meetings and discussions and in the organization of the pioneers' leisure activities – always following the prescriptions of different political and institutional authorities. They had to be near the children, pretending to be one of them, supporting their 'self activities' according to programs and plans. But their work was not visible – and their history remaines behind the scarlet scarf.

References

Bosev, Asen: 15 Years of the Septemvrijche Dimitrov Pioneer Organization, Sofia 1959

---

[24] Stanoev 1977, p. 298
[25] Paunova 2003, p. 208-219
[26] ibid.
[27] ibid.

Christova Donka: Ljato kraj Slaveevi gori, Razkazva edna otrjadna rukovoditelka (A Summer near the Nightingale Forests), Sofia 1962
Dzedzeva, Tamara: Palace of Dawn, Sofia 1962
Koen, Albert: Klassovo vuzpitanie (Class education). In: Bodra smjana, 2/1948, p. 4
Krupskaja, Nadezhda: Pionerdvizhenie i shkola (Pioneers movement and school). In: Pedagogicheskie Sochinenija, vol. 5, p. 213
Krupskaja, Nadezhda: Za vuzpitanieto i obuchenieto (about education and teaching), Sofia 1949
Markova, Violeta: Formirane na obshestvenoto mnenie v pionerskija otrjad (Origins of the Social opinion in the pioneer's troop), Sofia 1975
Oshanin, Dimitar: Samodejnost I rukuvodstvo v pionerskata organizatzija (Selfactivity and leadership in the pioneer organization), Sofia 1953
Parvanov, Petar: DPO Septemvrijche (MA thesis at 'Neofit Rilski' University) Blagoevgrad 2004
Svetlana, Paunova: Formirane na budeshtija socialisticheski grazhdanin (Opit vurhu DPO 'Septemvrijche') (Shaping the socialist citizen of the future). In: Sociologicheski problemi, 1-2/2003, p. 208-219
Stanoev, Ljuben et al: Theorija i metodika na pionerskata i komsomolskata rabota (Theory of the pioneer's and Comsomol's work) (Textbook), Sofia 1977
Trenev, Ivan: Zapovjadvajte na shastieto, Letopis na DPO 'Septemvrijche' (Order to the happyness. A chronology of DPO Septemvrijche), Sofia 1987
Zaimov, Purvan: Za disziplinata i svobodata (About dicipline and freedom). In: Bodra smjana, 9/1946

Periodicals:

Bodra smjana (New Shift)
Sociologicheski problemi (Sociological Problems)
Uchilishtna praktika (School Practice)
Pionerski rukovoditel (Pioneer Leader)

Lenka Kalinová

Conditions and Stages of Change in the Social Security System in Czechoslovakia (1945 - 1989)

In the Czech lands there exists a long tradition of social security. Its roots reach back to the end of the 18th century when pensions for state employees were granted and when, in 1887/88, obligatory accident and health insurance among workers was introduced. Since its founding as an independent state in 1918 the Czechoslovak Republic was one of the most socially-oriented states at that time on the European continent. It was the Social Democratic Party's strong representation until 1938, that contributed to this situation. In 1924 social security insurance was introduced according to categories: for instance state and public employees had their own social insurance. These features continued until 1948 when all types of insurance were combined within one single system by the Law of National Insurance.

The Establishment of a National Insurance Program

The establishment of a National Insurance derived from ideas prominent during the 1930s to avoid the causes of economic crises, especially the great crisis of the 1930s that threatened the very existence of free market economy. The ideas of Keynes brought a revolutionary change in the economic theory based on the idea that the elimination of wide-spread unemployment and poverty would make it possible to avoid unrest, revolution, and consequently state socialism. Thus, in 1941, the British government set up a special committee to prepare a reform of the social system. This project, submitted in 1942 by William Beveridge[1], attracted great attention in the world, and became the model for many countries and international organizations.

During the war, these ideas inspired the Czechoslovak foreign resistance movement, preparing the proposal for a future social insurance model. The democratic and communist resistance groups were active in initializing a government program for the reforms in the post-war era, the Revolutionary

---

[1] Social Report by Sir W. Beveridge: *Social Insurance and Allied Services*. London 1942

Labor Movement[2] (*Revoluční odborové hnutí – ROH*), in particular. The other political parties agreed, and thus it became part of the official program of the first post-war Czechoslovak government. The government committed itself to social security for all citizens in case of unemployment, illness, or old age. It also planned to provide free medical care to all citizens.

After the painful experience of the 1930s, when Czechoslovakia had one of the highest unemployment rates in Europe (reaching 20%, with 32% among the working class), the conviction prevailed among a great part of the population, especially the workers, that only a change in society could provide an assured level of income and social protection. At that time the idea of justice was connected to socialism, which was supposed to result in a fair distribution not only of income, but of property as well. This was also the idea behind the demand to nationalize industry and the banks, which was realized in the end of 1945. During the subsequent years nationalization was continued by including smaller businesses as well.

An important step towards a 'just distribution of income' was the manner in which a monetary reform was implemented at the end of 1945. Its goal was to eliminate 'starvation wages', which meant raising the income of lower-paid groups, especially workers. The lowest wages under index 442 and the middle income levels under index 141 were increased, while the highest wages were not raised at all. This wage adjustment created the basic wage structure, which, with minor changes, remained the same throughout the entire period of state socialism.[3] Similar to the leveling of wages, the system of social security was also reorganized. Compared to the pre-war state of affairs not only income, but pensions and sick pay in the state and public sector were lowered, and particularly the income of the working class was raised. At that time business income was lowered, as well as income from capital and real estate.

Between 1945 and 1948 the laws for National Insurance, was changed to eliminate existing differences in the retirement security for individual groups of the population. The proposed law was extraordinary for its time; it contained certain aspects of universality. It aimed at protecting children, mothers, and all citizens in case of illness, old age, disability, loss of a breadwinner and other social difficulties as well as the right to free education and medical care. It also included the institutional reconstruction of the earlier social insurance, the liquidation of many insurance companies, and the establishment of a National Insurance. Due to the opposition of some of the politi-

---

[2] Kalinová 2004
[3] Kalinová 2004, p. 70 -74

cal parties and officials of the former insurance companies, the proposed law was not passed before the takeover in 1948.

In the three years after the war deep changes took place under pressure from the working class movement, the labor unions and due to the initiative of the Communist Party. As a result of nationalization and land reform, property was redistributed and the differences between the incomes of high- and low-income groups should be adjusted.

The nationalization of industry, mines and banks, as well as the redistribution of land among small and medium-sized farmers became an important tool for the Communist Party in the 1946 elections. In the Bohemian part of the republic the Communist Party gained over 40% of all votes. The general politics under the conditions of revolutionary sentiments among workers, the weakness of the other political parties and the fact that the party was supported by most of the media and influential artists were factors that made it possible for the Communist Party to assume the command in 1948.

Immediately after the takeover in February 1948, the law on National Insurance was passed with great fanfare, meant to show the ruling party's will to fulfill its promises. In reality, it was never fully brought to life; already in 1949 it was officially criticized, afterwards it was gradually amended and then rescinded.

The Revocation of the National Insurance and the Move to a Nationalized Social Security

In the period between 1948 and 1953 the Soviet model of central planning was imposed, laid down in the five-year plan of 1951. As a result of escalating international tensions a change in the political course was made, based on the theory of the "intensification of class struggle in the process of building up the socialism". The application of this theory, not only in Czechoslovakia, but also in the other countries of the Soviet bloc, caused the liquidation of private small companies, both in urban and rural areas. Corresponding to the 'hard political course' a revision of social policy was introduced. The abolishment of social payments for private farmers and self-employed artisans, along with a ban on providing employment in private companies, became part of a program of 'limiting and repressing' private enterprises. These and other political measures forced private farmers and artisans to join agricultural and production cooperatives.

Under the constant threat of military conflict, Czechoslovakia became the 'industrial powerhouse of the socialist camp'. The plans required a fundamental restructuring of the economy, with far-reaching political and social consequences. The high costs of building up the heavy industry and the arms factories (the arms industry accounted for 10 % of the national product) produced a persistent shortage of the basic consumer needs.

When higher demands were made in the field of social politics, characterized by an extraordinary transfer of men into heavy industry and women into light industry, a reevaluation of social policies began. According to the ideology of the ruling party, there should be no poor or needy persons under socialism, and therefore no need for social welfare, which was regarded as a relic of the capitalist past. Therefore, institutions based on the initiative and solidarity of private activities were gradually closed down. In 1951, the Ministry of Labor and Social Affairs was dissolved, and in its place a Ministry of Labor, responsible for the organization of a social network, was established. Its task was to ensure the mobilization of workers, including temporary workers, for the mines, steel mills and heavy machinery industries in order to fulfill the excessively demanding plans for production in those sectors.

At that time the process of nationalizing the social institutions began: In 1951, health insurance was separated from retirement insurance and organized by the Labor Unions, which had to administer the funds from the state budget for sick pay. It had to be paid out by the enterprises, which in this way could control the validity of sick-leave claims. Financing for retirement security was taken over by the State Office of Social Security.

After 1952, the method of financing social security began to change. Contributions from employers and employees to social insurance became part of the income tax. Thus the insurance system was turned into a scheme of 'social security' that was centrally-directed. Officially this term was introduced in 1956, although the term did still not exactly describe reality. Social security was a catch-all phrase for the institutions that provide social payments and services to all citizens, in which payments are only partially tied to insurance. In reality, this kind of social security was restricted on the basis of the 'class' principle. For some members of the agricultural cooperatives and for the remaining private farmers, social security was limited.

After 1952, the health care system was organized according to the territorial principle. It was provided free of charge for employees, but members of agricultural cooperatives had only a right to limited health care and in case of illness did not receive sick pay.

The overall situation after the great changes in the social sphere and the reduction of previous benefits, for example a Christmas bonus and some other benefits, caused dissatisfaction and strikes of workers. Due to the general shortage of some kinds of foods and industrial goods, the rationing system was maintained for eight years after the end of the war. Free sale of some goods was introduced, but at a much higher price than on the market. The dissatisfaction of workers, especially in the large factories, produced increasing social tension.

The situation was to be solved through a monetary reform, according to which savings were exchanged at a rate of one to five, and greater amounts of savings at one to fifty, which affected the already modest savings of the working class. For this reason the monetary reform provoked a storm of unrest with strikes and demonstrations in several cities.[4] Against the background of the change in the social atmosphere, the government adopted a number of measures in the second half of 1953 designed to increase the income of the population. Lowering prices and increasing the production of consumer goods was one of the measures that improved the living conditions and the temper among the population.

At the beginning of the 1960s the speed of economic growth slowed down and in 1962 the economic expansion came to a halt. Consequently, in social policy a number of austerity measures had to be taken, such as lowering the subsidies on the prices of some services, which led to a reduction of children's facilities while the price of children's clothing rose, and placing a tax on retirement benefits above 700 crowns.

Since the end of the 1950s the ideological pressure had been eased to some extent. People began to lose their fears and room was given for spreading new ideas. As a result important works of literature and films were released, and there was some progress concerning new scientific and especially economic ideas. In this climate the project to realize more significant economic reforms was developed.[5] Its main goal was to reduce central planning and the corresponding directives to a certain extent, and to allow some market elements that would encourage the willingness of enterprises and employees to act on their own initiative. The first steps to introduce these reforms met with the citizens' interest and led to an increase in their activities.

---

[4] cf. Heumos 2006, p. 64/78/79
[5] Šulc 1998, p. 40-45

The Social Program of the 1960s

One part of the economic reform was a large-scale project of social improvements. It contained ideas of a conceptual nature as well as important suggestions for solving immediate problems. Among other things it included measures such as compensating for price changes, raising nominal wages and increasing the social income, especially with regard to supporting families with children in order to achieve a higher birth rate. In 1968 the lowest retirement payments were also raised to a certain extent.[6]

The most important document for economic, political and social reform was the Action Program of the Communist Party, adopted in April 1968. It emphasized that in order to take advantage of the citizens' initiative, it required a 'new type of democracy', which should also apply to the economic sphere. It confirmed the previously-discussed issue of creating democratic bodies in the enterprises. It was an important impulse, not only defending the interests of workers, but also dealing with the affairs of the enterprises and the society as a whole.

During the period of the so-called Prague Spring of 1968 the climate in society changed; discussions took place at large gatherings where mostly young people criticized the past problematical developments in the economy and society, and demanded change. The development towards more democracy came to a halt on August 21st 1968, when the country was occupied by the armies of the Warsaw Pact countries. Peaceful resistance by the population prevented an immediate political overthrow and change of the government. The striving for democratic reforms was really stopped by gradually curtailing the free press and by removing the party leadership led by Alexander Dubček and other reformist officials responsible for the Prague Spring from power.[7] Their replacement meant the gradual revocation of previous reform measures and the restoration of the former system. The new leadership called this process 'normalization', but in reality it was not able to silence society completely – even when, in November 1969, the resistance was partially paralyzed by the security forces.

---

[6] Kalinová 1998, p.268-270
[7] Kalinová 1999, p. 9-16

Social Security and the Agony of Communism

The process of silencing public resistance was accompanied by abolishing all legal and other norms. The greatest damage to society was done by the subsequent purge, the removal of all the political, economic and cultural elites whose representatives had taken part in the reform process. Less competent people who submitted to the new leadership and the anti-reform course took their places.

The only adopted document from the reform movement was the social program, without acknowledging its origin, however. It was an attempt to use the social benefits to regain the lost trust, especially of young people, whose resistance the new leadership feared most. Therefore several measures to support birthrates were adopted, since they had fallen during the previous years. In 1968, maternity leave was extended to 26 weeks and in 1970 a benefit payment of 500 crowns a month was introduced to support mothers caring for two children, if one of them was less than a year old. The benefit paid upon the birth of a child varied between 1000 and 2000 crowns. Family allowances were raised according to the number of children, from 90 cr. for one child to 1230 cr. for four children. Other measures designed to aid young people included subsidized loans for young married couples for a period of ten years, and even allowed partial forgiveness of debt upon the birth of a child.

The measures taken to increase the birthrate and an increased number of women of childbearing age born after the war led to a marked population boom. The number of live births per 1,000 people in the Czech Republic increased from 16 in 1970 to nearly 20 in 1974. In Slovakia the birthrate was higher and more consistent throughout the entire period, but in Bohemia the birthrate began again to decline in the 1980s. Retirement pensions which had fallen since 1964 as a proportion of the average wage from 57 % to 48.5 % were raised.[8]

It was possible to increase social payments during the first half of the 1970s, also because the economic growth achieved in the previous reform years continued, and for this reason the ruling party made efforts to win the population over by improving social conditions.

At the start of the 1980s, economic growth began to slacken again and real incomes stagnated; thus it was necessary in the mid-1980s to raise pensions and child contributions. Again for political reasons, major changes in

---

[8] Historická statistická ročenka 1985. p. 416- 417

the social security system were adopted, but they could not be put into practice before the radical political change in November 1989.

The social security of the population during the era of state socialism was closely linked to the development of the economic and political situation. At a time when political power felt threatened, it endeavored to appease the population by improving social security, through full employment and increasing incomes, as well as social payments and services. If we compare their quality with that of other countries on the basis of quantitative data (like the share of the GDR spent on social protection including health care) it was not very high. Retirement pensions in particular were low, whereas the degree of compensation in health care, housing and other services, being either provided free or at state-subsidized low prices, was higher. This system thus provided all of its citizens with modest housing, care for mothers and children, health care and other services.[9]

With reference to maintaining social guarantees and social welfare, employment legislation also played an important role. The law forbade enterprises to dismiss an employee without the agreement of the labor organization and adhering to the protections set forth in the Labor Law. High employment among women was made possible not only, perhaps, by the relatively broad range of child care facilities, but also by other social advantages. After a two- or three-year maternity leave, women could return to their original workplace, and draw sickness benefits if a child became ill.

In studying the history of the social system under state socialism, the question can be posed what effects social security had in maintaining the system – and provoking its end.

Over those 40 years there was a series of crises and dissatisfaction about the way the country was governed, but basically a large part of the population did not oppose the system of socialism itself. In the 1970s the issues causing much resentment were political, but unlike in Poland social crisis was not the main factor for the fall of the regime. Therefore the population did not expect any great changes. Some of the factors causing the fall of communism were the economy and the undemocratic political system, and above all the external situation at the end of the 1980s, i.e. the crises in the other countries of Central and Eastern Europe, especially the situation in the Soviet Union. Another factor contributing to the removal of Communism was an incompetent and politically discredited party leadership, which had played an important part in taking back the positive developments achieved during the Prague

---

[9] Turek 1995, p. 60-71

Spring, and therefore could not afford to allow any changes that would resemble its ideas.

Even though social policy was not particularly generous, it provided the citizens with social guarantees allowing them to feel moderately comfortable, which was of great importance for the generations which had experienced the economic crisis. This issue was still given priority even after 1989, when part of the older generation made it clear that these securities were essentially important to them. It was a different situation with the younger generation, to whom, as in other countries, social guarantees were not sufficient, and, as time passed, neither were the values of the consumer society.

After 1989 the population, feeling euphoric after the political changes and having illusions about the new system, accepted the fact that social guarantees were limited. During the process of transformation there was a willingness to adapt from a paternalistic welfare state and the social comfort it provided, to a more frugal situation with fewer social securities. People were less nostalgic for the 'good old times' than in Hungary, for example, where especially in the 1970s and 1980s communism was less discredited than in the Czech Republic.

Review of Basic Stages of the Social Security System

Social insurance was introduced in the Czech lands along with Bismarck's insurance laws of the 1880s. Retirement insurance for state employees was introduced in 1909. In Czechoslovakia a law on social insurance was adopted in 1924. After the Second World War, following the model of the English National Insurance, a comprehensive law was passed on a scheme also called National Insurance encompassing all citizens and all social risks.

The term social assurance or security is broader than social insurance and was increasingly used after the Second World War by the democratic systems providing social rights to citizens. It is based on the 'Agreement of the International Labor Organization' on the minimum norms of social security adopted in 1944. This concept of social security includes social insurance, social support, social assistance and social services. Social security provides payments and services to citizens not only in anticipated socially difficult situations like old age, but also in case of illness and disability, maternity and for child rearing.

In the Law on National Insurance from April 1948 the former differences concerning the social security of citizens were ameliorated. It encompassed the security of employees as well as self-employed citizens in the event of old age, illness, disability, work injury or loss of a breadwinner. Under this law new types of payments were conceived, such as family allowances and a retirement pension for wives. The retirement insurance was regarded as delayed consumption. The previous social insurance companies for individual categories of employees were integrated gradually, and a Central National Insurance was established with offices in every region and district. The complete unification of social insurance was to be implemented step by step. However, these principles of a social insurance which was progressive at that time were never put into practice.

The preparation of changes in the National Insurance began as early as 1949, when it was accused of "not fulfilling the line on limiting and suppressing private enterprise". According to the amendment to the law on the National Insurance, health insurance was separated from retirement insurance and health care facilities were nationalized. This law laid down that the social security of self-employed persons was to be significantly limited. Sick pay was not to be paid to them at all.

Since the existence of the National Insurance as a public institution was not in accordance with efforts to centralize the state administration, it was abolished. Afterwards retirement insurance was administrated by the State Office for Retirement Security, and the employers were assigned responsibility for sickness compensation administrated by the Central Council of Labor.

From January 1st, 1953 the way of financing social insurance was also changed. The insurance previously paid by employers, employees and the state was integrated into the income tax. Social and health insurance was increasingly financed from the state budget. Thus the National Insurance was nationalized and changed into a social security system. The state guarantee of insurance funds was changed into security funds, which changed their fundamental nature. While the earlier retirement and national insurance was regarded as an obligatory part of the social security of citizens, its nationalization made it possible to redistribute funds according to determined preferences and to limit the privately awarded benefits enjoyed by state and public employees.

In 1956 a law was passed, revoking the former privileges of state and public employees under sickness compensation and retirement security. According to this law, workers and employees received the same sickness compensation of 60-90% of their wages (previously, workers had received 50-60% of their wages and state employees 6-13 weeks of full pay).

In 1957 a differentiated system of retirement payments subdivided into three categories was introduced. Employees of the 1st category, working in the coal and iron mines, received higher pensions and could retire at the age of 55. The second category was made up of employees in occupations exposed to heat, surface mines and other workplaces hazardous to health. Other employees belonged to the third category. Under this law the retirement age was lowered for women according to the number of their children, and the earlier system of dependants' insurance was abolished.

In 1964 retirement pensions above 700 crowns a month were taxed as a reaction to the economic stagnation. This was a revocation of the previously granted amount and deepened its leveling effect. Due to the rise in the cost of living starting in 1967 it became necessary to raise the lowest levels of pension pay. Even so, in 1970 the average level of pensions compared to the rapidly-increasing wages declined. It can also be concluded that the attitude towards social security was skeptical because of the fact that despite the increase in the number of people receiving pensions the difference in outlay as a percentage of GNP rose less than one percentage point during the 1960s. In 1962 it was decided to start improving retirement security for agricultural workers at the larger cooperative farms.

According to the social program of 1966, all mothers and children were to be provided equal security and a minimum social support paid to those for whom it was the only source of income was to be introduced. Retirement security was expanded in the 1960s to cover all citizens. Thus the number of retirees at the end of the 1960s basically approached the number of people of productive age (in 1960 2.209 million persons received a pension; in 1970 the number was 3.033 m).

Pensions were sharply differentiated according to the defined category and the date of claim. In the third income category, covering nearly 90% of the retirees, the average pension in 1968 was 844 crowns, whereas in the first category it was 1,683 crowns. On July 1st, 1968 the lowest pensions were increased.

During the first years of 'normalization' from 1969 to 1989, a number of measures were taken for the benefit of young families with children. The raise of price was halted and the renewal of central planning resulted in guaranteed employment. Pensions were increased in 1975 (law 121/1975); however, their real value had declined significantly. The fact that a limit of 2,500 crowns was fixed for the highest pensions in category III was a serious drawback for higher-paid employees.

Though the lowest pensions were raised if they dropped below the minimum income level, a large proportion of citizens in the post-productive age group was forced to behave economically. In 1970 30% of people continued working after reaching retirement age. For those working while drawing pensions, however, a limit was set on a working income of 22.000 crowns a year for non-manual workers. This limit did not apply to manual laborers in those fields where a 'shortage of labor' persisted.

In the 1970s persons of post-productive age comprised 12% of all employees. Old age pensions were not the priority for the authorities, who tended to favor economically active citizens. For this reason retirees formed a reserve of inexpensive labor and most of them performed services at low wages. Health insurance payments were provided in the event of earnings lost during the period of being unable to work. These payments also included compensation during the period of pregnancy and cash assistance during maternity leave. Social events related to maternity and the raising of children were addressed by family allowances, bonuses upon the birth of a child, paid maternity leave and from the 1970s family stipends as well. Family allowances were extended to all families with children. From the 1960s they were graduated according to the number of children in a family. Important contributions to raising a child were free or subsidized services and products (inexpensive clothing, free school materials, low fees for children's facilities, etc.).

From the beginning of the 1970s subsidized loans for newlyweds were introduced, partly being written off upon the birth of a child. These measures had only temporary effect on raising the birth rate. In the 1980s the subsidized newlywed loans were increased from 30,000 to 50,000 crowns.

The majority of changes in the social security system during the era of state socialism was based on the current state of the economy and the political goals of the ruling party. Various preferences and discrimination violated the principles of social justice and were not based on the guaranteed rights of citizens.

References

Heumos, Peter: *Dělníci a státní socialismus (Workers and state socialism)*, Praha 2006
Historická statistická ročenka (Historical statistical yearbook). Praha 1985
Kalinová, Lenka: *Sociální reforma a sociální realita v Československu v šedesátých letech (Social reform and social reality in Czechoslovakia in the 1960s)*. Praha 1998
Kalinová, Lenka: *K sociálním dějinám Československa v letech 1969-1989 (On social history of Czechoslovakia in 1969 – 1989).* Praha 1999

Kalinová, Lenka: *Východiska, očekávání a realita poválečné doby (Origins, expectations and reality of the post-war period.* Praha 2004

Kalinová, Lenka: *Společenské proměny v čase socialistického experimentu (Social changes during the period of socialist experiment.* Praha 2007

Report by Sir W. Beveridge: *Social Insurance and Allied Services.* London 1942

Rys, Vladimír: *Česká sociální reforma (The Czech social reform),* Praha 2003

Šulc, Zdislav: Stručné dějiny ekonomických teorií (Concise history of economic theories). Brno 1996

Turek Otakar: *Podíl ekonomiky na pádu komunismu (Contribution of economy in the fall of communism).* Praha 1995

Marcel Boldorf

Social Welfare in East Germany (1945 - 1990)

In German history, social welfare traditionally consisted of the safeguarding of basic needs in cases where other means of the welfare state such as social security failed. It is an area of social security that considered itself as temporary and subsidiary, i.e. its aim was to eliminate its own necessity.[1] In that respect, social welfare, just as unemployment benefits, are in contrast to pension insurance and health insurance, which could not possibly render themselves superfluous in the same kind of way.

In Eastern Germany two concepts of social welfare were predominant after 1945: In a larger sense, the term social welfare was used synonymous with social policy, a term that was avoided in the official language of the GDR until the 1960s. According to this perception, social welfare included the whole of the social services and financial transfer of the state. In a narrow sense, it refers to welfare as individual financial support and means payments and services to those in need, or the poor, in case they could not claim support from different agencies, such as social security.

This contribution will focus on social welfare in the narrower sense, corresponding to the statutory provisions with regard to social welfare in the Soviet Occupation Zone (SOZ) and the German Democratic Republic (GDR). The following aspects of welfare will be discussed:

- financial support in cash;
- benefits depending on the inability to work;
- maintenance and recovery of the ability to earn one's income;
- field work by volunteers organised in a system of social committees.

The history of social welfare in the GDR can be described as a long process of marginalisation: As a consequence of World War II it started from a very high level and gradually lost significance. The following remarks will focus on the measures which led to the decrease in importance. At the same time it will show how welfare developed in a socialist system and how the elements of support diversified in reaction to different needs and claims from the people concerned.

---

[1] Hentschel 1983, p. 194

Welfare as Emergency Support (1945 - 1946)

Poverty is a phenomenon which has to be considered within its specific historical context. After the second World War not only a marginal group was affected, but the majority of the population, whose standard of living was below subsistence level.[2] In times of general destitution the number of welfare claimants rose to a peak level of 1.1 million at the turn of the year 1946/47, that is about five to six per cent of the total population.[3]

The reasons for this rise in claims were manifold: administrative and legal changes have to be distinguished from personal fates suffered due to the war. Parts of the administration of social welfare were unable to work properly even before the end of the war. Along with bureaucratic failure, financial shortages in the arrangement of social services occurred, because the organisational structure encompassing the whole of the *Reich* had collapsed. The reserves of the social security funds were exhausted and the still existing funds, e.g. of the local departments of health insurance, were lost in the turmoil of the last weeks of the war. The arising gaps, especially with regard to the payments of old age pensions, were provisionally covered by the municipal welfare agencies by very low-level support payments.[4]

On the level of the administrative regions of the former federal states and Prussian provinces (*Länder*), health insurance was re-established first, followed by the pension funds in the first half of 1946. But even when the social security offices in many places were working again, the shortage of manpower, bureaucratic obstacles and a lack of funds frequently caused arrears to build up in the disbursement of pensions and therefore a lot of people still had to rely on municipal welfare support. In the SOZ, the politicians responsible for social policy were convinced that they could do without the establishment of unemployment benefits. This delayed the reconstitution of an unemployment insurance until January 1947.[5] To a large extent, these initial difficulties explain the high number of welfare claimants in the post war period.

---

[2] Boldorf 1998, p. 19
[3] ibid., p. 34
[4] Hoffmann 1996, p. 45-52
[5] ibid., p. 53-54

The claims of a number of former beneficiaries of social welfare lost validity due to the changed statuatory provisions after the war.[6] The large number of National Socialist decrees and statutory provisions were annulled. Therefore, many groups of war invalids, which were formerly entitled to services related to their activities in the military, now depended on) social support. For a long time the Soviet occupying power did not allow the reconstitution of the support of war victims. Soldiers were not allowed to receive specific support as they were under general suspicion of supporting militarism. Only in July 1948, rudimentary parts of a support system for war invalids could be re-established and the payment of low pensions to former solders, invalids and surviving dependants was resumed.[7]

Related to personal fates two main reasons for poverty can be discerned:[8] Traditionally relevant poverty risks which only gradually became covered by social security were age, accidents, illness and widowhood,. Due to the general weakness of the population caused by deficient nutrition, illnesses such as tuberculosis increased. Besides, civilian victims of war, who had suffered bodily harm, were among the claimants. Single mothers as well as old people without old age pensions were groups of the society, which due to lacking funds often became dependent on welfare support.

The second reason which is to be considered as personal fate was the uprooting due to the war. It mainly based on forced migration of Germans from Eastern and Central Europe beginning in Winter 1944/45 – the main factor for the large scale of support needed. Roughly half of the welfare claimants were refugees from the East. Even though many of them had a higher rank they found themselves in a situation of dire poverty for a limited period of time and thus became the clients of social welfare.

The Decisive Years: Centralisation and Welfare Restrictions (1947 - 1949)

Following the re-establishment of social insurance, the administration responsible for the German Administration of Labour and Social Care (*Deutsche Verwaltung für Arbeit und Sozialfürsorge - DVAS*) in East Berlin, as well as the Soviet occupying forces pushed towards a centralisation of

---

6   Zank 1987, p. 133
7   Hudemann 1991, p. 269-293
8   Boldorf 1998, p. 22-23

welfare. This meant a breach with the traditional structure of the welfare state in Germany.[9] Social welfare was regulated by the Soviet decree No. 92 of 22 April 1947 about the measures to improve social welfare for the German population in the Soviet-occupied zone of Germany. The decree contained a set of welfare rules and regulations which had been devised almost completely by the *DVAS*. It followed the traditional system of German welfare in certain ways, but also introduced new aspects, especially in three areas in accordance with the guideline of centralisation:

a) The standardisation of the level of services by renunciating the principle of individualisation: The introduction of fixed benefit rates finalised the efforts towards the institution of uniform rates for support, which had already started in 1924.[10] Ration cards for food were used as the clue for the calculation of rates, as they offered a uniform criterion for the definition of minimum subsistence needs.[11]

b) Limitations to the entitlement of support and the distinction of different groups of claimants: The regulations excluded war criminals and active National Socialists from the welfare system. On the other hand, it allowed a privileged treatment for recognised victims of fascism. As the recognition of the status depended on discretionary criteria (especially on the attitude towards the Socialist Unity Party, the *SED*), only 36,200 victims of the fascist regime were recognised until August 1949.[12] Following the communist criteria of fascism, Jewish claimants, for instance, were not recognised as victims of National Socialism and were thus denied the entitlement to a privileged welfare treatment.

c) Welfare organisations between centralisation and affiliation with the municipality: Initially plans were made to locate the welfare administration on the district level of the districts (*Kreise*), just as the employment offices. This shift to a higher administrative level failed, because the districts proved to be inadequate to the task. Therefore, welfare administration remained the task of the municipalities.

The Soviet decree No 234 of 9 October 1947 intensified the arrangement of labour allocation. The employment agencies increased intervention by com-

---

[9] Wengst 2001, p. 982-983
[10] Sachße/Tennstedt 1988, p. 174
[11] Boldorf 1998, p. 94-96
[12] Goschler 1995, p. 182-183

pulsory measures to get all those capable of work into employment and order them out of the welfare system. The term to describe this was productive welfare (*produktive Fürsorge*). As far as the *SED* was concerned, this kind of welfare went beyond financial support and involved general arrangements for vocational training, especially for rehabilitation. As this kind of welfare served to activate the existing manpower – this argument presented by the *DVAS* – differed fundamentally from the idea of passive welfare (*passiver Fürsorgegedanke*) in capitalistic systems. It had abandoned the charitable nature of the old type of welfare.[13]

Essentially the measures of productive welfare were geared to implement an obligation to work. A restriction with regard to criteria for the exemption from work was decreed by the provisional government of the SOZ in autumn 1948: After a change in the implementing regulations only single mothers with children younger than three years of age or two children of less than eight were exempted from work and thus entitled to welfare support.[14] Before this change, the age limits had been one child younger than six or two children of less than 15.[15] As a consequence of this modification the total of eligible welfare beneficiaries fell to about half a million by the end of 1948.[16] The implementation of strict regulations remained typical for the GDR. Therefore, the employment agencies were significantly more successful with regard to a reduction of welfare claimants as well as the decrease in unemployment than comparable structures in West Germany.

The assessment of poverty was in the hands of social committees staffed by volunteers, which based on the traditional *Elberfeld System*. In 1949, 12,000 of these social committees existed in the SOZ, staffed by approximately 64,000 volunteers, which were recruited mostly in the *SED* and its mass organizations.[17] The prior restriction of the committee to towns and cities was overcome. Thus, rural areas could benefit from organized welfare for the very first time in German history. At the same time a trend towards less professionalization began, interrupting the development during the interwar period. The number of paid social workers gradually diminished. As they became more rare, social work was never institutionalised as a professional qualification in the GDR.

---

[13] cf. Matern 1948, p. 348-351 and Zumpe 1951, p. 327
[14] Zentralverordnungsblatt 1948, p. 469.
[15] Zentralverordnungsblatt 1947, p. 219.
[16] Boldorf 1998, p. 51-54
[17] Ibid., p. 162-167

Welfare in the Period of the 'Construction of Socialism' (1949 - 1961)

After the foundation of the GDR in 1949, Marxist ideas became increasingly important in the discussion of social policy. The discussion was aimed at a criticism of bourgeois social policy, which was considered a paternalistic appeasement strategy of capitalist states.[18] Accordingly, welfare was generally suspect in the GDR: Just as social policy as a whole, it was considered a relict of the capitalist system. After Stalin, the economic well-being of the people was to be considered as secured due to the advancement of the socialist economy. Therefore, in the construction of socialism, social policy should neither preserve the status quo, nor – according to the doctrine of uniformity – play an isolated role outside the policy oriented at society as a whole.

The expected consequence of the socialist way of working and production was that welfare would render itself superfluous. Contemporary statistics supported this optimistic assumption. The massive decrease in the number of beneficiaries was interpreted as the success of recruitment services. The debate of the first Five-Year-Plan gave rise to the belief, that the decrease in welfare could be regarded as a reflection of economic progress.[19] The reduction of the number of beneficiaries thus became a criterion of measuring the success of economic policy. The idea, that welfare would become unnecessary as soon as the transition into a socialist society was completed, gained importance. Especially the social politician Jenny Matern believed that this 'principle of welfare' could be accomplished within a short period of time.[20]

For social welfare this logic entailed the aim to work for its own supersession. The Ministry of Labour of the GDR planned to integrate not only the support of old age pensioners, but also of those unable to work into the social insurance system. The problem, however, was the continuation of what was left in responsibility of the local Social Welfare Offices. Still, as the group of people dependent on welfare remained large (at about 400,000 to 500,000 beneficiaries), the reform did not change the situation significantly. At the same time, difficulties resulting from the reform of budgetary and tax policy were to be expected and thus, the plans for the reform were dropped.[21]

---

[18] Koblitz/Ruban 1972, column 964
[19] Zumpe 1951, p. 328
[20] Matern, 1948, p. 350
[21] Boldorf 1998, p. 187-190

Effectively, the number of welfare beneficiaries stagnated at about half a million, a fact that even the Ministry of Labour of the GDR had to accept. Rigorous measures for getting people into work were exhausted. The remaining beneficiaries were difficult to place, especially people with serious disabilities as well as single mothers with children, i.e. groups, which had always been problematic in the history of welfare. To get these groups into work, more specialized measures for integration were needed.

Moreover, the increasing ideological nature of the debate had the effect, that a stagnation in the number of beneficiaries could be interpreted as a sign of failure of economic policy. Thus administrative pressure aimed at reducing welfare expenditures increased. In December 1952 the Politbureau of the SED finalized drastic financial cuts.[22] Along with the usual instructions to increase checks on the ability to work, the introduction of a time limit for support became a rule. In the year 1953, every welfare claimant was to receive payments for three months only. This confronted the executing local offices with difficulties, as part of their beneficiaries were neither entitled to social insurance nor able to work. In the first three months of 1953 payments remained unchanged, but in April 1953 many municipalities ceased to pay support. In Thuringia, demonstrations took place against those cuts in cities such as Erfurt, Weimar and Arnstadt.[23] The crisis was an early sign of social unrest preceding 17 June 1953. In the course of the reforms following the June crisis, the Politbureau of the *SED* was obligated to resume welfare payments.

The means by which the decrease in the number of welfare clients were achieved, were specific for the labour market policy of the 1950s. The welfare offices were closely linked to the agencies responsible for allocating labour. Only those proving that they were unable to work were to be eligible for the reception of welfare benefits. However, this could not be effected with absolute consistency, but still frequent checks were used to enlarge the number of people considered able to work or partly able to work. For instance, women, who were potentially able to work but exempted from work for specific reasons were subjected to special checks. Extensive programmes existed to train or re-train those of limited ability to work, especially the disabled, the number of which had increased significantly due to war-related injuries.[24]

---

[22] Staritz 1996, p. 100-101
[23] Boldorf 1998, p. 216-220
[24] Boldorf, p. 466-469

In order to administrate welfare successfully, exact information on statistical parameters relevant to the labour market with regard to welfare claimants was necessary. This information was collected on the lower administrative level and aggregated on the central level.[25] Along with this statistical information, the welfare agencies of the districts relayed information about the development of social welfare in their area to higher administrative levels, which was conductive to interregional recruitment services.

The amendment of the regulation about social welfare of 1956 fell into a period of general consolidation.[26] It codified the results of past politics without giving momentum to new developments. As tried and tested, principles of social welfare such as the prerogative of getting beneficiaries into work, the restrictive regulations for exemption from work of 1948 and the short-term assignment of labour, especially in agriculture, were laid down. The regulations safeguarded the continued application of the principles set in December 1952 and managed to continue the decrease in the number of welfare claimants. At the time, social welfare was a sector of social politics, which could not be abolished entirely, but was still strongly marginalised.[27]

In consequence, the importance of volunteer field work decreased. In some places social committees were dissolved completely.[28] Some areas of their work became part of general communal services. Social tasks became the responsibility of the so-called Social-Activists

Activists (*Aktivisten*), the new name for the former social committees, installed by the municipal administration. At the same time, mass organizations such as the People's Solidarity Organisation (*Volkssolidarität*) and the Democratic League of Women in Germany (*Demokratische Frauenbund Deutschlands*), took care of those in need. Especially in rural areas, however, some organisational improvements were lost and the Mayor once again became a central character in social welfare. Social welfare lost significance in the municipalities, at the same time, the allocation of labour became less important. When the Ministry of Labour was dissolved in 1958, the department of social welfare became part of the Ministry of Health.

---

[25] Hoffmann 2002, p. 437-443
[26] Verordnung über die Allgemeine Sozialfürsorge, 23.2. 1956, cf. Gesetzblatt der DDR I. 1956, p. 233-236
[27] Hoffmann/Schwartz 2004, p. 814-815
[28] Boldorf 2004, p. 491-492

The Re-Assessment of Welfare as a Result of the Wall (1961 - 1971)

The crisis of supply in 1960/61 set the priorities for future tasks of the GDR government.[29] The aim was the foundations for a long-term increase in the standard of living. This implied a stronger dependency of social politics on economic planning. At the same time, the building of the wall in August 1961 led to a consolidation of the GDR, as the citizens could no longer escape and had to accept the existing circumstances. On the whole, the focus of social policies remained on measures to get claimants into work, for instance in the health system by prevention and aftercare as well as rehablitation, paid by the state. The extension of day care for children, such as day nurseries, increased the opportunity of getting women into work. All these measures brought about a decrease in the number of welfare beneficiaries.

The marginal position of social welfare opened up the opportunity of new reforms. It based on the concept of 'social care', which gradually substituted welfare support. The term was now used to name the respective agencies in the social administration on municipal, district and the national level. The idea was directed towards the long-term problems of the welfare claimants:[30]

a) Old age pensioners: In the support for senior citizens, previously separate tasks were combined. Special committees coordinated the work of the different mass organizations. The most important of those was the *Volkssolidarität*. Predominantly volunteer work was sometimes assigned to paid nursing staffs.

b) Single mothers and families with many children: A regulation of 3 May 1967 was aimed towards ameliorating the living conditions of families with four children or more. The provision of adequate housing and granting of housing allowances along with the increase of child benefits were decreed at the same time, initializing a process which expanded the sphere of social support. This, too, was an area close to social welfare, because many children exposed to poverty.

As the number of supported people decreased, more support was available for other groups of claimants. This concerned (influenced, applied to) rehabilitation, which became more important in comparison to the 1950s. At this

---

[29] Steiner 2006, p. 84-86
[30] Boldorf 2006, p. 475-479 and 490

time measures had been regarded as aimed towards swift placement in a working environment; now they were regarded as a complex cross-functional co-operation of medical, social and pedagogical agencies. In 1961 a system of rehabilitation committees developed, taking responsibility for directing and guiding volunteer work.[31] They also coordinated and advised the state bureaucracy, to which they were closely linked. Members of the committees were delegated from administrative offices as well as from mass organizations, such as the official trade union organisation (*FDGB*), the *Volkssolidarität*, professionals of the field and the associations of those affected, such as the blind or the deaf and hard-of-hearing. The committees were closely linked to the state's administrations for economic, finance and labour market politics. Only on the municipal and district level were the members of the committees involved in practical work in the field of social support.

The Dissolution of Welfare in the 1970s and 1980s

In accordance with the marked decrease the sources for social welfare in the 1970s and 1980s were sparse.[32] What was left of the welfare system became part of the system of planned economy (*Planwirtschaft*). In 1974 and in 1976, it was again institutionalised in a central, cross-departmental coordination committee within the GDR government. Apart from this, welfare remained a marginal problem for social politicians and in consequence no serious intentions aimed at reforms arose. When finally the term 'social welfare' was deleted from the professional vocabulary of national administration in the mid-1980s, the Ministry's department for social care consisted in the following sections: a) day nurseries and homes (institutional welfare), b) comprehensive support of old people and families with three or more children, c) rehabilitation. The focus of the social activities in the 1980s were the areas of home care and the extension of nursery field work. Professional vocational training in social work was only promoted by one institution at the University of Applied Sciences in Potsdam in 1979. The deployment of paid welfare workers in the area of home care also put an end to the general reliance on volunteer work in this domain.

Towards the end of the GDR, the problem of social support can be considered as solved. Unemployment had been eliminated at the cost of in-

---

[31] Boldorf 2006, p. 456
[32] Boldorf 2008, p. 454.

creased underemployment. In most cases the requirements for social insurance were set for the risks entailed by age, accident, widowhood, etc., because the number of those self-employed and of workers without social insurance had decreased considerably.

The fact that social welfare could become a marginalised part of the social system was closely linked to measures of state and industry working towards an increased standard of living.[33] The subsidies of staple foods, rents, energy costs, children's clothing and public transport guaranteed a minimum standard for the majority of the population. Thus, the number of those in need of support with regard to basic provisions was kept low. Besides, the risk of unemployment was almost entirely passed on to the nationally-owned companies, the *VEB*, as employees could not be made redundant, even if there was no work for them to do. The companies were also urged to keep on employees of reduced productivity. Finally, a number of measures of social and family support, especially for families with many children as well as the provision of comprehensive child care, enabled single mothers or both parents to take part in working life. For many families this double income was also an economic necessity, still, this significantly decreased the risk of poverty.

Conclusion

After the collapse of the GDR only a short period of time was given to attempts to reform the welfare system. The Unification Treaty of 3rd October 1990 laid the legal foundations for the development of a uniform welfare state in Germany. Amongst other things it contained the clause, that the legal regulations for social support of West Germany were to come into force in the unified Germany on 1 January 1991.[34] In the course of the transition to a market economy and the institution of the corresponding legal and social system, the number of welfare claimants shot up. At the end of 1990 the number of welfare beneficiaries in East Germany was already 134,403, by the end of 1991 this number had risen to 254,000 recipients of continuous support.[35] In the course of only two years, welfare had left behind its margin-

---

[33] Maydell 1996, p. 345–346
[34] cf. Wienand/Neumann/Brockmann 1997, p. 34-48
[35] Statistical Yearbook of the Federal Republic of Germany 1992, p. 506, and 1993, p. 515. Backhaus/Olk 1993, p. 309-310

alised position and reached the level of the 1950s. This process, however, did not only take place in inverse conditions, but also under completely different economic and social circumstances. The increase of support is one of the main symptoms of the social decline of parts of the population in the course of the transformation.[36] The main cause was the development of widespread unemployment, which transformed high-risk groups protected in the GDR – unskilled workers, families with many children and single mothers – into welfare beneficiaries.

References

Backhaus, Holger/Olk, Thomas: Von der ‚staatssozialistischen' zur kommunalen Sozialpolitik. Gestaltungsspielräume und -probleme bei der Entwicklung der Sozial-, Alten- und Jugendhilfe in den neuen Bundesländern, in: Archiv für Kommunalwissenschaften 32 (1993), p. 300-330
Boldorf, Marcel: Sozialfürsorge. In: Kleßmann, Christoph (Ed.): Geschichte der Sozialpolitik in Deutschland seit 1945. Deutsche Demokratische Republik 1961-1971. Politische Stabilisierung und wirtschaftliche Mobilisierung (vol. 9). Baden-Baden 2006, p. 471-492
Boldorf, Marcel: Rehabilitation und Hilfen für Behinderte. In: Kleßmann, Christoph (Ed.): Geschichte der Sozialpolitik in Deutschland seit 1945. Deutsche Demokratische Republik 1961 - 1971. Politische Stabilisierung und wirtschaftliche Mobilisierung (vol. 9). Baden-Baden 2006, p. 449-470
Boldorf, Marcel: Rehabilitation und Hilfen für Behinderte. In: Hoffmann, Dierk/ Schwartz, Michael (Eds.): Geschichte der Sozialpolitik in Deutschland seit 1945. Deutsche Demokratische Republik 1949-1961 (vol 8). Baden-Baden 2004, p. 453-474
Boldorf, Marcel: Sozialfürsorge, in: Geschichte der Sozialpolitik in Deutschland seit 1945. In: Boyer, Christoph et. al (Eds.): Deutsche Demokratische Republik 1971-1989. Bewegung in der Sozialpolitik, Erstarrung und Niedergang (vol 10). Baden-Baden 2008, pp. 451-469.
Boldorf, Marcel: Sozialfürsorge in der SBZ/DDR 1945-1953. Ursachen, Ausmaß und Bewältigung der Nachkriegsarmut. Stuttgart 1998
Goschler, Konstantin: Nicht bezahlt? Die Wiedergutmachung für die Opfer der nationalsozialistischen Verfolgung in der SBZ/DDR. In: Buchheim, Christoph (Ed.): Wirtschaftliche Folgelasten des Krieges in der SBZ/DDR. Baden-Baden 1995, p. 169-191
Hauser, Richard et al.: Ungleichheit und Sozialpolitik. Opladen 1996
Hentschel, Volker: Geschichte der deutschen Sozialpolitik (1880-1980). Soziale Sicherung und kollektives Arbeitsrecht. Frankfurt/Main 1983

---

[36] Hauser 1996, p. 278-280

Hoffmann, Dierk: Sozialpolitische Neuordnung in der SBZ/DDR. Der Umbau der Sozialversicherung 1945-1956. München 1996

Hoffmann, Dierk: Aufbau und Krise der Planwirtschaft. Die Arbeitskräftelenkung in der SBZ/DDR 1945 bis 1963. München 2002

Hoffmann, Dierk/Schwartz, Michael: Gesamtbetrachtung. In: Hoffmann/Schwartz (Eds.): Geschichte der Sozialpolitik in Deutschland seit 1945. Deutsche Demokratische Republik 1949-1961 (vol. 8). München 2004, p. 799-829

Hentschel, Volker: Geschichte der deutschen Sozialpolitik (1880-1980). Soziale Sicherung und kollektives Arbeitsrecht. Frankfurt/Main 1983

Hudemann, Rainer: Kriegsopferpolitik nach den beiden Weltkriegen. In: Pohl, Hans (Ed.): Staatliche, städtische, betriebliche und kirchliche Sozialpolitik vom Mittelalter bis zur Gegenwart. Stuttgart 1991, p. 269-293

Hübner, Peter: Gesellschaftliche Strukturen und Sozialpolitische Handlungsfelder. In: Kleßmann, Christoph (Ed.): Geschichte der Sozialpolitik in Deutschland seit 1945. Deutsche Demokratische Republik 1961-1971. Politische Stabilisierung und wirtschaftliche Mobilisierung (vol. 9). Baden-Baden 2006, p. 77-145

Koblitz, Horst Georg/Ruban, Maria-Elisabeth: Soziale Sicherheit. In: Kernig, Claus D. (Ed.): Sowjetsystem und demokratische Gesellschaft, vol. 5, Freiburg et al. 1972

Matern, Jenny: Schulung und Beschäftigung als Faktoren positiver Sozialpolitik. In: Arbeit und Sozialfürsorge 3 (1948), p. 350.

Maydell, Bernd von et al.: Die Umwandlung der Arbeits- und Sozialordnung. Opladen 1996

Sachße, Christoph/Tennstedt, Florian: Geschichte der Armenfürsorge in Deutschland. Fürsorge und Wohlfahrtspflege 1871 bis 1929. Stuttgart et al. 1988

Staritz, Dietrich: Geschichte der DDR, 2nd edition. Frankfurt/Main 1996

Steiner, André: Von Plan zu Plan. Eine Wirtschaftsgeschichte der DDR. München 2004

Statistical Yearbooks of the Federal Republic of Germany

Verordnung über die Allgemeine Sozialfürsorge, 23 February 1956 (Gesetzblatt der DDR I. 1956)

Wengst, Udo: Gesamtbetrachtung In: Wengst, Udo (Ed.): Geschichte der Sozialpolitik in Deutschland: Die Zeit der Besatzungszonen 1945-1949. Sozialpolitik zwischen Kriegsende und der Gründung zweier deutscher Staaten. Baden-Baden 2001, p. 971-986

Wienand, Manfred/Neumann, Volker/Brockmann, Iris: Fürsorge. Opladen 1997

Zank, Wolfgang: Wirtschaft und Arbeit in Ostdeutschland 1945-49. Probleme des Wiederaufbaus in der Sowjetischen Besatzungszone Deutschlands. München 1987

Zentralverordnungsblatt 1947

Zentralverordnungsblatt 1948

Zumpe, Paul: Die Sozialfürsorge im Fünfjahrplan. In: Arbeit und Sozialfürsorge 6 (1951), p. 327.

Ingrid Miethe

Substituting Social Pedagogy – the Fight Against Disadvantage in the Educational System in the GDR

In the GDR, as in other Eastern Block countries,[1] the political landscape was dominated by a political agenda in which a de-professionalized social work programme remained only a subordinate concern. Social work, as it had been defined in contemporary western societies, had ceased to exist; moreover the concept was explicitly rejected, starting from the ideological premise that a socialist society (like the GDR), by definition, did not have a need of professional social work. By creating a socialist state, the necessity of professional social work had become void – at least from the ideological point of view. Social work was defined as an accompanying phenomenon of the dying capitalist, bourgeois society that would become more and more superfluous in the emerging socialist GDR society.[2]

While today scholars mostly agree that social pedagogy undeniably existed in the GDR, though known under a different name,[3] there has been little research concerning its exact practices.[4] This is due to the fact that up to now research on the history of social work in the GDR has been mostly the domain of historians who conduct research on social work issues without embedding the subject areas of their investigation in a scholarly discourse of social pedagogy.[5] In addition, the lack of material on social pedagogy in the GDR might be due to the fact that it is extremely difficult to discuss the field in an empirical and theoretical perspective that relates to the Western European theoretical discourse and yet retains the perspective of the specific issues and special logic of a socialist state. This dilemma characterizes the research in the former Eastern Block countries in general. However, it is especially relevant when discussing social work, since in this case researchers are interested in something that – according to the former official ideology – was not allowed to exist.

The concept of a 'surrogate structure' that Hering suggests for analyzing social work practices in the former socialist states proves to be helpful for the

1 cf. Hering 2007
2 cf. Hering/Münchmeier 2003
3 cf. Eckardt 1984; Bundesministerium 1998
4 compare the list in Belardi et. al. 1998
5 cf. Schulz-Krüdener 2007

further debate. Hering suggests to neglect the term 'social work' and recommends to distinguish instead between the concept of social policy on the one hand and social practice in the field on the other hand. The middle stratum in professional social work that is typical for Western European societies was virtually non-existent, by contrast. Since typical social work problems nevertheless existed - against all ideological premises - so-called surrogate structures were developed that provided aid in dealing with these problems and that were put in place by groups of non-professional people who had not undergone any relevant education.[6]

There was no unified framework for these surrogate structures; instead it can be observed that they assumed very different forms. We would do them little justice if we regarded them merely as deficient practice of social work in a western understanding. The first step has to identify these structures empirically and historically in order to take the second step, namely to analyse and interpret them within the general context. Scientists have started to search for historic traces in a number of former socialist states.[7] So far the GDR, which was very much an Eastern Bloc country during the period of the Cold War[8] and the European division between 1945 and 1989, has been neglected in this research. Therefore the aim of the following paper is to focus on the learning support initiatives of the former GDR in order to pursue the question of where similar surrogate structures of social work appeared, how they were described in Eastern Europe and which specific developments are recognizable.

This paper first depicts the general political framework and its relevance for social work practices. Then the limits of structural reforms are shown, becoming obvious at the time when it had been undeniably noticed that workers' and peasants' children were "lagging behind in educational progress". Taking the example of the Workers' and Peasants' Faculty (*Arbeiter- und-Bauern-Fakultäten, ABF*) as the most important counter-privileging educational institution of the former GDR, the discussion turns to the problems that learning support initiatives, aimed at promoting the children of educationally underprivileged families, potentially face and how these problems were dealt with pedagogically and politically. Based on this case example, the paper concludes with discussing to what extent the social practices at these educational institutions formed merely surrogate structures of social

---

6 Hering 2007: 244 f.
7 Hering/Waaldijk, 2006; Hering 2007
8 cf. Breckner/Kalekin-Fishman/Miethe 2000

work and whether or why this 'social work' may still have provided innovative initiatives.

Learning Support Initiatives as Part of Social Policy

By abolishing private ownership in the means of production the SED, i.e. the governing party, thought it had paved the way for creating a socialist society in which even social problems would more or less solve themselves since the causes of these problems had been eliminated. Despite this ideological premise, the immediate post-war period saw the emergence of social work structures that took up the practice of the era of the Weimar Republic (for example, the youth welfare offices and state youth welfare authorities). These early developments, however, almost completely stopped after 1950. Only marginal political interest had been shown in youth welfare work, whereas youth policies and youth support programmes were given a prominent status, i.e. they were re- organized and received explicit preferential treatment.[9]

As a consequence, educational work at schools and special youth programmes were closely intertwined, which in turn had far-reaching consequences concerning the issue of learning support initiatives as they are discussed in this paper. The social pedagogic areas of work therefore became part of the state-run general educational system. Thus schools and the state-run children and youth organisations turned into the main representative institutions for this work.

At an early stage educational policy was already one of the core areas of societal and social policy. The focus of educational policy in the 1940s and 1950s was on providing support to workers and peasants,[10] or, speaking in more general terms, policy focussed on the educational support of educationally underprivileged people. By implementing specific support initiatives for

---

9   cf. Hornstein/Schefold 1998
10 The discussion concerning the difficulty of clearly categorizing who was a "worker" and who a "peasant", in other words the categorization of a person's social origin continues to be the issue of criticism, quite justifiably so. However, there is not enough room for this discussion in this paper. The problem certainly existed in the GDR, in particular, but should not be overemphasized for the 1950s (see in more detail Miethe 2007: 105ff). The difficulty can be seen similarly before 1945 as well as in the old German Federal Republic (cf. Dahrendorf 1965).

this target group the SED, on the one hand, wanted to compensate for the inequality that had affected the education of this target group for centuries. On the other hand, the party clearly hoped to succeed in educating a new politically loyal elite.[11]

In order to implement this educational ideas a variety of political programmes was initiated, for example the preferential treatment of workers' and peasants' children concerning the admission to higher education facilities and universities, the introduction of a comprehensive school system, the provision of scholarships and the establishment of counter-privileging educational institutions. The best-known and quantitatively measured the most important counter-privileging educational institution in the 1950s was the Workers' and Peasants' Faculty, the ABF. This institution offered preparatory courses for entering universities to workers and peasants who, after attending junior school, had undergone vocational training and worked in a trade or profession. This educational policy of facilitating admission to an academic career succeeded insofar as the proportion of workers' and peasants' children entering university increased within a relatively short period of time. This successful development reached its peak in 1958 when 58% of the university students in the GDR gaining admission immediately after leaving school were workers' and peasants' children.[12]

The Limitations of Structural Reforms

During the 1950s it became obvious that the encouragement through educational policy was not sufficient to induce workers' and peasants' children to enter a path of further education. Firstly, it became obvious that the new structures did not respond to the existing demand, so that that this demand had to be induced before the policy could achieve its aims.[13] Experience

---

11 cf. Schneider 1998, Miethe 2007.
12 cf. 'Statistische Jahrbücher der DDR' (Statistical Yearbooks of the GDR). However, the term „workers' and peasants' children" used in the statistical yearbooks is misleading since the system did not succeed in increasing the share of peasants' children to the same degree as the share of workers' children. In addition, the share of women in the 1950s remained comparatively low and increased only in 1960 to approx. 30%. The term 'workers' and peasants' children' stands mainly for workers' sons.
13 Schneider 1998, p. 20

showed that the target group had to be persuaded to agree to a career path for higher education.

At an early stage another obstacle also became apparent: workers' and peasants' children did not necessarily meet the hopes of the SED and its expectations with regard to their success in higher education programmes. The higher education institutions as well as the ABF itself both quickly noted that especially workers' and peasants' children fell behind in academic achievement compared to children from other social backgrounds.[14] These problems can be explained relatively easily by referring to the categories of social and cultural capital as pointed out by Bourdieu.[15] The structural reforms alone were not sufficient to compensate for the sparse social and cultural capital that children inherited from their parental homes. Therefore workers' and peasants' children tended to be less successful than children from other social classes.

Of course, this result was highly inconvenient to the SED because of its ideological premises. Therefore the socialist state failed to establish remedial pedagogic programmes, although education administrators had, early and unceasingly, pointed out the problem. It was only at the end of the 1950s that the difficulties were acknowledged and interpreted in the official scholarly journals.[16] Pippig, for example, noted:

"Many workers are not yet capable of guiding their children's educational development. In addition, specifically the politically self-confident workers have not enough time to spare for their children due to their active participation in shaping our society and their eagerness to further educate themselves. Thus many workers' and peasants' children are in fact still underprivileged; they are initially in a worse situation than children from bourgeois parents or from intellectual circles. How important the role is that the home environment, the milieu at home plays in this respect, has been clearly described in our research about the fact that certain children were lagging behind in educational progress."[17]

---

14 cf. Geißler (2000) for higher education institutions, Miethe (2005, 2007) for ABF institutions.
15 cf. Bourdieu 1983
16 In the pedagogic journal (Zeitschrift für Pädagogik) published by the German Pedagogic Center (Deutschen Pädagogischen Zentralinstitut) the issue is raised about the slower progress of certain children, namely in articles by Pippig (1958), and the discussion is continued by various practitioners in their reflections on educational experiences (Pippig 1959; Lompscher 1959; Perlick 1959; Lange 1959).
17 Pippig (1958, p. 893)

In this quotation the phrase "lagging behind in educational progress" was coined for the first time.[18] In order to solve this problem different strategies were developed and discussed. Teachers as well as parents were active in this fight, which took place at the workplaces of the parents and in child and youth organisations. For example, some programmes included parent-oriented initiatives that went as far as providing pedagogic instruction to special groups. In some cases even the workplaces of the mothers were contacted to negotiate family-friendly working times for the mothers. Of course, the main objective was to bring up children collectively by activating them; this was implemented through closely intertwining youth pioneer organisations, FDJ groups and the target-oriented organisation of school outings and holiday camps for children. Activities smoothly changed from being school-related to being extracurricular and vice versa. This shows that education and upbringing were very close connected in the GDR.

A further look at the initiatives that were realized to "fight against lagging behind in educational progress" proves that actually only a small portion was school-related, such as didactic approaches, for example. By far the major part of these initiatives referred to extracurricular pedagogical/educational work, i.e. they actually covered fields of social pedagogy. This fact merely highlights the dilemma caused by the different terminology and ideological premises of both democratic and socialist societies.

As will be shown in more detail within the context of describing the ABF, the contents and methods applied to "fighting against lagging behind in educational progress" may easily be compared to what we define today as social pedagogy. Apart from that, the way in which the SED used the phrase "lagging behind in educational progress" also always implied a political deficit, not only the obvious educational deficit resulting from insufficient cultural and social capital. This second connotation meant that the workers' and peasants' children, more often than not, disappointed the SED because against expectation they did not automatically become politically active. Talking about the "fight against lagging behind in educational progress" therefore always implied additional ideological efforts to influence workers' and peasants' children politically, in a way that would hardly have been acceptable in a democratic society. To equate these efforts to influence children with social pedagogic initiatives typical for western countries would therefore involve a simplification, though contents and methods are, to a large extent, comparable to the practical field of social work. However, we must not overlook the fact that the social work as it had been practised by teachers

---

18 The German term in the documents is "Kampf gegen das Zurückbleiben."

at schools included social pedagogic and social work practices that cannot merely be reduced to adhering to the ideological premises of the SED.

The SED deliberately avoided delving further into the extent of the problem and the options to solve it. Although the protagonists in the field of education policy were careful to describe and document the problem of "lagging behind in educational progress", they did not ask for conducting empirical research that would have analysed the problem scientifically.[19] As a consequence, today only scarce data is available about the extent of the problem and also about the effectiveness of the initiatives. It is equally difficult to reconstruct the actual fieldwork, which in any case was not reduced to realizing political objectives. For this reason the example of the ABF will be described on the following pages in order to elucidate the "fight against lagging behind in educational progress". The ABF has been analyzed in greater detail in a recent research project. Empirical data for this project was collected in all the relevant archives, concerning the GDR in general, in 14 narrative interviews with graduates (male and female) and in 28 interviews with teachers of the ABF Greifswald. Additional information was gained in group discussions with graduates of this ABF, in particular, and through using a standardized questionnaire concerned with the life stories of former ABF students (n=207).[20] As the data also included biographical interviews, we are in a position to address the personal experience of the students with respect to the initiatives.

The 'Fight Against Lagging Behind' at the ABF

The ABF and its education administrators knew the problem of "lagging behind in educational progress" well at least since 1954.[21] The teachers had been aware of the problem for much longer in their professional practice, so that they had long since developed pedagogic counter-measures, even with-

---

19 The only empirically based research of the problem was published in 1959 (Mendyk/Holz 1959). This survey was intended to collect pre-sampling data of the problem in preparation of a larger research project that was, however, never realized.
20 see biographic project on the ABF Greifswald: "Die ABF Greifswald. Eine biografische Institutionenanalyse" supported by the German Research Foundation (vgl. Miethe 2007; Miethe/Schiebel 2008).
21 cf. Miethe 2007, p. 168ff.

out having any specific instructions. In the "fight against lagging behind in educational progress" the ABF mostly took similar initiatives as those discussed for schools.[22] In addition, the fact that students were nearly all housed in student residencies provided circumstances that were comparatively favourable to learning support initiatives targeting workers' and peasants' children.[23] For that reason the work in the student residences formed a central part of the specific programmes the teachers of the ABF were involved in. On the following pages those dimensions will be delineated that formed a fundamental part of the extracurricular special initiatives, supplementing the core curriculum.[24]

Creating and Maintaining Motivation

As already noted above, it was difficult to convince workers and peasants of the usefulness of taking up a university course. Therefore, the task ahead was not so much to maintain the motivation for higher education; instead the key task was to create motivation from scratch. This task to persuade workers and peasants to follow a course of higher education fell first and foremost to the party organisations, the unions and the socialist youth organisation *(FDJ)* at the workplaces. Since not enough workers and peasants registered at the ABF due to these campaigns – not least because at their workplaces people were not particularly eager to lose their best workers to universities – the ABF instructors themselves became active in campaigning at the workplaces. More specifically, they had long conversations with potentially suitable young workers about the usefulness and purpose of a university degree. At agricultural workplaces these conversations had to take place primarily with the parents of the young people. "We sometimes grabbed them while they

---

22 In contrast to the debate about schools there was no public debate with respect to the ABF about the experiences and initiatives concerning the "fight against lagging behind in educational progress".

23 With respect to the educational reforms Schelsky (1961, p. 158) pointed out that rather than leaving the student residences to "stupid, rich people", it would be far better to reserve them "for workers' children attending higher education facilities", so that "in addition to normal school attendance" they would have the benefit of "educational support and of a culturally knowledgeable environment, both of which they lacked in their parental homes."

24 cf. Schafhirt 2006.

were milking their cows and explained the ABF and university courses to them", one ABF instructor said about these campaigns.

However, even if they succeeded in motivating the young people to register with the ABF, there was still no guarantee that somebody's initial motivation would be sufficient to finish the course. When academic problems occurred, there was a great danger that the young person would drop the course and leave. Equally, the decision to study at the ABF often caused severe conflicts with the parents, so that this aspect also needed careful pedagogic attention. The instructors spent time outside classes to discuss such problems with the students and the parents. In addition, the student residences had the huge advantage that students with similar problems lived together. As a consequence the students experienced their educational career (and the related conflict with their parents) less as an individual choice, but rather as a collective choice that was politically promoted and for which they found support among their peers.[25]

At the same time, it was common practice at the ABF to conduct specific evaluation interviews with the students who had academic difficulties in order to "fight against lagging behind in educational progress". Students, representatives of the FDJ and instructors took part in those interviews and together they tried to find appropriate means of support to help the student to achieve the (academic) goal. There were cases where the students doubtlessly felt to be under severe pressure through these interviews and cases where they were driven to strive for goals that were far beyond their abilities. More frequently, though, these interviews would be regarded as helpful and the educational career in general as a profit to the student's biography.

Targeted Learning Support Initiatives – Learning to Learn

Even if the motivation to start an educational career existed, many ABF students did not have sufficient cultural capital to be successful in their chosen career. The students from educationally underprivileged homes first had to be taught how to learn, especially because the school attendance had been interrupted by going to work for a varying number of years. In those cases the instructors appointed specific 'learning support mentors', which meant that a student with better academic abilities was obliged to support a student who had academic deficits. Also there were 'learning support collectives', mostly

---

25 cf. Miethe 2005a

consisting of the occupants of a room at the student residence; they were obliged to study together and support each other. Thus the students learnt to form networks and to provide learning support for others.[26] "To create such a setting and to establish a relevant/respective formal structure implies that a social pedagogical approach was employed to deal with the problem."[27]

The student residences were also the places to which the instructors came – after finishing their normal teaching obligations – in order to 'supervise'[28] the independent study time or to support certain students, even outside of class. Due to these extracurricular remedial lessons the instructors were under so much additional pressure that even the state secretariat demanded a reduction in hours, since they feared that the instructors would not be able to work for a long period under such pressure.

Development of a Positive Self-Image

Another central element is the pedagogical support to help students in developing a positive self-image. An educational career in the GDR always caused an estrangement from the original parental milieu. Despite the abundant ideological support during their educational career it was by no means natural for students to move self-confidently, in an assured manner, in a university/the environment of higher education. Therefore it was always part of the instructors' duties to discuss with the students, in accordance with the intention of the FDJ, why the educational career was the right choice and why it was important for them.

The neutral term 'positive self-image' was chosen to describe this important dimension that the ABF also strived to develop. However, the documents as well as the interviews clarify that the path taken to develop a positive self-image was tinged with political ideology. According to the political jargon the definition of the "fight against lagging behind in educational progress"

---

26 See the fictional description of this learning context in the novel by Hermann Kant (1965) "The Auditorium" (Die Aula), which is set at the ABF Greifswald in its first academic year.
27 Schafhirt 2007, p. 37
28 The term 'supervise' is the official term in connection with the independent study time to be found in the written sources. In actual fact the instructors did not so much 'supervise', as they provided learning support to students where the latter were not able to manage it on their own.

partly implied the "development of pride in one's own proletarian class".[29] The argument was not addressed to the individual person with his or her abilities and dreams, but rather to the 'collective person' belonging to a political group. The aim was not to develop a neutral positive self-image. It was first and foremost to create self-confident socialists. Nevertheless, the aspect gained great importance when it came to evaluating a student's success, and for this reason it should not be reduced to its political intention, but should instead be regarded as a general dimension for a successful educational career.

Transfer of Incorporated Cultural Capital

Apart from transferring cultural capital in the form of academic titles, the ABF also transferred incorporated cultural capital. Such a transfer of incurporated cultural capital was in part explicitly set out in the ABF curriculum in which teachers were instructed to organise excursions to places of cultural interest or to arrange theatre outings with the students.

To a large extent, however, the transfer of this form of resource was achieved through informal ways of educational processes, mostly outside regular classes. This informal transfer was mainly effected by those teachers who were themselves educationally influenced by bourgeois ideas[30] and who – whether consciously or subconsciously – passed them on to their students. Sometimes the transfer consisted of simple messages, such as that "there may be more than one shirt to wear during term time" or "knife and fork are to be handled in a certain way".[31] The mingling of private and public spheres[32], which is so typical of societies in socialist states, had a positive effect on the development of incorporated cultural capital, since (private) issues that would hardly find a place in the ABF curriculum were included as a matter of course in the pedagogical extracurricular work. "They moulded us into human beings" was a shared consensus in the group discussion with former ABF students. This description definitely did not only refer to the transfer of academic knowledge at the ABF, but also to the access to incorporated cultural capital in the form of behaviour and lifestyle.

---

29 Pippig 1958, p. 898
30 cf. Miethe/Schiebel 2008
31 Interview with an instructor of the ABF Greifswald
32 cf. Shlapentokh 1989; Miethe 2000.

Gender-Specific Blind Spots

Although, during the whole time that the ABF existed, the proportion of women at the institution was too low and especially women tended to neglect to follow up their ABF education by a university degree, no special learning support initiatives were developed in this respect. In 1952 women-specific education programmes were implemented that for a short while increased the proportion of women. These programmes, however, focused mainly on structural improvements (more advertisements, preferential admission).[33] There were no pedagogic initiatives that focussed on the relevance of gender.

The internalised bourgeois codes of the teachers – their positive effect has been described before – proved to have a negative effect with respect to gender. Contrary to the official female ideal of the well-educated working woman,[34] the teachers subconsciously transferred gender stereotypes to the students. As the interviews with the instructors show, the internalized conception of female virtues resulted in disparate treatment and a different view on women as opposed to men at the ABF.

Teachers as Social Pedagogues?

As the analysis of the ABF above illustrates, the work of an ABF instructor comprised much more than merely the transfer of knowledge. It also involved activities that may be classified as social pedagogic or social work tasks - although the instructors had not received any specific training to carry out these tasks.[35] They either implemented the pedagogic work outside (academic) classes themselves or they initiated and supported its (self-) organisation. The youth organisations and workplaces, too, provided additional support, but the largest burden remained with the instructors.

Sometimes these extracurricular tasks were part of an instructor's official job description. It was, for example, a normal part of an ABF instructor's job to supervise the independent study time in the student residences, just as it

---

33 cf. Miethe 2008 for more detail.
34 cf. Merkel 1994
35 To a large extent the ABF instructors did not even hold the entitlement to teach in higher education classes so that they had to obtain the entitlement while on the job via distant learning courses.

was deemed part of the instructor's job to conduct the supporting interviews with students or to organise class outings. The campaign to reach potential students was part of the instructor's responsibilities, too. The instructors sometimes did much more social pedagogical work as they were officially expected to do. Thus, the extent of the extracurricular remedial learning support often went beyond the expectations. Similarly, the instructors often took on the task of counselling their students in matters as diverse as an (unwanted) pregnancy, sorting out financial problems or accompanying students to meetings with their parents. All instructors refer to the pressure they felt due to these additional social pedagogic tasks.

The question arises why the instructors were willing to take on not only those extracurricular tasks that were dictated to them, but also the additional ones. There are two possible answers to this question. First of all, the ideas underlying their conceptualisation provided a strong source of identification for many instructors. As a consequence, they saw their work at the ABF not merely as their profession, but also as the focus of their lives, involving a high biographic relevance.[36]

Secondly, the instructors were exposed to direct pressure from higher positions in the hierarchy to take on additional 'voluntary' work. Since the SED ideology refused to acknowledge the problem of "lagging behind in educational progress", the Central Committee (ZK) of the SED ascribed the causes of the problem not to the deficient cultural and social capital as the students from educationally underprivileged backgrounds had obtained at home. Rather, the cause was seen in an alleged insufficient enthusiasm on the side of the instructors. The strong commitment of the instructors was at least in part an attempt to protect themselves from anticipated accusations of providing insufficient support for their students.[37]

---

36 See case reconstructions of instructors of the 'NS-differentiation-type' (NS-Abgrenzungstypus) and the "Justice type" (Gerechtigkeitstypus) in Miethe/ Schiebel 2008.
37 This becomes important when looking at the debate on revisionism in 1957/58. The problems the ABF faced were interpreted in this context as insufficient willingness on the part of the instructors and resulted in the campaign to "educate the educators" (see Miethe 2007: 188ff. for more detail)

The 'Fight Against Lagging Behind' – A Substitution of Social Pedagogy?

So how should the social practice of specific learning support in the first years of the GDR be evaluated? Is it a substitution of social work? The answer can be affirmative or negative, depending on the perspective.

Seen from the perspective of the present understanding of social work the thesis of a surrogate structure finds support. The social practices at the ABF were far from the professional practice as we define it today. The activities were carried out by employees who had not received any training in this area of work (de-professionalizing), were rarely implemented as part of an explicit conceptual approach, and they were, most importantly and due to their official "non-existence", not embedded in any professional scholarly discourse.[38] In actual fact, the activities were part of a "social pedagogical tangle" that aimed at coping with current problems as the situation demanded and that did not exist according to the official ideology of the GDR.

The evaluation is different if seen against the historical background of the 1950s. Even Western authors concede that the GDR in the 1950s was ahead of West Germany at the time, as far as the reduction of social inequalities in education was concerned.[39] In actual fact it was more than a decade ahead compared with West Germany. This also means that the GDR was confronted with problems that concerned West Germany only twenty years later. West Germany developed the profile for school social work only in the late 1960s and early 1970s. Apart from the fact that this field of work was discussed within the context of social pedagogy, looking for theoretical and methodical orientation with respect to pedagogy, the actual practical fieldwork featured a tangle similar to that of the GDR and was equally often carried out by non-qualified persons.[40] The degree of professionalization in school social work was not more advanced at that time than in the GDR of the 1950s. According to this perspective it is hardly possible to regard the social work practices described in this paper merely as "surrogate structures". Within this comparative perspective the practices should rather be evaluated as one possibility to address current problems that were noticed in West Germany only twenty years later.

---

38 To a large extent reference was made to A.S. Makarenko's pedagogic approach – therefore a relevant social pedagogical discourse is apparent.
39 compare Froese 1961; Geißler 2002.
40 cf. Streblow 2009

Contrary to the situation in the GDR, the situation in West Germany allowed the professionals to put the proper name to the problem so that it became possible to develop a professionalized social work practice. The experiences of the 1950s in the GDR with respect to demolishing social inequalities in the educational system would have greatly enriched the discussion here, not only in terms of linking youth work and school work, but also on the level of practical field work. The practitioners in the GDR could have contributed their experience gained during a decade of providing learning support to people from educationally underprivileged homes to the discussion. The GDR chose to miss this chance for ideological reasons, since nothing was acknowledged that was ideologically unwanted. The innovations that might have been possible were degraded to a surrogate structure and the professionalization of social work in Western Germany developed without a contribution from the GDR.

References

Belardi, Nadno/Bindrich, Peter/ Fankhänel, Thomas (Eds.): *Die ostdeutsche Sozialarbeit im Spiegel der Fachliteratur*. Hamburg 1998
Bericht vom 2. Deutschen Jugendhilfetag in Köln: *Jugendhilfe und Bildungspolitik*. München 1966
Bourdieu, Pierre: *Ökonomisches Kapital, kulturelles Kapital, soziales Kapital*. In: Krecket, R. (Ed.): *Soziale Ungleichheiten*. (Soziale Welt, Sonderband 2) 1983, p. 183-198
Breckner, Roswitha/Kalekin-Fischmann, Devorah/Miethe, Ingrid: *Introduction*. In: Dies. (Eds.): *Biographies and the Division of Europe*. Opladen 2000, p. 7-20
Bundesministerium für Familie, Senioren, Frauen und Jugend: *Neunter Jugendbericht. Bericht über die Situation der Kinder und Jugendlichen und die Entwicklung der Jugendhilfe in den neuen Bundesländern*. Bonn 1994
Dahrendorf, Ralf: *Arbeiterkinder an deutschen Universitäten*. Tübingen 1965
Eckardt, Peter: *Sozialistische Sozialpädagogik – dargestellt an der Jugendhilfe der Deutschen Demokratischen Republik* (Dissertation an der Fakultät für Geistes- und Sozialwissenschaften der Universität Hannover). Hannover 1984
Froese, Leonhard: *Bildungstendenzen in der modernen Welt*. In: Froese, Leonhard (Ed.): *Bildungswettlauf zwischen Ost und West*. Freiburg/Basel/Wien 1961, p. 7-36
Geißler, Gert: *Geschichte des Schulwesens in der Sowjetischen Besatzungszone und in der Deutschen Demokratischen Republik 1945 bis 1962*. Frankfurt am Main u.a. 2000
Geißler, Rainer: *Die Sozialstruktur Deutschlands. Die Gesellschaftliche Entwicklung vor und nach der Vereinigung*. Wiesbaden 2002

Hering, Sabine: *Traditionen, Utopien, Destruktionen – die Sozialstaatskonzepte des „Ostblocks' (1945-1990).* In: Seibel/Otto/Friesenhahn (Eds.): *Reframing the Social. Social Work and Social Policy in Europe.* Boskovice 2007, p. 241-259
Hering, Sabine/ Münchmeier, Richard: *Geschichte der Sozialen Arbeit. Eine Einführung.* Weinheim/München 2005[3]
Hering, Sabine/ Waaldijk, Berteke: *Guardians of the Poor – Custodians of the Public. Welfare History in Eastern Europe 1900-1960.* Opladen/Farmington Hills 2006
Hornstein, Walter/ Schefold, Werner: *Sozialpädagogik.* In: Führ/ Furck (Eds.): *Handbuch der deutschen Bildungsgeschichte.* Band VI, 1945 bis zur Gegenwart. Zweiter Teilband Deutsche Demokratische Republik und neue Bundesländer, München 1998, p. 281-315
Kant, Hermann: *Die Aula.* Berlin 1965
Lange, Gerhard: *Über die besondere Förderung der Arbeiter- und Bauernkinder. Erfahrungen aus der Arbeit Leipziger Schulen.* In: Pädagogik, Heft 7/1959, p. 567-575
Lompscher, Joachim: *Über die Arbeit mit den Zurückbleibern.* In: Pädagogik Heft 5/1959, p. 368-380
Mendyk, Inge/Holz, Hans-Joachim: *Grundsätze und Erfahrungen zur Förderung der Arbeiter- und Bauernkinder.* Herausgegeben vom Pädagogischen Zentralinstitut. Berlin 1959
Merkel, Ina: *Leitbilder und Lebensweisen von Frauen in der DDR.* In: Kaeble/Kocka/ Zwahr (Eds.): *Sozialgeschichte der DDR.* Stuttgart 1994, p. 359-382
Miethe, Ingrid: *Biografie als Vermittlungsinstanz zwischen öffentlichen und privaten Handlungsräumen: Das Beispiel von Frauen der DDR-Opposition.* In: Miethe/ Roth (Eds.): *Politische Biografien und sozialer Wandel.* Gießen 2000, p. 163-188
Miethe, Ingrid: *„Die Universität dem Volke!". Der Beitrag der Vorstudienschule Greifswald zur sozialen Umschichtung an der Universität (1946-1949).* In: Deutschland Archiv Heft 6/2005, p. 1050-1056
Miethe, Ingrid: *Bildung und soziale Ungleichheit. Bedingungen für einen erfolgreichen Bildungsaufstieg am Beispiel der Arbeiter-und-Bauern-Fakultäten (ABF) der DDR.* In: Bender-Junker/ Mansfeld (Eds.): *Bildung und Bildungsanlässe. Pädagogische und gesellschaftliche Anlässe.* Darmstadt 2005a, p. 175-194
Miethe, Ingrid: *Bildung und soziale Ungleichheit in der DDR. Möglichkeiten und Grenzen einer gegenprivilegierenden Bildungspolitik in der DDR.* Opladen/ Framington Hills 2007
Miethe, Ingrid: *Widersprüchliche Gegenprivilegierungen. Bildungspolitik der DDR im Korsett unterschiedlicher ideologischer Prämissen.* In: Geißel/Manske (Ed.): *Kritische Vernunft für demokratische Transformationen.* Opladen/Framington Hills 2008, p. 145-163.
Miethe, Ingrid / Schiebel, Martina: *Biografie – Bildung – Institution. Die Arbeiter- und Bauern-Fakultäten der DDR.* Frankfurt/ New York 2008
Perlick, Kurt: *Über die besondere Förderung der Arbeiter- und Bauernkinder. Einige Probleme aus der bisherigen Diskussion.* In: Pädagogik, Heft 6/1959, p. 469-474
Pippig, Günter: *Über die besondere Förderung der Arbeiter- und Bauernkinder. Gedanken und Erfahrungen.* In: Pädagogik, Heft 12/1958, p. 893-902
Pippig, Günter: *Kampf gegen das Zurückbleiben heißt richtig erziehen.* In: Pädagogik, Heft 9/1959, p. 777-787

Schafhirt, Stephanie: *Bildungsaufstieg und Soziale Arbeit. Sozialpädagogisches Handeln im Bildungswesen der frühen DDR* (Diplomarbeit an der Evangelischen Fachhochschule Darmstadt), Darmstadt 2006

Schelsky, Helmut: *Anpassung oder Widerstand? Soziologische Bedenken zur Schulreform. Eine Streitschrift zur Schulpolitik.* Heidelberg 1961

Schneider, Michael: *Bildung für neue Eliten. Die Gründung der Arbeiter-und-Bauern-Fakultäten.* Dresden 1998

Schulz-Krüdener, Jörgen (2007) Rezension zu Pitzsch, Henning: *Jugend zwischen Kirche und Staat. Geschichte der kirchlichen Jugendarbeit in Jena 1970-1989.* Köln/Weimar/Wien 2005

Shlapentokh, Vladimir: *Public and Private Life of the Soviet People. Changing Values in Post-Stalin Russia.* New York/Oxford 1989

Streblow, Claudia: *Schulsozialarbeit: Entwicklungen und empirische Einblick.* In: Bock/Miethe (Eds.): *Handbuch qualitative Methoden in der Sozialen Arbeit.* Opladen/Farmington Hills 2009 (forthcoming)

Sven Korzilius

The Repressive Side of Social Policy in the GDR: Penal Laws against 'Asocials' and 'Parasites'

The aim of this article is to give a survey of the repressive aspects of social policy, especially the criminal sanctioning of certain kinds of deviant behaviour in the GDR during three different periods: until 1961, from 1961 to the end of Ulbricht's reign, and finally, under Honecker. This shall be done by analysing legal and stereotypical continuity, general lines of criminological discussions, the development of the intensity of persecution and the interference of state and society in the construction of a marginal social group through processes of negative labelling.[1]

In respect to the aspect of continuity it is necessary to begin with a short glance at the development of the interference in social and criminal policy up to 1945. It has a long tradition in the early modern state to react to social problems related to poverty, such as begging, homelessness or prostitution, by resorting not only to charitable measures, but also to policing.[2] One of the culminating points of development during the 18th and 19th century (especially in Prussia[3]) was the German Empire's penal code of 1871 (*Reichsstrafgesetzbuch, RStGB*). In a chapter on 'asocial behaviour', it dealt with minor offences like begging, homelessness and vagabondage, prostitution, failing to provide alimony, excessive gambling and the unwillingness to do work serving the public good while receiving welfare aid[4]. Because of the principle of commensurability between offence and punishment the penalties provided by law for the aforementioned offences could not be very harsh: the worst possible sentence was imprisonment for a few months. In the eyes of many politicians this was not enough. They argued that for reasons of public safety these persons had to be put under arrest for longer than only a few months.

Conservative bourgeois ideology tried to ignore economic causes for those offences, but developed the idea that the offenders' inappropriate be-

---

1 It offers a synthesis of some of some central aspects of the author's PhD thesis (Korzilius 2005); cf. also Zeng 2000, and Windmüller 2006.
2 Sachße/Tennstedt 1980
3 Allgemeines Landrecht, Part II, title 19/20.
4 Rudolph 1995

haviour was due to cultural deficiencies which could be 'cured' through austere disciplinary education. As a consequence the legislators used a trick to achieve sentences for long detention, without openly giving up the doctrine of commensurability. The authors of the Prussian penal code had already introduced this trick: the law provided a special form of disciplinary detention (*korrektionelle Nachhaft*) in workhouses, institutions of detention exclusively designed for those guilty of 'asocial behaviour'[5]. This legal construction corresponded to a tripartite view of crime, most clearly formulated by von Liszt in 1882[6]. According to this view a large number of offences were committed by 'normal' citizens who only needed to be deterred by penal law. Apart from that there were two special groups of offenders: those who were inimical to society (*Gemeinschädliche or Anti-Soziale*[7]) whose pernicious behaviour had to be prevented in case of doubt even by death penalty. And those who were a burden to society (*Gemeinlästige/ Asoziale*), but capable of being reformed.

After 1871 there were a lot of workhouses. During the more liberal first years of the Weimar Republic the number of detentions in these establishments was rather low, whereas at the end of the Republic, in the shadow of the Great Depression, the discourse sharpened and propaganda against 'asocials' became harsher.[8] In the early thirties, when the Republic drifted into the National Socialist regime, the workhouses filled up again, but not for long, because the National Socialists radicalised the measures against 'asocials'. Asocial behaviour was now seen as a consequence of genetic deficiencies and the offenders were considered unable to be reformed. Two biological metaphors became dominant: that of a rotten branch of a tree which had to be cut off, or that of parasites exploiting and damaging the plant. This meant that for part of the group the interpretation changed from being a burden on society to being alien to society (*gemeinschaftsfremd*). Eugenic arguments were used for justifying the well-known mass sterilisations[9]. The en-

---

5   For the history of the institution of the work-house in a diachronic perspective cf. the exemplary studies of Ayaß 1992 and Daners 1996.
6   Liszt 1882/1883, known as the 'Marburg Programme' (Liszt developed these ideas in his inaugural address when he came to the University of Marburg as a professor of law)
7   This is the reason why I prefer to use the term 'asocial' in English as well. The duality of 'anti-social' and 'asocial' gets lost if 'asozial' is translated as 'anti-social'.
8   Korzilius 2006
9   Bock 1986

deavours to achieve social rehabilitation (which was the objective of the workhouses in the Weimar Republic, at least as a fig leaf for the long detentions) were now regarded to be too expensive and useless.

The Nazis sent 'asocials' to concentration camps (they formed the category of prisoners recognizable from the black triangle), where they had to do the hardest work, while accommodation and food supply were very meagre. In their ideology of selection, the Nazis theoretically promised those who proved to be 'worth returning to society' that they might be released (remember the notorious, cynical 'Arbeit macht frei!' slogan), but in practice the overwhelming majority was considered to be not worth living and had to be exploited until death (*'Tod durch Arbeit'*).[10]

Repressive Social Policy in the Soviet Occupation Zone and the Early GDR

How did the occupation powers react when it turned out in 1945 that a radicalisation of repressive social policy measures could lead to inhumanities and cruel mass-murder? The Americans were the only holders of power who decided that the workhouse system had been corrupted to such an extent during the Nazi regime that they decided to abandon it completely. In the other three occupation zones the legal instrument (§§ 361, 42 RStGB) continued to exist, but a lot of the workhouses were damaged or used for more urgent purposes. Detention figures were negligible. The Soviets, but also the other victorious powers added new regulations, mostly at the regional level, to the outdated German law. As the public administration was in the hands of the military, these regulations had the character of ad hoc instructions. In a lot of cities labour camps were set up, where homeless people or beggars, for example, were often kept imprisoned together with people arrested for political reasons[11]. A lot of these camps had been established for women with venereal diseases, which were very common after the war. Their purpose was

---

10 cf. the fundamental study of Ayaß 1995
11 E. g. the 'Kommandohaft' in Dresden, as described by Max Opitz in: Bundesarchiv, SAPMO, SgY 307EA 0001/2 (Max Opitz), 499 et sqq. or the 'Vorbeugungshaft' in Thuringia, documented in: Municipal Archive of Nordhausen.

to combine medical treatment with moral education.[12] This unstable, transitory phase did not provide the opportunity to develop any remarkable perspectives of social policy or criminology.

After the foundation of the two German republics, the politicians of the young socialist state could begin to discuss the perspectives of further social development more thoroughly. Three major currents can be distinguished: one which I would like to call optimist or abolitionist, a second one which I refer to as Stalinist, and finally a conservative one. The optimists and the Stalinists both took their starting point from Marxist ideas, according to which the kind of offences called 'asocial' were typical signs of the corruption and foulness of capitalist society. The optimists therefore claimed that those negative remnants of the old society would somehow automatically disappear a few years after establishing the new society (*Rudimententheorie*). As a consequence they considered legal sanctions against asocial behaviour to be superfluous and were in favour of cancelling such norms in the projects for a new 'socialist' penal code. The Stalinists (at least in their ideologically correct pronouncements) believed in the disappearance of such residues of bourgeois society as well, but nevertheless they wanted legal sanctions against such forms of behaviour to be maintained, because in their view the existence of petty crimes was a more threatening phenomenon. They thought that some of the offenders were not mere relics of capitalism, but rather their importance was blown up as enemies of socialism. For this reason Stalinist interpretations added these offences to the wider range of political crimes (*Freund-Feind-Theorie*). The conservatives, who could more frequently be found at the practical level of public administration and police than on the nomothetic one, were not much interested in socialist ideology. They did not believe in the sudden disappearance of those offences, but they did not dramatise their existence either. They expected judicial practice concerning 'asocials' to continue as before.

In everyday judicial life, conservatism was rather strong. A lack of distance from antebellum law and even from Nazi decisions became apparent in several areas. In the course of the discussion on acknowledging different groups as victims of fascism (*Opfer des Faschismus, OdF*) those people who had worn the black triangle in the concentration camps were not admitted to

---

12 Falk 1998, Naimark 1995, here especially chapter 2: Soviet Soldiers, German Women and the Problem of Rape, p. 69-140, cf. the instructions of the Soviet Military Administration in Germany (SMAD) no. 030 and 273

the official organisations of the victims.[13] In the reasons given for actual criminal judgements, especially against prostitutes, during the forties and fifties the courts sometimes even took sterilisation by the Nazis as evidence justifying the verdict.[14] The sentences or reports on inmates were full of old stereotypes. Even before the foundation of the GDR some of the governments of the states in Germany discussed the reopening of workhouse[15]. During the fifties, due to decisions made by the central authorities some of them were even reconstructed and some new ones were opened, so that by the end of the 1950s about twenty of these facilities existed throughout the GDR. The only novelty was the invention of a new name for them - asylums for social mentoring (*Heime für soziale Betreuung*). This conservatism was not only recognizable in the area analysed here, but also in the wider area of social welfare.[16]

But in various other fields the ideologically correct optimistic view of the future development of socialism in the GDR had its consequences, e. g. within the field of social care. In the early 1950s, the aim of abandoning institutions of social welfare completely became dominant because they were perceived as being of no use anymore.[17] Another important sector to suffer from this ideological optimism was the social sciences: a large number of institutes and chairs in the field of social sciences were not re-established or were even abolished during this period. Most branches did not come into existence again in the GDR before the end of the 1950s or even 1960s[18].

---

13   Groehler 1993, cf. the cases in Thüringisches Hauptstaatsarchiv, Ministerium für Wirtschaft und Arbeit (Department of Economy and Employment), files 4025-4029, 4040, 4057, or in Landesarchiv Berlin, C Rep 118, 1058

14   cf. the files in: Thüringisches Hauptstaatsarchiv, Ministerium für Wirtschaft und Arbeit, 3945, p. 16-18 or in: Bundesarchiv, DP 1 VA 504.

15   For Sachsen-Anhalt cf. Landeshauptarchiv Magdeburg, Rep K 4, MdJ, 906; for Mecklenburg-Vorpommern cf. Landeshauptarchiv Schwerin, Rep. 6.11-19, Sozialministerium, 2075 and MP HA Justiz 508.

16   Boldorf 1998, p. 236: "Die Fürsorgepolitik beschritt keine neuen Wege, sondern war in vielerlei Hinsicht in der repressiven Tradition der Armenfürsorge verhaftet.

17   Boldorf shows that the ideological claim of a better society was combined with fiscal necessities; for both reasons social welfare suffered a systematic neglect (p. 235).

18   Kessel 1991, p. 17. But the optimism was not the only reason for this neglect of the social sciences: another important reason was that social stratification of socialist society was a taboo under Stalinism.

Above all it was the group of the abolitionists whose arguments became prevailing in the field of legislation. The work on drafts for a new socialist penal code had already begun in 1951. Closely referring to von Liszt's division into three types of offenders, the first drafts aimed at deterring everybody from crime, of neutralising the enemies of socialism and of educating the backward people. They contained norms sanctioning prostitution, absenteeism and a lack of work discipline.[19] But the latest draft of the new penal code of 1959/60 did no longer refer to asocial offences and workhouses were not provided either.

Two main reasons for this success against the hard-line politicians are to be mentioned. The first one results from the area of international politics, namely the de-Stalinisation of the Khrushchev era (cf. the Twentieth Party Congress of the CPSU in 1956). The second one results from conditions within the society of the GDR. The 1950s were an era of social relaxation and openness. On the one hand there were outstanding opportunities of social advancement due to the gaps left by the numerous victims of war and Nazism, the brain-drain towards the FRG and, last but not least, the ideologically motivated affirmative action towards working class youths. On the other hand the struggle for social advancement was not very strong, since – also as a result of the ideologically motivated transformation of the society – being a worker did not mean belonging to the lowest social stratum any more, neither economically nor symbolically, whereas the former privileges of other social strata were reduced at the same time.

Consolidation During the Ulbricht Era

But the progressive tendencies did not last. At the end of the 1950s, a wind of change was blowing from the USSR, creating new anti-parasite laws.[20] The novelty of this legislation was that according to these laws two formerly rather distinctive groups were concerned: Begging, prostitution and other forms of petty crime were sanctioned as parasitic (not very differently from western European legal tradition)[21]. At the same time, more 'bourgeois' be-

---

19 cf. the drafts, Bundesarchiv, BA DP 1 VA 1326, fol. 65-73 and fol. 326.
20 Raschka 2005, p. 323-344
21 Schroeder 1961, p. 292-305.

haviour was covered by these laws, such as living on rental income or doing skilled work illicitly.[22]

Like most other states of the Warsaw Pact, the GDR more or less copied these laws in the form of an ordinance creating the possibility of restricting residence (*Verordnung zur Aufenthaltsbeschränkung*) from August 1961.[23] Because of two facts this ordinance is a good example of the legislative processes in this type of dictatorial state (*Maßnahmestaat*). Since it meant a severe restriction of personal freedom, in a constitutional state this kind of a penal regulation would have had to pass through a parliamentary legislative process. This was not the case in a state where the aim of fighting for socialism was considered to be more significant than the fundamental freedoms and rights of the citizens. As a result this ordinance was passed by the Council of Ministers of the GDR instead of the parliament. The second characteristic is the vague and extensive definition of the constituent elements of crime. According to § 3, 2 of the ordinance the courts had the possibility to sentence people who were work-shy to work camps, a new kind of punishment.

As the ordinance did not specify who would be guilty of unwillingness to work, a discussion arose among politicians and legal experts concerning the question against which people they should use this newly forged, sharp weapon. Lekschas and Renneberg, at that time young and ambitious professors of law and communist hard-liners (for them every crime was an act to be seen within the context of class struggle, and therefore every criminal was a foe of socialism) wanted to interpret it along the lines of the Soviet example.[24] But Ulbricht himself called them off and forced them to criticise themselves.[25] The reason for Ulbricht's reluctance was his economic policy and his strong desire for inner consolidation, which led him to declare the class struggle inside the GDR to be over[26] and to forbid the interpretation of crime inside the GDR as a form of class struggle (*Klassenkampftheorie*). As a result only in the very first months of its existence the ordinance was used against the 'bourgeois type' of offender. Later on, the term 'parasite' as a negative topos was only kept on a very abstract, ideological level, whereas in the eve-

---

22 Beermann 1961, p. 111-146; Bilinsky 1957, p. 803-808; Maurach 1964, p. 185-195

23 The thesis of some authors that this ordinance has to be seen as being closely related to the construction of the Wall lacks convincing proof.

24 Lekschas./Renneberg 1962, p. 76-91

25 ibid., p. 500-505

26 As some scholars state convincingly, as early as the notorious conference of Babelsberg, 1958.

ryday life of legal authorities and experts the old stereotype of talking about an asocial person was dominating.

During the last months of 1961 and in 1962 the situation was still chaotic. In many places the law enforcement agencies started to use this new ordinance to sentence quite a huge number of cases in comparison to the late 1950s. There were some more than 300 convictions during the third quarter of 1961 and about the same number in the following three months. The Minister of Justice and the State Attorney General were appalled and tried to contain this uncontrolled development. One problem was that nobody knew where to imprison the more than 750 new convicts, because the planned boot camps had not been established yet. At the very beginning they were committed to ordinary prison institutions, which was heavily criticised, because the experts claimed that work camps should be different from normal imprisonment. Living conditions in the newly opened camps were meagre. The inmates had to sleep in (sometimes rotten) shacks and they lacked the most commonplace items like cutlery, bed linen, socks or shoes. They were obliged to work hard, e.g. in open-cast mining, railway construction, brickyards or in the textile industry, for between 48 and 60 hours a week. The measures for achieving social rehabilitation were often reduced to harsh discipline, order, tidiness and cleanliness, sometimes combined with lessons in Marxism-Leninism.[27] During the following years the situation improved with regard to both the inner organisation of these camps and the proceedings preceding the convictions. According to the Departments of Justice and of the Interior, a sentence on the basis of the ordinance should be passed as a last resort only. In about 1965 a procedure comprising three stages had been developed. During the first stage the state did not want to intervene, but a serious intervention in the collective at work or in the neighbourhood should help. If necessary, it was combined with some mentoring by colleagues or neighbours. If these measures failed, the local authorities for the Interior (*Rat des Kreises*) should intervene and force the person concerned to undergo measures of supervision and care. Only after all of these measures had failed a criminal trial should be initiated. This system was codified in an ordinance added to the Penal Code of 1968 (*Verordnung über die Gefährdetenfürsorge*).

In the course of the sixties the social sciences in the GDR began to develop, starting with the first participation of a GDR delegation at the world congress of the International Sociological Association (ISA) in 1959 and the participation of a large GDR delegation at the conference of editors of philo-

---

27 cf. the reports in Bundesarchiv, BA DO 1.11/108 and 1580

sophical reviews of the Warsaw Pact countries in Leipzig in 1962. Institutional frameworks were generated[28] and scientific work became increasingly prolific[29]. Scientists aimed at a more realistic and less dogmatic approach to their own society. The consequences for the area analysed here were manifold. Sociologists and criminologists did not interpret offences like vagabondage, begging or prostitution as facets of class struggle anymore, therefore the 'parasite' variant of offender did not find its way into the GDR penal law of 1968. The focus was on the former asocial offences, complemented by absenteeism and a lack of working discipline. These occurrences were also no longer regarded as atavisms of an outdated society to be replaced soon, but they were regarded as social problems to persist for a yet incalculable period of time. The abolitionist trend of the late fifties was revised. After some years of research and debates, the commissions creating the draft for the penal code reform finally reintroduced an article (§ 249) in the Criminal Code of 1968 which sanctioned 'asocial behaviour' with at least one year in a work camp (*Arbeitserziehungslager*). In these debates the experts had to decide which institution was better suited to reform the convicted – the asylums for social mentoring, emanating from the old workhouses, or the boot camps, established after 1961. They decided in favour of the latter. The workhouses were closed down completely during the 1960s. With their integration in the criminal code, work camps as a special kind of imprisonment received a legal basis.

As ideology still forbade blaming society at large for the continuance of petty crimes, the discussion on the causes of crime was restricted to the searching for causes at the individual or micro-social level (family problems,[30] drinking etc.). The difference from western criminology became smaller; on both sides of the Iron Curtain, criminological apologists of the respective established society tried to avoid the question of macro-social causes of crime.[31] In the descriptions of 'asocial milieus' in studies of the

---

28 Ludz 1972. After 1963, sociology in the GDR showed more and more characteristics of an autonomous science. An important step was the resolution of the Politburo to launch a sociological research programme. During 1964/65 sociological departments were opened at the universities of Berlin, Dresden, Greifswald, Halle, Jena, Leipzig and Rostock, as well as the Institut für Gesellschaftswissenchaften beim ZK der SED in Berlin. Also in 1964, a scientific council was founded for sociological research.
29 For the criminology cf. Rode 1996
30 See for example Ludwig 1983
31 cf. Korzilius 2001, p. 587-608

1960s, 1970s and 1980s the authors referred to numerous old and long-lasting clichés formed during the German Empire or Weimar Republic.[32] The main traits cited[33] were laziness and a lack of ability to delay gratification. Thus "asocial behaviour" in a broader sense meant the eagerness to earn a living easily, without working (therefore prostitutes remained the prime example of female 'asocials'[34]), the unwillingness to study or to improve professional skills and a lack of cultural interests or sporting ambition. 'Asocials' were described as unable to maintain stable partner relationships, preferring to spend their time in loose peer-groups, lingering around and drinking excessively[35]; with respect to their sexual behaviour they were characterized as promiscuous. In a nutshell, they were said to be unable to live their lives in a methodical, planned way, as analyzed in Max Weber's 'Protestant work ethic'.[36] The criminal sanction of work camps, especially designed for those whose deviance from this ethical norm became too apparent, should teach them a self-disciplined lifestyle. This is very important for a comparative analysis of socialist and capitalist societies: their common denominator is the fact that they are both work-oriented societies. Both social concepts despised social welfare and claimed instead that those who wanted to work could earn their own living by working. Those who did not adapt to a rigid labour discipline in both societies were not only not helped willingly, but even held responsible themselves and finally punished.

---

32 Lindenberger 2005, p. 227-254
33 E. g. in academic monographs like Rudolf 1979, Wolf 1978, Horbank 1975, Jackwerth 1985, Lehmann 1978, Pfennig 1989. For stereotypical descriptions in the materials of the draft-commissions for the penal code cf. above all Bundesarchiv DP 1 VA 2424 and 2425
34 For comments on prostitution cf. a report of the prosecutor of the disctrict of Dresden from 28th of Dezember of 1972: Bericht über die Untersuchung der Delikte nach § 249 StGB, Hauptstaatsarchiv Saxonia, RdB 33051, and Fehr 1983
35 For the close relation of drinking and 'asocial behaviour' cf. Baatz 1975, Szewczyk 1978 and 1979; Hauptstaatsarchiv Thüringen, Weimar: BdVP Erfurt 20.1. (1961-1975), Nr. 236, fols. 101-105: Bericht zur Alkoholkriminalität vom 24.08.1970
36 cf. Neumann 1988, pp. 160-171. Gorz 1988, p.172-192 describes socialist work ethics as an attitude that goes back to this ethical concept.

Escalations Under Honecker

During the 1970s and 1980s, clichés about 'asocial behaviour' did not change significantly; but nevertheless the 1970s started with some optimism. An interpretation of the legislation on criminal prevention of 1968 shows that the government credited the society with the ability to play a decisive role in the process of social reintegration of 'asocials' (and other deviants). But suddenly an important change took place: the conviction rates increased dramatically. Such an explosion of criminal persecution is unquestionably a sign of a systemic crisis which needs profound elucidation. The rising paranoia of Honecker and his entourage is firstly to blame. They required a more totalitarian approach to solve, or at least to hide, social problems. This development led to mass persecutions, aiming especially at presenting a "clean" GDR to an international public, as for example shortly before and during the 10th World Festival of Youth and Students in 1973, when the figures of detentions based on § 249 Penal Code of the GDR exceeded 14,000 for the first time (nearly ten times as many as 1967!), namely[37] because of a lot of spontaneous apprehensions in the Berlin area.[38]

The paranoia of the Honecker government may account for some peaks in the statistics, such as that of 1973, but it is not sufficient to explain the fact that the detention figures stayed on a very high level throughout the last twenty years of the GDR. To give a second explanation, I want to propose a very important reason which requires taking into account the development of the East German society,[39] – in other words: its closure and the negative impacts it had. The GDR's own sociologists had already begun to investigate social stratification and processes of closure. Because of the justifying nature of the allegedly egalitarian character of East German society, the government

---

37   Whereas during the 1960s, sentences based on § 361 of the old Penal Code had nearly ceased to exist and sentences based on the ordinance of 1961 only in 1967 began to rise above 1000 a year, sentences based on the new § 249 rose up to 4161 in 1969, they continued as follows: 1970: 3756, 1971: 5061, 1972: 5686, 1973: 14164, 1974: 7414, 1975: 6498, 1976: 5850, 1977: 5200, 1978: 7507, 1979: 11528, 1980: 13292, 1981: 10299, 1982: 10930, 1983: 9329, 1984: 7703, 1985: 5460
38   Raschka 2000, p. 67-7
39   This fact is sometimes neglected by some older, Cold War-influenced studies, which concentrated on the asserted 'totalitarian' character of the GDR.

ordered some of these studies to be kept secret[40], but western scientists were also investigating the society of the GDR. These studies prove that a social stratification existed, and that the working class was not at the top. Unskilled workers were considered to be a stratum at the lower end of society. And this stratification was cemented over generations, meaning that the descendants of unskilled workers had very little chances of ascending socially, whereas children of the intelligentsia and especially of the new political elites could easily follow their parents.[41] This closure[42] caused frustration, for a lot of, primarily younger, GDR citizens in two respects: they did not see any chance of advancing socially and economically in their own society[43], but dreamed of such chances in a western society, which was what western television and other media promised. At its best this frustrated struggle for social advancement led to sharper social distinctions,[44] at its worst it resulted in aggressions towards the weakest or most inferior people, who slid into the role of scapegoats. Whereas during the fifties working collectives showed strong solidarity (remember the outburst of strong dissatisfaction on June 17th, 1953) and tried to hide weaknesses of individual colleagues from supervisors, this solidarity fell apart later. Victims of such growing social aggression were not only those stigmatised as

---

40 Thieme 1996
41 Geißler 1992; Merkens 2000
42 On social enclosures in general see Parkin 1983. Parkin states that during phases of social closure this closing mainly operates via strategies of exclusion, by which one social group tries to preserve or even to augment its privileges through the subordination of another group, i. e. by excluding another group as standing beneath its own. In fact, I believe this is what happened in the GDR under Honecker when the mass-production of 'asocials' via marginalisation, discrimination, denunciation, criminalisation and stigmatisation. But what I do not like is Parkin's notion of strategy: strategy implicates a rational, planned action. This is what does not happen in such social processes (at least not in my case study of the GDR), they occur more unconsciously and very often not in bad faith on the part of social actors. On social closure
43 This is no contradiction to the findings of some social historians on the GDR which prove that a lot of people did not want to get into higher positions. (Solga 1995 and 2001, p. 35-52) People did not renounce these positions, because they did not want to pay the price for this kind of ascension, namely to get closer to the party and the state, with the consequence of being obliged to show more loyalty and therefore lose personal freedom.
44 cf. Bourdieu 1979

'asocials', but also foreigners such as immigrant workers[45] and other minorities[46].

Since the fall of the Wall, contemporary witnesses have tended to deny this. There are mainly two reasons for this denial. The first one is what creative spirits called '*Ostalgia*', a special form of nostalgia of former GDR citizens. The second one is that the marginalised, as the term already implies, were only a minority. A lot of witnesses, however, belonged to the core of a collective and do not remember a lack of solidarity with some of their colleagues. Only after more intensive questioning do witnesses often admit that special brigades for 'drunkards' (*Trinkerbrigaden*) existed and that some colleagues were expelled from work as 'asocials' or 'work-shy'. In fact, the social discrimination[47] and the willingness to denounce 'asocial behaviour'[48] rose significantly. The reports are full of complaints from workers asking the officials to free them from 'asocials' in their collectives and of citizens demanding harsher punishments for these offences.[49] 'Asocials' became outsiders in processes very similar to those described by Elias and Scotson.[50] It is an important peculiarity that in the GDR under Honecker criminal law was used as one of the weapons in this 'battlefield' of social distinction. In French society, as analysed by Bourdieu, the process of establishing distinctions worked rather informally, at a symbolic level, based on the central role of habitus. But criminalisation can play a role in such processes, as Fritz

---

45 cf. Behrens 2003; Elsner/Elsner 1994
46 Maaz 1990
47 cf. Zeng, p. 148-152 and Jackwerth, p. 35 and 68 for discrimination in the neigbourhoods.; cf. also: Friedrich-Ebert-Stiftung 1977, p. 40
48 Jackwerth, p. 69.
49 See, for example, reports on the elections of judges and lay judges from 1972 and 1974, Bundesarchiv DP 1 SE 1588. Cf. also a report of the municipal council of Blankenburg (Bezirk Magdeburg), in: Landeshauptarchiv Magdeburg, Rep. M1 RdB/BT Nr. 7666), and the reports of the district courts of Frankfurt (Oder), Suhl, and Cottbus from 1986 in Bundesarchiv DP 1 SE 1587/2. Cf. also Backhaus 1984, p. 98 and 104. He states that collectives would ask for harsher punishments of those with a bad labour discipline, and that they wanted to get rid of them. Neubert 1973, p. 266 ff. comes to very similar conclusions. The development in the USSR resembled that of the GDR, cf. Connor 1972, p. 256 u. S. 266-268. For rising conflicts at work cf. also the report: „Arbeitseinsatz und Integration in den Arbeitsprozeß von kriminell Gefährdeten/Asozialen", Landesarchiv Berlin C Rep. 104, Nr. 236, p. 16.
50 Elias/Scotson 1965

Sack convincingly showed: just as school diplomas can contribute to differentiation in a positive way, a criminal sentence has the opposite effect for the convicted.[51] In this respect the unqualified legal definition of 'asocial behaviour' bore far-reaching consequences within the GDR. In the field of law the term 'asocial' did not have its colloquial meaning, but the colloquial term rather unconsciously found its way into the administrative and judicial procedures which 'asocials' had to undergo, via the sense of justice, intuition or experience of judges, other officials and lay people involved,[52] via the statements of the public prosecutor, of the representatives of collectives, who often painted an extremely negative image of the accused[53], or of officials of the institutions which had dealt with an asocial person before he reached the last stage of a trial, and finally via the criminological literature, which, as we have seen, teemed with pseudo-scientific clichés. As a consequence the social stigmata[54] were acknowledged as formal, judicial labels, a fact that contributed to reproducing the social structure.[55]

The rising number of denunciations must have aggravated the paranoid anxieties of the government; and at the same time the apparent unwillingness of society to reintegrate people with social problems led to disillusion concerning solidarity in a socialist society. Politicians had to accept that they could not force people into a feeling of fraternity towards their fellow citizens. Due to both factors the criminal policy became increasingly harsh. The persecution was intensified steadily, law enforcement agencies were extended, Stasi staff had to investigate the 'asocial milieus', and even new legal projects to permit the hospitalisation of certain persons in a special kind of asylum were discussed.[56] In some of the larger factories special brigades for socially deviant people, like alcoholics, people released from prison etc., had to be created, because the regular collectives were not willing to accept them. This development could only end up in a vicious circle.

---

51   Sack 1968, p. 469ff. According to Sack, the crime confirmed by a sentence becomes one of the 'negative goods' analogous to positive goods like assets, income or privileges.
52   This is not peculiar to the GDR, but happens in all judicial processes. Cf. Sack, p. 461ff.
53   Backhaus 1984, p. 120
54   For social stigmatisation cf. Goffman 1963
55   Lamnek 1994, p. 193
56   cf. BStU MfS HA IX 15946, fol. 5-22 and BStU MfS HA IX 13067, fol. 13-24.

Conclusion

Throughout modern history, the approach to social problems has been Janus-faced: a helping, caring face always found its complement in a disciplining, castigating face. This fact was not different in the GDR. Even the provisional arrangements of the military government after the war concerning prostitutes, beggars, homeless and the 'work-shy' showed this duality. The officials tried to organise the food and medical supply, but at the same time demanded that everybody should dedicate his or her strength to reconstruction. These measures did not establish the preconditions for further development. A political discussion on the role of social care in a socialist state on the one hand and of criminal law on the other hand only began in the 1950s. The ideological mainstream held the opinion that the most important step in solving social problems had already been done by having founded a socialist state. There were two different consequences of this attitude. Social care was neglected and some politicians hoped soon to be able to abandon it completely. Criminal laws against asocial behaviour were also regarded as unnecessary, because they were interpreted as a rather innocuous relic of the old bourgeois society. The concurring ideological view which interpreted crime, and even petty crime, as an offence showing a hostile attitude towards the new society did not gain acceptance and it was finally abandoned by its protagonists under pressure from Ulbricht in 1962.

But abolitionist views did not triumph either. At the end of the 1950s, the USSR enacted 'anti-parasite laws', which, due to the coercion within the alliance, had to be introduced in the other states of the Warsaw Pact as well. With the ordinance of 24th August, 1961, the GDR fulfilled this task in a very simple way. The text was not edited carefully (unintentionally or on purpose?). The formulation concerning punishing the 'work-shy' could have meant anything. It could have been meant as a weapon in the last stage of class struggle, or merely as a means of educating undisciplined workers. Ulbricht interpreted it in the latter sense. After a rather chaotic phase at the very beginning of the 1960s, in about the middle of the decade the most deplorable circumstances in the newly installed boot-camps were improved, though even then the 'education' or 'social rehabilitation' in these facilities was reduced to very hard work and harsh discipline.

At the same time, social sciences developed in the GDR. However, as the results of their investigations were not meant to describe persisting structural inequalities of the socialist society (Ulbricht had postulated equality, but not achieved it) as one possible reason of deviance, they concentrated on micro-social and individual problems as causes of crime and thereby came very close to the coeval conservative criminology of western states. Their studies did not overcome the negative stereotypes of their predecessors of the last decades of the 19th and the first of the 20th century; their approach did not develop any really innovative ideas, neither did the new Criminal Code of 1968. But the legislators of 1968 still showed a certain confidence in the capacity of socialist society to deal with social problems in a fraternal, non-discriminatory way. The three-stage treatment of deviants labelled as 'asocials', which had been developed during the 1960s and codified in 1968, showed that particularly the collectives at work were expected to reintegrate deviant and other people with social or comparable problems.

Under Honecker, these hopes proved to be illusions. The system, as in many other fields of the GDR economy and society, showed serious signs of crisis. The most striking one was an explosion of the convictions based on § 249 of the East German Criminal Code. They rose above 14,000 in the course of 1973 and never sank beneath 5,000 again (in contrast to only some 1,500 cases in 1967). This alarming symptom may be explained by two major reasons: growing paranoia of the government under Honecker, which also became apparent in the enormous expansion of *Stasi* staff and '*IMs*', and a double closure of the GDR society. This closure was felt strongly because of the contrast to living conditions in the west, which were idealised by the media and seemed to promise good chances of advancement, and a lack of possibilities of advancing socially even within their own socialist society. This led to frustrations, to stronger attempts to distance oneself from people supposed to be inferior and even to open aggression towards minorities or deviants. In this phase, the tendency to denounce people with a less disciplined *habitus* as 'asocial' rose. Together with the quasi-totalitarian paranoia of the Honecker regime, this led to a vicious circle of criminalisation, which GDR citizens could not really escape until the system collapsed.

References

Adler, Frank: *Ansätze zur Rekonstruktion der Sozialstruktur des DDR-Realsozialismus*, in: Berliner Journal für Soziologie, 1991, p. 157-175
Ayaß, Wolfgang: *Das Arbeitshaus Breitenau*. Kassel 1992
Ayaß, Wolfgang: *"Asoziale" im Nationalsozialismus*. Stuttgart, 1995
Baatz, Gerhard: *Psychiatrische Probleme der Alkohol- und Sexualkriminalität sowie Asozialität*. In: Staat und Recht 24 (1975), pp. 1617-1620

Backhaus, Klaus: *Die effektive Ausgestaltung des Strafverfahrens bei Straftaten Asozialer gemäß § 249 StGB*. Potsdam 1984
Beermann, R.: *The Parasites Law*. In: Soviet Studies 1961/62, p. 191-205
Behrens, Jan: *Fremde und Fremd-Sein in der DDR: zu historischen Ursachen der Fremdenfeindlichkeit in Ostdeutschland*. Berlin 2003
Bilinsky, Andreas: *Parasitengesetze in der Sowjetunion*, in: Jahrbuch für Ostrecht 1961, p. 111-146
Bock, Gisela: *Zwangssterilisation im Nationalsozialismus. Studien zur Rassenpolitik und Frauenpolitik*. Opladen 1986
Boldorf, Marcel: *Sozialfürsorge in der SBZ/DDR 1945-1953. Ursachen, Ausmaß und Bewältigung der Nachkriegsarmut*. Stuttgart 1998
Bourdieu, Pierre: *La distinction. Critique sociale du jugement*. Paris 1979
Connor, Walter: *Deviance in Soviet Society. Crime, Delinquency and Alcoholism*. New York/London 1972
Daners, Hermann: *"Ab nach Brauweiler...!" Nutzung der Abtei Brauweiler als Arbeitsanstalt, Gestapogefängnis, Landeskrankenhaus*. Pulheim 1996
Elias, Norbert/Scotson, John Lloyd: *The Established and the Outsiders. A Sociological Enquiry into Community Problems*. London 1965
Elsner, Eva-Maria/Elsner, Lothar: *Ausländerpolitik und Ausländerfeindschaft in der DDR (1949-1990)*. Leipzig 1994
Falk, Uta: *VEB Bordell. Geschichte der Prostitution in der DDR*, Berlin, 1998Korzilius, Sven: *"Asoziale" und "Parasiten" im Strafrecht der SBZ/DDR. Randgruppen im Sozialismus zwischen Repression und Ausgrenzung*. Köln/ Weimar/Wien 2005
Fehr, Gerhard: *Zu einigen Aspekten der Entwicklung der Risikogruppe der männlichen Homosexuellen und der Risikogruppe der kriminell gefährdeten, nicht lesbischen weiblichen Jugendlichen und Jungerwachsenen in der Hauptstadt Berlin*. Berlin 1983
Friedrich-Ebert-Stiftung (Ed.): *Kriminalität, Strafvollzug und Resozialisierung in der DDR*. Bonn-Bad Godesberg 1977
Geißler, Rainer: *Die Sozialstruktur Deutschlands. Ein Studienbuch zur sozialstrukturellen Entwicklung im geteilten und vereinten Deutschland*. Opladen 1992
Goffman, Erving: *Stigma. Notes on the Management of Spoiled Identity*. Englewood Cliffs 1963
Lamnek, Siegfried: *Neue Theorien abweichenden Verhaltens*. München 1994
Gorz, André: *Jenseits von Arbeitsutopie und Arbeitsmoral*. In: Zoll, Rainer (Ed.): *Zerstörung und Wiederaneignung der Zeit*. Frankfurt/Main 1988, p. 172-192
Groehler, Olaf: *Integration und Ausgrenzung von NS-Opfern. Zur Anerkennungs- und Entschädigungsdebatte in der Sowjetischen Besatzungszone Deutschlands 1945-1949*, in: Kocka, Jürgen (Ed.): Historische DDR-Forschung. Aufsätze und Studien (Zeithistorische Studien). Berlin 1993, p. 105-127
Horbank, Horst: *Untersuchungen zum Tatbestand der Gefährdung der öffentlichen Ordnung durch asoziales Verhalten gemäß § 249 Abs. 1 StGB 1. und 3. Alternative*. Berlin 1975
Jackwerth, Gerald: *Zur sozialen und rechtlichen Situation Strafentlassener und kriminell gefährdeter Bürger. Eine empirische Untersuchung ihrer finanziellen Gesamtsituation zu Beginn der Resozialisierung*. Berlin 1985

Kessel, Carsten: *Rechtssoziologie in der Deutschen Demokratischen Republik.* Berlin 1991
Liszt, Friedrich von: *Der Zweckgedanke im Strafrecht.* Berlin 1882/83
Kocka, Jürgen: *Ein deutscher Sonderweg. Überlegungen zur Sozialgeschichte der DDR.* In: Aus Politik und Zeitgeschichte 1994/40, p. 34-45
Korzilius, Sven: *Kriminalitätsursachenforschung in Ost und West. Die DDR-Kriminologie im Vergleich mit Michael R. Gottfredson/Travis Hirschi: A General Theory of Crime,* in: Timmermann, Heiner (Ed.): *Die DDR in Deutschland: ein Rückblick auf 50 Jahre.* Berlin 2001, p. 587-608
Lehmann, Christel: *Die Entwicklung von Kindern aus desorganisierten Familien.* Berlin 1969
Lekschas, John/Renneberg, Joachim: *Lehren des XXII. Parteitags der KPdSU für die Entwicklung des sozialistischen Strafrechts der DDR.* In: Neue Justiz 1962, p. 76-91
Lekschas, John/Renneberg, Joachim: *Zur Überwindung von Dogmatismus und Sektierertum in der Strafrechtswissenschaft,* Neue Justiz, 1962, p. 500-505
Lindenberger, Thomas: *„Asoziale Lebensweise". Herrschaftslegitimation, Sozialdisziplinierung und die Konstruktion eines „negativen Milieus" in der SED-Diktatur.* In: Geschichte und Gesellschaft 31 (2005), p. 227-254
Ludz, Peter Christian (Ed.): *Soziologie und Marxismus in der Deutschen Demokratischen Republik,* vol 1. Neuwied/Berlin 1972
Ludwig, Heike: *Gestörte Familienbeziehungen und psychische Auffälligkeiten bei fehlentwickelten Jugendlichen (Untersuchungen in einem Jugendwerkhof).* Jena 1983
Maaz, Hans-Joachim: *Der Gefühlsstau. Ein Psychogramm der DDR.* Berlin 1990
Maurach, Reinhardt: *Der Tätertyp im Wandel des Sowjetstrafrechts,* in: Recht in Ost und West (ROW) 1964, p. 185-195
Merkens, Hans (Ed.): *Übereinstimmung und Differenz – Jugend in der DDR.* Hohengehren 2000
Naimark, Norman: *The Russians in Germany. A History of the Soviet Zone of Occupation, 1945-1949.* Cambridge, Mass./London 1995
Neubert, Werner: *Bemerkungen zur Erziehung kriminell Gefährdeter.* In: Der Schöffe, 1973, p. 266ff.
Neumann, Enno: *Das Zeitmuster der protestantischen Ethik.* In: Zoll, Rainer (Ed.): Zerstörung und Wiederaneignung der Zeit, Frankfurt/Main, 1988, p. 160-171
N. N.: *Zur Rolle und Funktion der Täterpersönlichkeit in der Strafzumessung,* in: Bolck, Franz (Ed.): *Täterpersönlichkeit, Straffälligkeit, Strafzumessung.* Jena 1982, p. 23-38
Parkin, Frank: *Strategien sozialer Schließung und Klassenbildung.* In: Kreckel, Reinhard (Ed.): Soziale Ungleichheiten. Göttingen 1983, p. 121-135
Pfennig, Heike: *Zur Analyse und Bedeutung wesentlicher Sozialbeziehungen sozial auffälliger Bürger.* Berlin 1989
Raschka, Johannes: *Justizpolitik im SED-Staat. Anpassung und Wandel des Strafrechts während der Amtszeit Honeckers.* Köln/Weimar/Wien 2000
Raschka, Johannes: *Mobilisierung zur Arbeit. Die Verfolgung von „Parasiten" und „Asozialen" in der Sowjetunion und in der DDR 1954-1977.* In: Zeitschrift für Geschichtswissenschaft 53 (2005), p. 323-344

Rode, Christian: *Kriminologie in der DDR. Kriminalitätsursachenforschung zwischen Empirie und Ideologie.* Freiburg im Breisgau 1996

Rosin, Wolfgang: *Asozialität – eine der auffälligsten Abweichungen von der Grundnorm sozialistischer Lebensweise.* Berlin 1978

Rudolph, Andrea: *Die Kooperation von Strafrecht und Sozialhilferecht bei der Disziplinierung von Armen mittels Arbeit.* Frankfurt/Main u.a. 1995

Rudolf, Gottfried: *Zur Diagnostik asozialitätsrelevanter Einstellungen.* Berlin 1979

Sachße, Christian/Tennstedt, Florian: *Geschichte der Armenfürsorge in Deutschland. Vom Spätmittelalter bis zum Ersten Weltkrieg.* Stuttgart u.a. 1980

Sack, Fritz: *Neue Perspektiven in der Kriminologie,* in: Sack, Fritz/König, Réné (Ed.): *Kriminalsoziologie.* Frankfurt/Main 1968, p. 432-475

Schroeder, Friedrich-Christian: *Gesellschaftsgerichte und Administrativjustiz im vorrevolutionären Rußland. Ein Beitrag zum Problem der Kontinuität des russischen Rechts.* In: Osteuropa-Recht 1961, p. 292-305

Solga, Heike: *Aspekte der Klassenstruktur in der DDR in den siebziger und achtziger Jahren und die Stellung der Arbeiterklasse.* In: Hürtgen, Renate/Reichel, Thomas (Ed.): Der Schein der Stabilität, DDR-Betriebsalltag in der Ära Honecker. Berlin 2001, p. 35-52

Solga, Heike: *Auf dem Weg in eine klassenlose Gesellschaft? Klassenlagen und Mobilität zwischen Generationen in der DDR.* Berlin 1995

Szewczyk, Hans: *Untersuchungen und kritische Beurteilung der Entwicklungsbedingungen zum Alkoholstraftäter,* in: Kriminalistik und forensische Wissenschaften 1978 (34), p. 51-55

Szewczyk, Hans (Ed.): *Der Alkoholiker. Alkoholmißbrauch und Alkoholkriminalität.* Jena 1979

Thieme, Frank: *Die Sozialstruktur der DDR zwischen Wirklichkeit und Ideologie: eine Analyse geheimgehaltener Dissertationen.* Frankfurt/Main u.a. 1996

Volkstribunale für "Parasiten". In: Ost-Probleme 1957, p. 803-808

Windmüller, Joachim: *Ohne Zwang kann der Humanismus nicht existieren- „Asoziale" in der DDR.* Frankfurt/Main 2006

Wolf, Matthias: *Ursachen und Mitbedingungen der Asozialität. Typenanalytische Untersuchungen zu Dissozialen sowie typenanalytische Auswertung von Nachuntersuchungen der späteren Entwicklung der begutachteten Probanden.* Berlin 1978

Zeng, Matthias: *„Asoziale' in der DDR. Transformationen einer moralischen Kategorie.* Münster 2000

Heike Wolter

Farewell / Well-Fare to the Beach – the GDR's Recreational System

"One cottage here is more beautiful than the other, the service is very good." This was written by Marlies Baumann from a trip to Greifswald in 1986. The mentioned service – organized by the trade union *(Freier Deutscher Gewerkschaftsbund, FDGB)* included accommodation, full board and an extensive sporting and cultural programme during her two-weeks-holiday. The expenses (in the best category!) were approximately 300 Marks – about a third of the genuine price. If she had travelled with a child, she would only have to pay 30 Marks more.[1]

This is one example of Erich Honecker's visions, when he declared at the 8. party convention of the Socialist Unity Party *(SED)* in 1971: "We only know one goal, which signifies our party's general politics: to do all we can for the people's well-being, for the happiness of the people, in the interest of the working class and all working people. This is the aim of socialism. For that we work and struggle."[2]

The Idea of the Comprehensive Welfare System in GDR

In the GDR, the idea of public welfare was – in opposite to the present-day understanding of welfare politics in Germany – imbedded into the target of social security for all people. Therefore the GDR tried to provide a widespread well-being of the whole population – even though on a relatively low level. Doing so, they extended the idea of 'welfare' on one hand, on the other hand they attempted to avoid the traditional understanding of the term, because full employment and work obligation were installed to make welfare benefits superfluous.[3]

The development of social tourism, which will be treated in the following contribution, shows that these kind of 'socialist' strategies were not only

---

[1] cf. FDGB-Bundesvorstand 1980
[2] ZK der SED 1975, p.134
[3] cf. Boldorf 1998, p.187

meant and realized to take care for the people, but also to control and to patronise them.

'Tourism' as a Welfare Strategy?

It is obvious that holiday arrangements can only marginally be counted among the classic parts of social security systems. While health resorts, recuperative holidays for children as well as the cures for disabled people may be a prevalent part of the welfare system, comprehensive recreation proposals for the whole population are normally situated outside the traditional understanding of public welfare. In the GDR however, the interest in people's recreational activities was based on Marxism/Leninism, where tourism is ideologically regarded as a strategy to recreate manpower for the working progress. Thus, all employees, and eventually also their families, had the entitlement to join the benefits of tourism, although the name itself was not very 'politically correct'. In the official GDR terminology 'recreational system' was the elementary term for the whole official holiday programme,[4] because the capitalistic term 'tourism' should be completely repelled. The word 'recreational system' was chosen to demonstrate the socialist understanding of social security as a basic instrument to heal the people's distress, protect them against life's discomfort – and to guarantee their work power.

The Genesis of Social Tourism in the GDR

In the first period it was not possible to build up a comprehensive public recreational system in the GDR. There were, however, early attempts of the Soviet Military Administration (*SMAD*) and, later, of the government to offer affordable holiday arrangements for all people, as a part of substantial living standards. Important strategies to realise these ideas were: The confirmation of paid holiday entitlements for workers and employees in the first GDR constitution in 1949; the set up of the FDGB's holiday service in 1946/1947; and – partially illegal – the acquisition of holiday capacities using existing buildings by takeovers and expropriation.

---

[4] cf. Oehler 1989; Uebel 1968

In the beginning only trade union members and their families had the privilege to spend this kind of inexpensive holidays. But the promised advantages motivated more and more people to join the trade union (in 1989 97,4% of the working public were members of the FDGB) – and the recreational benefits soon became a common property.

However, the FDGB was not the only institution that offered social tourism opportunities in the GDR, even though the trade union understood itself as the main provider for recreation until the end of the GDR. Additional recreational institutions were youth tourist *(Jugendtourist)*,[5] the ministry for the people's education *(Ministerium für Volksbildung)* in the department of child recreation and other mass organisations.[6] Only the GDR travel agency, founded in 1957, worked cost-covering and was thus not part of the GDR's welfare institutions.

In the 1960s the domestic travel opportunities extended, and the travel facilitation into socialist states created a higher demand for journeys abroad. This new framework of tourism brought the GDR government into conflicts: The low-level domestic holiday offers (which were originally meant as a welfare provision) were increasingly perceived as insufficient. Especially since the extension of tourism in the 1970s, the people's desires could not be fulfilled any more.[7] Although some administrative units for recreation were installed on the level of departments and districts, the demand was much higher than the supply, which was characterised by a low quantity, a lack of quality and insufficient coordination.

The intension of Erich Honecker to combine economic and social policy, definitely produced a more distinct perception of the recreational requirements of the people, but on the other hand it boosted the public expectations – and could only marginally been carried out.

---

[5] 'Jugendtourist' was the youth travel agency of the GDR. It belonged to the general GDR travel agency, since 1973 it was independent.

[6] The GDR's cultural federation *(Kulturbund)*; the German gymnastic and sporting federation *(Deutscher Turn- und Sportbund)*; the society for German-Soviet Friendship *(Gesellschaft für deutsch-sowjetische Freundschaft)*; the society for sport and technology *(Gesellschaft für Sport und Technik)*; the garden plot holders, settlers and small animal breeders unit *(Verband der Kleingärtner, Siedler und Kleintierzüchter)*; the committee for tourism and trekking *(Komitee für Touristik und Wandern)*.

[7] The holiday travel capacities rose according to Heike Bähre between 1975 and 1989 from 3.1 million journeys to 8.6 million journeys a year (Bähre 2003, p. 271).

Limitations of Welfare Tourism

Until 1989 the demand continued to be extremely higher than the supply. Because of the FDGB allocation quotas, people could only avail a trade union holiday once every five to six years. Further on the travel opportunities were not, as pronounced by the propaganda, open to everybody. People of economically important enterprises, state institutions and the National Army (*NVA*) were preferentially considered.

Although being in serious economical difficulties, the GDR government could not claim for any consumers renouncement – especially not for reduced recreational offers. Thus, the existing potential had to be used as effectively as possible – a fact that could not remain concealed to the citizens.

Even in case these efforts would have been successful, they were not made to care for the people, but to legalize a system which systematically restricted some of the people's rights. But, supported by extensive propaganda strategies, the GDR's welfare policy realized itself as the executor of a 'conservative system management.'[8]

The Clients of the Recreational Policy

The concept of recreational policy – introduced at the FDGB conferences – demonstrated without ambiguity, who were the target groups of social care, and which parts of the population were regarded as undeserving. Apart from the general development of the capacities of the holiday camps and the improvement of the hygienic standards, the concepts underlined the fact that especially families, children and youth should be included into the recreation offers.

The typology of welfare entitlement is exemplified by the criteria of the FDGB's holiday awarding:[9] Travel offers were assigned according to work efficiency and work conditions,[10] the family situation – especially families with many children were considered - the number of obtained FDGB holidays in recent years, and the degree of social activity inside and outside the

---

[8] Meyer 1989, p. 30
[9] cf. Informationsblatt des FDGB. Each year the 'assignment of FDGB holidays' for the following year was published.
[10] Shift workers, and people who were working under hard conditions, were preferentially chosen.

FDGB. Certain destinations abroad and privileged kinds of travelling – such as cruises – were only assigned to a small part of the population or as an award – strictly outside allocation key.

For the normal programme everyone was eligible, who was an FDGB member for at least one year. People could apply for a holiday for themselves, their partner and their underage children. Also eligible were young professionals and trainees independent of the length of their membership; active members at university or basic military services; members who were temporarily occupied abroad – and since the mid 1970s: also pensioners.[11]

A typical notification of acceptance might read: "In the previous year, colleague Meier has worked very well. She is conscientious and cooperative. She was prepared to work overtime in order to fulfil the department's duties. In her function as the trade union official for culture, she has done a very good job. She has two children, and though she worked here for the last five years, she never received a trade union holiday."[12]

Areas of Classic Welfare Policy in the Recreational System

The official welfare policy in the GDR showed a particular interest in ill and old people, as well as children and adolescents. These groups were supported continuously – also in the recreational system.

Among others, comprehensive measures were taken for people with special needs by taking them on FDGB holidays for the deaf, haemophile, blind, handicapped, families with mentally disordered children, patients suffering from celiac disease and nephritic diseased diabetics.[13]

Physically handicapped children and adolescents – though only a small number – had also the opportunity to spend holidays in the specialised "International Rehabilitation Camp for the Physically Handicapped" in Pepelow, others in accordingly equipped youth hostels. Despite these efforts, which were based on a fundamentally generous support by the state as well as the personal engagement of custodians, also in this area the basic and finally overstraining problems of the socialist state's welfare structures became obvious. The necessary expansions could not be made, and the hardly acceptable demands to the according hostels and professional attendance suf-

---

[11] cf. FDGB 1975, p. 8
[12] Kante 1999, p.110f.
[13] cf. Grossmann 1988, p. 170

fered from a lack of professional helpers.[14] Individual agreements with local contractors to find a pragmatic solution were not wanted, because they did not fit into the ideas of socialist centralism and the aspired comprehensive programs.

Even graver deficits became obvious in the interaction with mentally ill people, whose tourist mobility frequently remained their family's concern. A comprehensive cooperation with the Youth Association (*FDJ*) and other mass organisations was mere propaganda. Therefore affected families founded so called '*rehab clubs*', which offered youth hostel journeys to the mentally disabled. Their state support was limited to financial allowances (all participants could travel for free). But the search for support staff and other operative requirements remained difficult.[15]

The GDR child and youth welfare service included anyone of these target groups, because the GDR's youth policy, youth protection and youth care were regarded as a unity. All these responsibilities were unified within the sector of 'people's education' - declaring them as FDJ's 'youth assistance'. Beyond the narrowly defined area of classic youth welfare service for 'delinquent', 'ineducable' and 'antisocial'[16] adolescents (in which recreational questions did not play any role), the state regarded himself as a promoter of socialist education and thus as an advocate for reasonable leisure and holiday offerings.[17]

For pensioners, the '*Volkssolidarität*' functioned as the competent welfare institution, although they offered no recreational holidays, because the vast majority of aged people were provided by the FDGB, based on their membership during their employment. Each former FDGB member was eligible to off-rate journeys, because they belonged to the lowest income group with a monthly revenue of less than 500 Marks.

The GDR's prophylactic and rehabilitative curing system was open to all citizens and comprehensively developed.[18] The cures were assigned by the GDR social insurance, which was since 1956 centrally managed by the FDGB. A certain number of 'cure cheques' were assigned to each enterprise, to pass them on to individual employees.

---

[14] cf. Sommer 1989 (youth hostel ‚Adolf Hennecke' in Hormersdorf)
[15] cf. Barsch 2007, p.181ff.
[16] The pejorative term continually appears according to Marcel Boldorf in contemporary documents (cf. Boldorf 1998, p.236).
[17] cf. Eckardt 1984, p.56ff.; Bernhardt/Kuhn 1998
[18] cf. Bähre 2003, p.264ff.

Functions of Recreation and Tourism

In 1985, Margita Grossmann identified the function of recreation and tourism in socialism as a conglomerate of social, political and economic missions.[19] Until 1989 the GDR regarded itself as a society with different social classes and groups, which cultivate different ways of living. Considering tourism, these groups showed differences in dependency to their income, education and further factors. The aim of social policy was, however, to create social homogeneity and to reduce the effects of social differences – not least – with the help of recreation welfare strategies: "A major feature of social tourism is it's being open to all groups of the population, who spend their work capacity in the reproduction process or constitute the labour potential of the future."[20] In reality a lot of privileged groups existed whose living conditions differed obviously from those of the mass population. Therefore, the contradiction between the socialist idea of mankind, in which all individuals are equal members of the society – and the conservation and stabilisation of the reigning class' leading position, could not be resolved.

The Recreational System as a Part of GDR Social Policy

The studies on the recreational system in GDR reveal the basic contradictions of GDR social policy. In the 1950s the character of socialism included predominantly the idea to make social and welfare policy superfluous. But since the 1960s social policy was appreciated as an important area of political action. In the mid 1960s experts analysed a deep conflict inside the theoretic fundament of the socialist social policy when arranging social security in the GDR. This was caused by exogenic (most COMECON states turned to rather consumer oriented politics) as well as endogenous factors (the population's protest against certain living conditions). In the GDR which was by now recognised as a developed socialist society, the different groups were supposed to enforce their social interests by actively dealing in the according representative institutions.

Concerning these changes social tourism was no longer acknowledged as a temporary type of holiday, whose function would soon be overtaken, but

---

[19] cf. Grossmann 1985, p.773
[20] cf. ibid., p.781

became a widely accepted form of travelling. Fights rather took place within the arrangement of the different social tourism providers who tried to substantiate their social function. The main question was now, how the deprivileged image of social tourism could be improved.

These processes led to the development of new institutional structures such as the foundation of a *FDGB* social policy department or a number of social political research facilities. An increasingly pragmatic tourism policy emerged, which attached importance to the protection of tourist needs and, above all, to fulfil the self-set provisioning claim. Thereby, the GDR government recognized that tourist needs would not alter in isolation but accordingly to the international development.

Together with the increasing lack of appreciation towards full employment for all in the GDR as a 'work-fare-state',[21] a process of delegitimisation arose. The population considered social tourism offers no longer as the stately propagated 'social achievement'. The SED had to face the irresolvable conflict between welfare aims and the lack of the necessary economic resources. The year 1989 consequently proved to be the 'consumer revolution' which was dominated by unsatisfied welfare aspirations.

Dictatorship of Welfare, Relief of Provisioning?

Beyond the narrow understanding of welfare structures, in the area of recreation it seems appropriate to describe the GDR as a 'welfare dictatorship' (*Fürsorgediktatur*) like Konrad Jarausch did,[22] although this is a rather generalising term for the different stages in 40 years of GDR history. The GDR had a welfare system, which was less concerned with special needs of the disadvantaged but tried to create general benefits – a kind of a 'hypertrophic relief'. Beatrix Bouvier, however, advocated the term 'provisioning dictatorship'[23] to describe the concept of social security in the GDR. Independent of the choice of the term, the GDR's recreational system widely fulfilled the features of classic welfare criteria: basic provisioning, recreation of work power and the validation of minimal life standards. On the other hand the economics functions of tourism suffered, such as giving and taking an impe-

---

[21] This characterisation was rightly made by Manfred Schmidt, who identified the GDR as a „mixture of welfare state and workfare state" (Schmidt 1999, p.303).
[22] cf. Jarausch, 1998, p.43f.
[23] Bouvier 2002, p.337

tus to the economic and societal development as well as being the motor of individual differentiation. Although this may be a strange perspective today – it was an effective part of the GDR welfare system – welfare to the beach.

References

Bähre, Heike: Tourismuspolitik in der Systemtransformation. Eine Untersuchung zum Reisen in der DDR und zum ostdeutschen Tourismus im Zeitraum 1980 bis 2000. Berlin 2003
Barsch, Sebastian: Geistig behinderte Menschen in der DDR. Erziehung – Bildung – Betreuung. Oberhausen 2007
Bernhardt, Christoph/Kuhn, Gerd: Keiner darf zurückgelassen werden! Aspekte der Jugendhilfepraxis in der DDR 1959-1989. Münster 1998
Boldorf, Marcel: Sozialfürsorge in der SBZ/DDR 1945-1953. Ursachen, Ausmaß und Bewältigung der Nachkriegsarmut. Stuttgart 1998
Bouvier, Beatrix: Die DDR – ein Sozialstaat? Sozialpolitik in der Ära Honecker, Bonn 2002
Eckardt, Peter: Sozialistische Sozialpädagogik. Dargestellt an der Jugendhilfe der DDR. Hannover 1984
FDGB-Bundesvorstand (Ed.): Grundsätze für die Verteilung der Erholungsaufenthalte des FDGB für den Zeitraum 1976-1980. Beschluß des Präsidiums des Bundesvorstandes des FDGB vom 8. August 1975. In: Informationsblatt des FDGB. Beschlüsse und Informationen des Bundesvorstandes des FDGB 12/1975, p.4-8
FDGB-Bundesvorstand (Ed.): Programm für die Entwicklung des Kur- und Erholungswesens der Gewerkschaften im Siebenjahrplan der *DDR* von 1959 bis 1965. Markranstädt 1960
FDGB-Bundesvorstand (Ed.): Richtlinie zur Neuregelung der Finanzierung des Feriendienstes. Berlin (ca. 1980)
Grossmann, Margita: Funktionen des Fremdenverkehrs in der sozialistischen Gesellschaft. In: Wissenschaftliche Zeitschrift der Hochschule für Verkehrswesen Dresden vol. 4/1985, p.771-786
Grossmann, Margita: Zur Entwicklung des Sozialtourismus in der DDR unter den Bedingungen der intensiv erweiterten Reproduktion. In: Mitteilungen aus der kulturwissenschaftlichen Forschung. In: vol 24/1988, p. 168-173
Hering, Sabine /Münchmeier, Richard: Geschichte der Sozialen Arbeit. Eine Einführung. Weinheim/München 2005
Jarausch, Konrad H.: Realer Sozialismus als Fürsorgediktatur: Zur begrifflichen Einordnung der DDR. In: Aus Politik und Zeitgeschichte 20/1998, p.33-44
Kante, Edgar: Deutschland – ein Schauermärchen. Aufstieg und Fall der DDR selbst erlebt. Berlin 1999
Meyer, Gerd: Der versorgte Mensch. Sozialistischer Paternalismus: bürokratische Bevormundung und soziale Sicherheit. In: Landeszentrale für politische Bildung Baden-Württemberg (Ed.): Politische Kultur in der DDR. Stuttgart/Berlin/Köln 1989, p.29-53

Oehler, Ellenor et. al: Erholungswesen. Leitung, Organisation, Rechtsfragen. Berlin 1989

Rothaar, Erich: Die Feriendienstkommission. Berlin 1975

Schmidt, Manfred G.: Grundzüge der Sozialpolitik der DDR. In: Kuhrt, Eberhard (Ed.): Die Endzeit der DDR-Wirtschaft – Analysen zur Wirtschafts-, Sozial- und Umweltpolitik. Opladen 1999, p. 273-319

Sommer, Eckhard: Wandern im Stuhl. In: Neues Leben. Jugendmagazin, vol. 8/1989, p. 56f.

Uebel, Horst: Zur begrifflichen Systematik des Fremdenverkehrs. In: DDR-Verkehr, vol. 8/1968, p. 307-310

Vortmann, Heinz: Soziale Sicherung in der DDR. In: Aus Politik und Zeitgeschichte vol. 32/1988, p. 29-38

Weinert, Rainer/Gilles, Franz-Otto: Der Zusammenbruch des Freien Deutschen Gewerkschaftsbundes (FDGB). Zunehmender Entscheidungsdruck, institutionalisierte Handlungsschwächung und Zerfall der hierarchischen Ordnungsstruktur. Wiesbaden 1999

Wolff, Hans-Jürgen: Die Fremdenverkehrspolitik der DDR. Ein Ausdruck und Mittel zur Erfüllung der Hauptaufgabe des VIII. Parteitages der SED. In: Lehrstuhl für Ökonomik des Fremdenverkehrs an der Hochschule für Verkehrswesen ‚Friedrich List', Dresden (Ed.): Beiträge zur Fremdenverkehrswissenschaft, Bd. 5, o.J., p. 7-26

Wolter, Heike: „Ich harre aus im Land und geh, ihm fremd" Die Geschichte des Tourismus in der DDR. Frankfurt/Main, 2009

ZK der SED (Ed.): Für das Wohl des arbeitenden Menschen all unsere Kraft. Bericht des Zentralkomitees an den VIII. Parteitag der Sozialistischen Einheitspartei Deutschlands. In: Honecker, Erich: Reden und Aufsätze. vol. 1, Berlin 1975.

Dorottya Szikra

Social Policy under State Socialism in Hungary (1949 - 1956)

Similarities and Differences between Welfare Policies in State Socialist Hungary and Capitalist Democracies in Western Europe (1949 - 1990)

The similarities between state socialist and capitalist countries have rarely, if ever, been analyzed.[1] The most important similarity is probably the constant growth of public expenditure in general, and within that, welfare expenditure in particular within the whole period. At the same time, it is not easy to make such a comparison, because the structure of expenditures was very different.[2] Another similarity is that the growth of expenditures and a real boom of welfare states took place in both parts of Europe in the 1970s. This was the period when earlier reforms and extensions of, for instance, the pension insurance schemes came to maturity. Also, a more extensive growth of family policies, and within that, the setting up of caring institutions for children and the elderly took place in most of the countries. As the 1980s in Western Europe are marked by the debate on the welfare state being in 'crisis', the same problems arose in Eastern Europe, although accompanied by a complete lack of professional or public debates.

The major differences included those arrangements that would not be present in Western European capitalist democracies, but were of central importance for state socialist countries. The most important of all these was the full-time employment as a right and as an obligation. Although capitalist countries also aimed at full employment after World War II, it was mainly meant for men, on the one hand, and it was not compulsory, on the other hand. Because full employment belonged to the fundamental commitments of the state socialist countries, there existed no unemployment insurance, although the problem could not be systematically extinguished. Furthermore, the generally low levels of both incomes and social transfers were kept in place for the entire period, although differences rose by the 1980s. This also

---

1 One of the few exceptions is the book of Goran Therborn, 1995.
2 Tomka 2004

meant that a two-earner family model was not only a must but also a necessity.

A second difference was the major role of price subsidies. Although this was not an unknown feature of capitalist democracies in the period under research, it was not applied to such an extent as in state socialist countries. A third feature was the relatively central role of firms, and especially of heavy industrial firms, in welfare provision. Although it is true that most fringe benefits were provided to people (mainly to men) in managerial positions,[3] blue-collar workers also had the possibility to take their children to the kindergarten operated by their firms, receive cheap meals and drinks at their firms or benefit from distributions of scarcely available goods via their employers. Thus, low-paid compulsory employment, a high level of price subsidies and an extensive set of fringe benefits can be detected as the most important state socialist features of welfare provision.

The period of state socialism can be divided into three main parts. These sub-periods would not be the same in all of the state socialist countries of course, but they would somewhat be similar. Also, the level of payments and the measures taken differed substantially from country to country.[4] Although we will mention some facts about other Central and Eastern European countries, our focus is on Hungary and the periods are presented according to the Hungarian case. These are the following: 1. From the communist take-over until the early 1960s; 2. From the mid-1960s to the mid-1980s; 3. From the mid-1960s to the systemic changes of 1990.

The Political Background of 'Welfare' Politics

The structure and mechanisms of social policy in early state socialist Hungary cannot be grasped without taking a brief look at the tremendous political and economic transformations that took place in the country between 1949 and 1956. The short seven years that passed between the onset of the single party system in 1949 and thereby the establishment of the communist regime in Hungary and the outbreak of the 1956 revolution saw the rise and fall of a Stalinist dictatorship. This meant: the complete restructuring of the work and function of the Parliament, the government, the local administration and the country's economic and social life. Subordinate to Moscow-directed political

---

3   Kemény 1990.
4   Szikra/Tomka 2009

goals a catch-up industrialization dominated the economic, social as well as educational policy making.

By 1949, the Hungarian Workers' Party (*Magyar Dolgozók Pártja, MDP*) gained hold of full political power in Hungary and a single-party communist regime was established. The secretary general of the Hungarian Communist Party and from 1948 of the Hungarian Workers' Party, Mátyás Rákosi, acted as the country's deputy prime minister and in 1952-53 as its prime minister. During the Rákosi era, between 1949 and 1956, political pluralism ceased to exist and with the annihilation of political and personal freedom the country was transformed into a totalitarian regime. The Central Committee, the Politburo and the Secretariat that formed the head of the party dictated and oversaw the work of the Parliament, the government and local administration. The State Security Authority (*Államvédelmi Hatóság ÁVH*) established in 1948 and from 1950 onwards existing under the direct heading of the Council of Ministers and Rákosi himself functioned as a state secret police. Before it was dissolved following the 1956 Revolution, it not only controlled the issuance of passports, documents that were hard to obtain in the tightened political control of the early 1950s, but also operated four internment camps and organized the forced removals of 'class enemies' from their homes to various locations in the country. The members of ÁVH also played an active role in the construction of political trials, one of the largest of which in Hungary took place in 1949 when then Minister of Foreign Affairs, László Rajk and several high ranking army officials were sentenced to death and executed.

The early phase of state socialism was also characterized by extensive industrialization with an emphasis on the establishment of Hungary's heavy industry and the expansion of the labor force. The country was governed along five-year-long economic plans subordinate to Moscow-directed politics. In spite of the entrance of middle class women to the labor force and the constant redesign of the educational structure to meet the industry-driven regime's efforts to produce sufficient numbers of workers to its shifting types of employment needs the country was struggling with both unemployment and a lack of properly trained work force. A figure from 1953 illustrates the problem well. There were about 150,000 unemployed professionals, ironically, mostly in the field of heavy industry.[5]

---

5   Vámosi 2009

Steps in Welfare Provision: 1945 - 1975

In the first period of state socialism, contrary to the aggressive propaganda, there was not much improvement in the level of welfare provision. Important measures were taken, like the extension of social security to formerly excluded social groups, most importantly the agricultural workers, but levels of payments stayed very low. Although family allowance was also extended to all those who were in full-time employment, this, just like other measures, only applied to those working in the state-run sectors. Agricultural workers, even those who worked in the state sector, received lower payments, and in Hungary, for instance, they were not covered by free health care. This way, social insurance and also family policies were designed to drive people into the heavy industry, the growth of which was the ultimate goal of the communist leadership.[6]

Although state propaganda claimed that 'the greatest treasures' of communist states were their children, the Hungarian state hardly put any effort into the creation of an extensive system of child care institutions, such as crèches or kindergartens. The social historian Éva Bicskej has shown that the central state actually withdrew from such tasks, and – compared to the situation in the late 1930s and the early 1940s – it passed the responsibility of opening up such institutions much more into the hands of municipalities and parents themselves.

This was not so different in the early 1950s in Western Europe either where child care services were also started to be extended in the 1960s. At the same time there were two important differences: One was state propaganda concerning the ultimate paternal responsibility of the central state and its leaders in sharp contrast with reality. The second important difference was that the complete lack of political and civil rights made it impossible for people to react to what was being or not being done to them. Also, constant fear from being penalized for minor political or civil actions indeed worsened the level of people's well-being. Due to the low level of payments and the lack of welfare institutions the living standard of the Hungarian people actually decreased by the mid 1950s.[7]

Widespread poverty and the lack of political rights suggest that sociologist Lynne Haney's description of the first two decades of state socialism in

---

6   Szalai 1998
7   Ferge 1986

Hungary as a period of 'welfare society' might be only partially supported.[8] Suppressed dissatisfaction with the system, including the lack of welfare, led to protests and uprisings all over the Eastern bloc. The year 1956, the revolution in Hungary and the uprisings in the same year in Poland had major consequences for the development of social policies in the region. An unspoken consensus between the state and the people was settled by the late 1950s in which political leaders realized that there was no way to stay in power without providing more extensive welfare measures for people. This means that in case of state socialist countries the famous Marshallian concept (1952) on the development of rights was successfully turned upside down: The state provided welfare rights, sometimes quite extensively, but expected the population to give up the slightest hope for having civil or political rights in return.[9]

This compromise opened the way for a new wave of social policy legislation throughout the whole region. The most important of these changes concerned women: The introduction of extended parental leaves in all the East-Central European countries in the late 1960s. This move was markedly new and different both from previous policies about female labor market participation and from the short-term maternity leaves that remained in place in Western Europe. Apart from Poland, where the long-term maternity leave was unpaid until the 1980s, it provided a reasonable payment for mothers staying at home with their children until the ages of two or two and a half, later until three. The reasons for its introduction included the surplus of female labor force by the time of slower industrialization, and also, increasing concern about extremely low fertility rates. Psychologists of the time also suggested that it was best for children if they remained with their mother in first three years of their lives.

Another important change was the move towards universalism concerning the inclusion of agricultural workers into the welfare schemes from which they were either excluded previously or unfavorably treated. Since 1975, finally, free health care and the same level of family allowances and pensions became also available for the agricultural workers in Hungary. In Poland, farmers were included into existing social insurance schemes in the late 1970s too.[10]

This did not mean 'real' universalism, because those who had no full-time employment or who were not employed at all, like, for instance, some

---

8   Haney 2002
9   Szikra/ Szelewa 2008
10 Inglot 2008

Romany mothers with big families, were excluded from both the extended parental leave and other social insurance schemes.[11]

'Optional Familialism'

Although mothers were meant to stay at home with their children in their first years, the 1970s and early 1980s were the times of the creation of social services focused on child care. We thus see a situation where mothers really had the choice between staying at home and relying on institutions. This opened the way to the so called 'optional familialism'[12] in Hungary, where, although the primary caring activities were done by the family and thus overwhelmingly by mothers, the state provided some help for care-work. In other countries, like Poland, the state refrained from 'intervening' into the lives of families and thus left the caring responsibilities almost exclusively with mothers and female relatives. In Czechoslovakia, at the same time, a lack of welfare services and an extremely long parental leave (four years) meant that the state explicitly wanted mothers to stay at home and care for their children. At the same time, because of the unequal distribution of domestic tasks between men and women and because of the persistence of patriarchal relationships such state actions increased the dependence of women on their partners.[13]

In the middle of the 1980s it became increasingly obvious that the socialist countries were not able to finance their expenses themselves. The loans that Hungary received from the World Bank from the middle of the 1980s made its situation rather complex at the eve of the systemic changes. The World Bank not only demanded political democratization but also widespread welfare reforms. Most of all it was propagating the cutback on family allowances in Hungary and privatizing the pension systems all over the region.[14] Thus the end of state socialism and the introduction of market economies in the region not only meant the loss of millions of jobs and with that the loss of social security but also a struggle for welfare arrangements that were built up under the era of an unspoken compromise between communist leaders and the people.

---

11 Varsa 2005
12 Leitner 2003; Szelewa/Polakowsky 2008
13 Saxonberg/Szelewa, 2007
14 Müller 2000; Orenstein 2008

Conclusion

In this paper I summarized the most important features of state socialist social policy and provided examples from the Hungarian development. The system of (almost) full employment, and within that, the full-time employment of women was the most important bases for state socialist social policy. As welfare rights were mainly linked to full-time employment, social policy became a means to fulfill the political and economic aims of the regime. We also described the three main periods within state socialism: Early social policies were mainly restrictive and did not provide significant welfare to people. It was not until the middle of the 1960s that state socialist social policies became an important source of welfare for people in Hungary. The 1956 Revolution in Hungary played an important role in this.

The renewed social policy of the 1960s was carried out partly through family policy measures which had long lasting effects on the Hungarian welfare system. An 'optional familialist' system was built up by the middle of the 1980s which provided a possibility for mothers to choose between subsidized care at home or kindergarten care for their children.

From the end of the 1980s there were several attempts to change the system of long maternity leaves and the relatively generous family allowance in the country, but these attempts met severe public resistance. This is all the more interesting that the partial privatization of the pension system could be carried out without such resistance.

References

Bicskei, Eva: Our greatest treasure is the child. The Politics of Child Care in Hungary between 1945-1956. In: Social Politics, 13/2006, p. 151-188.
Ferge, Zsuzsa: Fejezetek a magyar szegénypolitika történetéből. (Chapters from the History of the Hungarian Poor Policies). Budapest 1986.
Fodor, Éva: Working Difference: Women's Working Lives in Hungary and Austria 1945-1995. Durham 2003
Haney, Lynne: Familial Welfare: Building the Hungarian Welfare Society, 1948-1968. In: Social Politics 7/2000, p. 101-122.
Inglot, Tomasz: Welfare States in East Central Europe, 1919-2004. New York 2008
Kemény, István: Velünk nevelkedett a gép. (The machines were growing up with us). Budapest 1990

Leitner, Sigrid: Varieties of Familialism. The caring function of the family in comparative perspective. In: European Societies, 5/2003, p. 353-375

Müller, Katharina: From the State to the Market? Pension Reform Paths in Central-Eastern Europe and the Former Soviet Union. In: Social Policy and Administration, 36/2002, p. 156-175

Orenstein, Mitchell A: Privatizing Pensions. The Transnational Campaign for Social Security Reforms. Princeton University Press 2008

Saxonberg, Steven/Dorota Szelewa: The Continuing Legacy of the Communist Legacy? The development of family policies in Poland and the Czech Republic. In: Social Politics 3/2007, p. 351-379

Szalai, Júlia: "A társadalombiztosítás érdekviszonyairól." (The interests and the stake-holders of the Hungarian social security system). In: Szociológiai Szemle 1992/2, p. 27-43

Szikra, Dorottya/Dorota Szelewa: Passen die mittel- und osteuropäische Länder in das ‚westliche' Bild? Das Beispiel der Familienpolitik in Ungarn und Polen. In: Christina Klenner/Simone Leiber (Eds.): Wohlfahrtsstaaten und Geschlechterungleichheit in Mittel- und Osteuropa. Kontinuität und postsozialistische Transformation in den EU-Mitgliedstaaten. Wiesbaden 2008, p. 88-123

Szelewa, Dorota/M. Polakowski: Who cares? Patterns of Care in Central and Eastern Europe. In: Journal of European Social Policy, 18/2008, p. 115-131

Szikra, Dorottya/ Béla Tomka: Social Policy in East Central Europe. Major Trends in the 20st Century. In: Cerami, Alfio/Pieter Vanhuysse (Eds): Post-Communist Welfare Pathways: Theorizing Social Policy Transformations in Central and Eastern Europe. Basingstoke 2009

Therborn, Goran: European Modernity and Beyond. The Trajectory of European Societies 1945 - 2000. London and Thousand Oaks 1995

Tomka, Béla: Welfare in East and West: Hungarian Social Security in an International Comparison, 1918-1990. Berlin 2004

Varsa, Eszter: Class, ethnicity and gender - structures of differentiation in state Socialist employment and welfare politics, 1960-1980. In: Schilde, Kurt/Schulte, Dagmar (Eds.): Need and Care, Opladen 2005, p. 197-217.

Vámosi, Tamás: A Gazdasági Szerkezet és Szakképzési Rendszer Kapcsolata 1949 - 1956 (The Connection between the Economic Structure and the Educational System, 1949-1956). Pécs 2009

Eszter Varsa

Child Protection, Residential Care and the 'Gypsy-Question' in Early State Socialist Hungary

The protection of children by the state was a constitutionally declared right of citizens in the Hungarian People's Democracy. The post-1949 restructuring of child welfare and child protection emphasized the new state's commitment to the protection and education of its youth. Two landmark legal documents, the 1949 Hungarian Constitution and the 1952 Law on Marriage, the Family and Guardianship, testify state efforts to use childhood as a means to express a radical departure from the past. An enforced projection of the 'happy childhood' in state socialist Hungary served as an emblem of the success and self-justification of the state socialist enterprise.[1]

Protection by Law

Child protection was embodied in the law, and was linked to gender equality. The 1949 Constitution, which was not only Hungary's first codified constitution but also a declaration of the governing principles of the new Hungarian People's Democracy, specifically addressed the issue of the protection and education of Hungarian youth. In its introduction, the Constitution expressed the opening of a new era in which, together with "the leadership of the working class" and "reliance on the support of the Soviet Union, people have begun to lay down the foundations of socialism" and "the country, on the road of the people's democracy, is heading towards the realization of socialism."[2]

This document placed "the structure of institutions for the protection of mothers and children" among policies intended to support "women's equal rights with men," and also declared that "the Hungarian Republic pays special attention to the development and education of youth, and protects their rights consistently."[3]

---

1 cf. Kirshenbaum on the use of the image of the "happy childhood" in the context of Soviet Russia, pp. 133-159.
2 Law 20 of 1949
3 ibid.

The Law on Marriage, the Family and Guardianship expressly followed up the constitutionally declared protection of youth: "The purpose of the Law on Marriage, the Family and Guardianship is, based on §§ 50-52 of the Constitution and in line with our People's Democracy's social order and socialist moral understanding, to regulate and protect the institutions of marriage and family, ensure women's equality and children's protection in the marriage and the family, and forward the development and education of youth."[4] Decrees directly dealing with the issue of child protection and guardianship, issued in the same year, dealt also with the new regime's radical departure from "the anti-people state power of landlords and capitalists" that preceded Hungary's 'liberation.' In 1952, the Council of Ministers, for example, banned the official use of the term "abandoned children" which had been in use since the origins of charitable and state-supported child protection in pre-World War II Hungary, and introduced instead the notion of "children under state care," "endangered children" and "endangerment" to refer to youngsters between ages zero and eighteen who could be considered in need of state care. The decree hereby also raised the age limit for state care from 15 to 18.

Such documents show that child protection and education had gained official standing among the welfare responsibilities of the state and expressed ambitious goals for the society's children. But at the same time, state socialist Hungary, caught up in rapid industrialization and modernization, failed to fulfill these ideals. Residential care, a key institution of child protection in state socialist Hungary, not only formed part of the malfunctioning social and educational services of the state and made its residents especially vulnerable to the state's economic needs but it was also built on existing gender, ethnic and class differentiation in society.

Residential Care

According to data by the Hungarian Central Statistical Office, the size of the country's population was about nine million people in 1949. Children aged 0-18 comprised 31.6 % of the entire population out of whom 1.37 %, about 31-32 thousand children, were in state care. Describing the limited number of available facilities and the extent of poverty in Hungary, historian Ferenc

---

4   Law 4 of 1952 on Marriage, the Family and Guardianship

Gergely places the estimated number of children in need of state care to 2000-3000 cases.[5]

The preferred form of institutional provision for children in state socialist Hungary was residential care, which encouraged the placement of children under state care in large children's homes. A shift towards institutionalisation is well-illustrated by the following figures: With nine new Child Protection Institutions, built in the year 1950, there were altogether 70 children's homes in the country, housing more than 5,000 children.[6] The percentage of children placed in institutions grew quicker than those in foster care.[7] There was a shift toward building up and extending the children's homes structure in Hungary to care for children perceived to be 'abandoned' or 'endangered' in state-owned residential homes rather than in families.

Efforts towards the Assimilation of the Roma in State Socialist Hungary

Historical analysis has pointed out long-existing discriminatory and assimilationist attitudes towards the Romany population in Hungary whose earliest groups are documented to have lived in the country since the Medieval Ages.[8] Efforts towards the forced assimilation of the Roma with use of national policy measures appeared first in the Habsburg Empire in the middle to the end of the 18th century. Although state socialist Hungary voiced and constitutionally declared the equal rights of nationalities, it denied nationality rights to the Roma.[9] The first Central Committee decree on the situation of the Romany population in Hungary in 1961 stated the Roma "did not constitute a national minority" identifying them as a social rather than an ethnic

---

5   Gergely, 1997
6   Kurucz 1971, p.7
7   While in 1950 more than 50% of the about 25, 000 children under state care were placed into foster care, by 1955 this proportion had declined to 38 %, with only 7, 500 children placed in foster families out of the officially declared about 20.000 children under state care.
8   Mezey 1986
9   The Roma in Hungary comprise around 5-10 % of the population today. The first representative data collection in state socialist Hungary from 1971 identified their number around 3% of the population, but the data varied according to the methods of collection.

layer to be assimilated into the working-class.[10] The description of The birth of black identity cards for the Roma instead of the regular colour in 1953,[11] the existence of forced-bathings in Hungary between 1940 and 1985,[12] or Romany women's reduced access to Hungary's most generous motherhood benefit, introduced in 1967,[13] are only some of the well-documented discriminatory measures against the Roma in state socialist Hungary.

Banning Placement with Biological Relatives in 1950

In 1950, in the last year of its operation, the Ministry of Welfare brought out a decree in which the Minister of Welfare "strongly draws the attention of the directors of Child Protection Institutions to the fact that [...] only in exceptionally well-founded cases should they place children under the age of three and twins, without an age limit, who belong to Child Protection Institutions under their leadership, into the care of their biological relatives (*vérszerinti hozzátartozó*)."[14] In the background of this decree demanding a strict evaluation of the circumstances of children in state care for material reasons and eligible for placement with their biological relatives, there were serious concerns about the misuse of state support. In the following, I highlight an ethnicity-based differentiation behind the introduction of this decree in its intersection with gender and class:

I am using reports sent by various institutions in the country to the Ministry of Welfare leading to the introduction of this and a previous version of this measure in 1949 as well as the results of a nation-wide inquiry by the Ministry into the execution of the requirements demanded by the decree conducted between 1949 and 1950.

I show that especially Romany women and families were accused of an inclination to misuse and take advantage of state-provided support for their children.

---

10 Stewart 2001, p. 71
11 Purcsi-Barna 2004
12 Bernáth 2002
13 Varsa 2005
14 Decree 3.365-42/1950 (IV.6.) of the Ministry of Welfare, National Archives of Hungary (MOL), XIX-c-1-g, 3365/42/1950 (144.d.). Just prior to the introduction of local municipal councils the decree still refers to the pre-World War II administrative structure and makes use of its terminology.

In order to fully understand the Ministry of Welfare's call for the re-evaluation of children's eligibility for placement with biological relatives it is necessary to take a short look at the history of decrees around the end of World War II that allowed such placements. Following the end of the war the country's economic as well as national and international political situation motivated an increase in public-political attention to child protection. The rebuilding of welfare services, and among them, especially services for the welfare and protection of children, gained more and more political weight with the growing influence of the Communist Party and the concomitant struggle among parties for political power. It was not only the country's undeniable poverty, weak public services and a lack of public supply but also the seizure and rebuilding of the Ministry of Welfare by the Communist Party in 1945 that must be taken into account when explaining the history of decrees allowing for the placement of materially abandoned children with their biological relatives. A pre-war state provision of the Ministry of Interior from 1938 let twins, if officially declared materially abandoned, stay with their biological relatives.[15] In 1945, a decree by the Ministry of Welfare added that all materially abandoned children up to the age of three might stay with their biological relatives.[16] State support, otherwise used for the provision of children with foster parents or in a children's home, was to be given to the biological relatives and be spent for looking after the child.

At the time of its introduction the decree of 1945 was generally seen as a way to support poor, war-stricken families. This is reinforced by a letter to the Ministry of Welfare written by the head of the 9th Department of the Municipal Government of Budapest, responsible for social political affairs. Social Democratic Party member, Mrs. Pollák Szerén Stern, addressed the Ministry in September 1945 asking for the reintroduction of placements with biological relatives and "the raising of children in their families."[17] She pointed out that such a decree already existed in the early 1920s, preventing children from being "placed in another village or town or to the care of foreign (*idegen*) care takers. Placement into an orphanage was only formal and, in fact, turned into the welfare support of poor children."[18]

A further temporary extension of the decree of 1945 to so-called "new settler (*új telepes*) families" in 1947 underlines the class-differentiated struc-

---

15 Decree 271.000/1938 of the Ministry of Interior. Reference to this decree by the Ministry of Welfare, MOL, XIX-c-1-g, 3365/53/1950 (144.d.).
16 Decree 100.290/1945 N.M. Ibid.
17 Mrs. Pollák Szerén Stern, MOL, XIX-c-1-g, 117.446/1949 (96.d.)
18 Ibid.

ture of this provision and thereby strengthens the political undertone of state-provided child protection and welfare support given to families.[19] New settlers were usually poor, landless, working class families who were moved into the houses and farms formerly inhabited by ethnic Germans, forced to leave the country between 1945 and 1948. For a period of eight months, between March and October 1947, new settlers could receive state support if their children were declared materially abandoned and the child could be kept with biological relatives. The age limit was fixed much more generously than in other cases; it covered children up to fifteen in case the family had three or more children. Authorities were nevertheless careful to declare that families had to prove "they were otherwise competent to support the child."[20] Furthermore, in case children stayed in state care beyond October 1947 they were to be removed from their families and be placed with "foreign foster parents."[21] Introduced partly in 1947 and partly in 1948 another two decrees also allowed for the placement of officially abandoned children with their biological relatives without an age limit if parents were either yet unreturned prisoners of war or war widows.[22]

Against this background, it is interesting to see that in 1949 and 1950 authorities were beginning to express concern about both "a lack of attention to current legal measures" by institutions that placed children with their biological relatives "even when that would not have been permitted by law," and relatives taking advantage of this situation.[23] The degree of state-concern is demonstrated by the fact that the decree of 1950 is basically a reiteration of a similar decree from 1949.[24] In 1950, however, measures in support of war veterans and widows were also abolished. The introductory passages of both decrees reveal signs of alarm concerning "certain biological relatives" who, "as it has been found out" spend the money they received by the child protection institution for the "proper nutrition and support of children" for their "own purposes."[25] A following passage, also formulated exactly the same

---

19 Decree 88.661/1947 (III.1.), Reference to this decree by the Ministry of Welfare, MOL, XIX-c-1-g, 117.446/49 (96.d.).
20 Ibid.
21 Ibid.
22 Decree 86.070/1947 N.M and decree 114.479/1948 N.M. Reference to these decrees by the Ministry of Welfare, MOL, XIX-c-1-g, 131.100/1949 (99.d.).
23 Decree 3.365-42/1950 of the Ministry of Welfare, MOL, XIX-c-1-g, 3365/42/1950 (144.d.).
24 Decree 131.100/1949 (IX.10.) MOL, XIX-c-1-g, 131.100/1949 (99.d.).
25 Ibid and decree 3.365-42/1950 of the Ministry of Welfare, MOL, XIX-c-1-g, 3365/42/1950 (144.d.).

way in the two decrees, clearly shows that the state discourse at this point already constructed the need of children and their relatives as two separate entities: "Since children's placement with biological relatives, that only takes place in exceptional circumstances, serves not the interests of relatives but the interests of the child, the child care support can also not be viewed as a social aid or welfare measure in support of relatives but as serving solely the advancement of the subsistence and development of the child."[26]

By 1950 it was already squarely stated that placement with biological relatives was to be understood as "preferential treatment" that might be allowed "only in the interest of the child" and that was to be "revoked immediately in case of misuse."[27] The Minister of Welfare also demanded municipal governments, regional notaries, and mayors of districts in Budapest to recommend the placement of materially abandoned children with biological relatives only following "a thorough assessment" of the child's milieu (környezettanulmány).[28] Drawing on a decree from 1912, the decree of 1950 also established that children in Child Protection Institutions "may neither be placed in the same village or town where their parents reside nor in the same village or town where the circumstances of their abandonment originate from."[29] Finally, it also abolished the support for families of unreturned prisoners of war or war widows.

What motivated authorities at the national level to alter the regulation of child protection is revealed when looking at the institutional level. Reports from Child Protection Institutions to the Ministry show that directors were unhappy about how parents, and especially Romany mothers, were handling state-provided support.

A report written in April 1950 to the Ministry of Welfare by the director of the Budapest State Child Protection Institution, Mrs. Dési-Huber, shows against whom the decree was directed. The same month the decree about the renewed regulation of the placement of children in state care with biological relatives took effect, Mrs. Dési-Huber summed up the lesson from an "experiment" she made with altogether 24 children in a small town situated on the borders of the Great Plain: "As an experiment I denied the execution of the order of placement of nine children in the care of their mothers. I asked the Orphan Guardianship Authorities to review these decisions as well as

---

26 Ibid.
27 Decree 3.365-42/1950 of the Ministry of Welfare, MOL, XIX-c-1-g, 3365/42/1950
28 Ibid.
29 Ibid.

some previous ones there [in the small town] that in most cases concerned [the placement of] Gipsy children, and if they found our suspicion well-founded I asked them to terminate the status of abandonment or remove the child from the care of their parents." Mrs. Dési-Huber could boast about the success of her experiment since not only did she find out that out of the nine children there was only one who was thought to be rightfully placed with his or her parents but she also discovered another fifteen "almost without exception Gipsy children" who "were to be taken away from their parents or in case they were unwilling to give them to us their abandonment had to be terminated."[30]

Mrs. Dési-Huber closed her letter to the Ministry by stating that she will call on all small towns "having similar conditions" in the official district under the supervision of the institution directed by her to do such a revision and she recommended the same action to be taken by institutions in the countryside.

Another report to the Ministry of Welfare written by the Child Protection Institute of Kecskemét, a town in the South-West of Hungary, illustrates a similar differentiation of Romany mothers when revising cases of state care and placements with biological relatives. The Ministry of Welfare sent out a call in the spring of 1950 to all Child Protection Institutions in the country to revise and potentially decrease the number of children in state care. Making use of these reports on how many and what age children were left in state care the Ministry called on all directors in June 1950 who "have not executed" the ministerial decree on terminating the placement of children with their biological relatives. In answer to this call, that was threatening directors with punitive measures unless they abided, the director of the institute at Kecskemét confidently stated that there were no more children above the age of three left with biological relatives. He added that also the cases of children under the age of three and twins in state care raised by biological relatives "had to be on most occasions terminated." He identified in his report three main reasons for such terminations: "a lack of proof for material abandonment, the inappropriate placement of children with their relatives" because the money received was "not spent on the child," and finally, "the impossibility of controlling how the money was spent."[31] He attached a letter as well, written by one of the overseers of foster parents and such biological relatives, as "illustrative of the problem." In this letter the overseer reported that in her district parents were unwilling to let their children be raised by "a foreign

---

30 Mrs. Dési-Huber, MOL, XIX-c-1-g, 3365/42/1950
31 Tivadar Kesztler, director, MOL, XIX-c-1-g, 3365-53/1950

foster parent" and that therefore cases of state care had to be terminated. "As a matter of fact," she continued, "with one or two exceptions, there were mistakes with all [biological relatives]. Either the inappropriate nutrition [of the child], or the improper use of the support, or the environment is inappropriate. The latter of which, especially with the Gypsies, is impossible to avoid."[32]

The above case about the alteration of a regulation on the state care of children shows that national policy-making in the field of child protection was built around a presumption about the misuse of state-provided support to families and the inappropriate care given by parents of Romany origin. Dissatisfaction voiced at the local institutional level by heads of Child Protection Institutions was well-taken at the national level by the Ministry of Welfare and the placement of children with biological relatives was practically terminated. This action, in line with historical practice concerning the assimilation of the Romany population into the majority culture and population in the territory of Hungary, sheds light on its continuity under state socialism. Romany children were assumed to receive a better upbringing by the state than by their biological relatives. This case illustrates on two occasions that, not unlike in previous decades, various actors at both local and national levels shaped welfare measures so as to exercise gender, ethnic and class differentiation. The generous extension of the option to remain with biological relatives to the materially abandoned children of new settlers in 1947 supported the politically motivated population exchange that took place with the forced removal of the ethnic Germans from Hungary following World War II. This differentiation along ethnic and class lines was carried further with the termination of the regulation that was initiated on basis of anti-Romany discrimination. Since caregivers were understood to be mothers, both the introduction and the termination of the regulation were therefore connected to ethnic and class-based differentiation in intersection with gender differentiation.

Conclusion

In this paper I analysed gender-, ethnic- and class-based differentiations inbuilt in state welfare provisions supporting poor families whose children

---

32 ibid

were declared to be "abandoned" and "endangered" in the late 1940s and the early 1950s in Hungary. In the first years of the new, communist political system the country's welfare structure, and within that, child protection was substantially reformed. The main characteristic of the reform was the forced move away from the pre-World War II practice of foster care as the most popular form of state care to the institutional residential care of children. This reform in the field of child protection was motivated, among others, by the fact that in consequence of the war and the unequal distribution of resources after the war, mass poverty struck hundreds of thousands of families in Hungary. Also, many children lost one or both their parents. Political factors, such as the forced removal of the ethnic Germans from the country between 1945 and 1948, also played an important role. Although placing children with "biological relatives" was used as a means to provide poor families with extra resources in order to prevent them from starvation and secure their children with the minimum of subsistence in the late 1940s, it was suspected to be misused by some local and national level authorities. As a consequence, this measure was re-evaluated and by restricting it to strictly limited cases, practically terminated. This was a quite open anti-Romany move by the state that shows the racist character of state socialist welfare politics in the Hungary of the early 1950s.

References

Bernáth, Gábor (Ed.): *Kényszermosdatások a cigánytelepeken (1940-1985)* (Forced Bathings in Hungary, 1940-1985). Budapest 2002
Bicskei, Éva: *"Our greatest treasure the child." The Politics of Child Care in Hungary between 1945 - 1956.* In: Social Politics, vol. 13, 2006/2, p. 151-188
Gergely, Ferenc: *A magyar gyermekvédelem története, 1867-1991* (The History of Hungarian Child Protection, 1867-1991). Budapest 1997
Kirshenbaum, Lisa A.: *Small Comrades: Revolutionizing* Childhood in Soviet Russia, 1917-1932. New York 2001
Dezső Kurucz: *Statisztikai Tájékoztató 1970.* (Statistics 1970, Child Protection and Guardianship). Budapest 1971
Mezey, Barna, Tauber, István, Pomogyi, László. (Eds.): *A magyar cigánykérdés dokumentumokban* (The Hungarian Gypsy-Question in Documents). Budapest 1986.
Purcsi-Barna, Gyula: *A cigánykérdés 'gyökeres és végleges megoldása'* (A 'Radical and Final Solution' to the Gipsy-Question). Debrecen 2004
Stewart, Michael: *Communist Roma Policy, 1945-1989, as seen through the Hungarian Case.* In: Guy, Will (Ed.): *Between Past and Future: The Roma of Central and Eastern Europe.* Hertfordshire 2001, p. 71-92

Varsa, Eszter: *Class, Ethnicity and Gender – Structures of Differentiation in StateSocialist Employment and Welfare Politics, 1960-1980.* In: Schilde/Schulte (Eds.): *Need and Care, Opladen 2005*, p. 197-217

Barbara Klich-Kluczewska

Social Policy and Social Practice in the People's Republic of Poland

"Social policy as a science concerned with the ways of deliberate transformation of social structure has more opportunities than ever to develop. The revised socio-economic system will pose the great challenges to the discipline." (Krzeczkowski 1947)

Just after the Second World War some Polish scholars shared the opinion that reflection on outstanding prewar traditions of social policy in Poland would become an important point of reference for the new political authorities. They did not predict how quickly this notion would be blacklisted as undesirable, being in contradiction to the Stalinist state model. Social policy as a scientific discipline and as practical socio-political activities disappeared for almost six years from the public sphere and returned to official language only on the wave of the thaw of 1956. Then it was rehabilitated and a gradual comeback of the 'Polish social policy school' connected with the 'National Institute of Social Economy' (*Instytut Gospodarstwa Społecznego*), established in 1920, took place.

The special interest in social issues during the 1970s was accompanied with the attention to the ideas of prewar theoreticians:[1] Their thoughts influenced the works of numerous scholars of the post-1956 era,[2] who tried to formulate the new definition of social policy. Jan Rosner described social policy "in conditions of the socialism in 1972 as the activity of the state and social organizations in the field of shaping conditions of the existence and the work aimed at satisfying individual and social needs and based on principles of the socialist egalitarianism."[3]

The Transitional Period 1945 - 1948: Social Rescue

"Today the living standards in my village are very low. Not everyone has its Sunday's best. Everyday shoes are clogs. We eat bread and milk if there's a cow; otherwise, black coffee. Eggs, butter and cheese are only used to buy

---

1 Konstanty Krzeczkowski, Ludwik Krzywicki and Stanisław Rychliński
2 Wacław Szubert, Jan Rosner, Antoni Rajkiewicz, Jerzy Olędzki, Jan Danecki
3 Auleytner 2004, p. 92

salt, matches and paraffin. We always have potatoes, cabbage and noodles for lunch. Meat only for Easter or Christmas. Some are better off, but there are few of them, mostly those with a horse or a cow."[4]

This description provided by a villager from Central Poland, recorded in 1948, perfectly illustrates the situation among many residents in war-ravaged Poland, and also demonstrates the tasks faced after the Second World War by the new communist authorities. The new responsible leader fought against political opposition and, at the same time, introduced the programme of changes in the social and political system.

The agricultural reform, which, theoretically, had to solve the problems of the Polish – mostly rural[5] – society assumed obligatory and unpaid plotting of land properties. Therefore, the landed gentry was eliminated as a social group, but: the small land allowances received by peasants (on average three ha) did not significantly reduce the Poland-specific break-up and overpopulation of villages. In early 1946, all companies owned by Germans or Nazi-collaborators were nationalised without charge, while compensation was provided to all companies in the 17 most important branches of industry and enterprises employing more than 50 workers. Others were liquidated as a part of the so-called 'trade battle' in the years 1947until 1949.[6]

Facing the tragic economic devastation of Poland and prevailing the physical and psychical exhaustion of the society, social care was the essence of the social policy in the first years after the war. Immediate actions concerned, in the first place, orphans, disabled war veterans, people returning from concentration camps and repatriates from behind the eastern border. Social support institutions focused on satisfying the basic needs: providing additional food, clean clothes, sanitary means, and prevention and treatment of diseases that could spread into epidemics.[7] Ultimately, the support included 26.5% of population.

The actions were taken within legal frames of the pre-war social care act of 1923 that described "use of public resources to satisfy living needs of those that cannot do the same permanently or temporarily using their own funds or work; and also prevention of generation of the circumstances specified above."[8] This obligation was in the hands of municipal unions and of the state, if costs exceeded the municipal funds.

---

[4] Wieś polska 1968, p. 23
[5] 63% of the population lived in the country
[6] Trade battle, cf. Landau Z./ Roszkowski W. 1995, p. 231-235
[7] The risks of tuberculosis, typhus fever, dysentery, cf. Miernik 2007, p.167
[8] Ustawa o opiece społecznej, 16. 04. 1923

However, the charitable activities were not completely eliminated in the interwar period or replaced by modern social care policy. The social support market in the Second Republic of Poland - dominated by associations and funds of nationalist and religious nature - still existed after 1945.[9]

The variety of social support forms in early People's Republic of Poland resulted from reviving pre-war traditions. Provision of additional food, clothes and shelters was handled by local government and social organisations, laicist and religious foundations, congregations, state foundations and offices. An important role was played by the Polish Red Cross (*Polski Czerwony Krzyż*) and the Central Social Care Committee (*Centralny Komitet Opieki Społecznej*), established in 1944, forming a branch of state administration, to advocate more generosity for the needy. The flow of support in the form of cash and necessities also came from abroad via numerous organisations.[10]

The developed administrative model of social policy management also referred to interwar traditions. A separate Ministry of Labour and Social Care (*Ministerstwo Pracy i Opieki Społecznej*) was established, becoming the central body of social administration.[11]

Social Provisions and Full Employment?

Officially, the Ministry dealt with the following problems: the so-called 'social provisions' (social care, social security and some problems related to health protection) and the employment, which was of key significance owing to social and ideological reasons.

The full employment policy was strictly coordinated with the revitalisation policy of the Western Territories and the nationwide restoration. Labour surplus, as unemployment was officially referred to from this point, was reduced by employing people to clear debris in the cities and to reconstruct buildings.

Popular training courses improving qualifications were organised to provide for the loss of skilled labour borne by Poland during the war.[12] Con-

---

[9] Wódz 1982, p. 15; Krzyczkowski 2005, p. 53
[10] For example: UNRRA, CARE, YMCA, YFCA etc., cf. Jarosz 2002, p.15-16 or Miernik 2007, p.160
[11] Rosner 1975, p. 65
[12] Auleytner 2004, p. 119

trolled employment rose very quickly. Despite constant existence of 'surpluses', the campaign aimed at increasing productivity among women was commenced for ideological reasons. However, the strategies that seemed beneficial from the social viewpoint triggered economical losses. Owing to the disorder, expanding bureaucracy and low salaries, the average productivity was very low. The idea of labour competition and socialist discipline of work, transplanted to Poland in 1947, should have been a way to improve productivity. The real effects of these actions proved to be opposite to the intentions.

In 1946, only every fourth Pole used the support managed by the Social Security Office (*Zakład Ubezpieczeń Społecznych*) reactivated after the war. However, citizens did not pay their premiums by their own as this was the employer's obligation since 1945. At the same time, within the next four years, the state gradually became the employer of 80% of working Poles, which resulted in the practical nationalisation of the social security system. The simplification of the premium calculating system completely destroyed the dependence between premium payment and the resulting benefits.[13] As a consequence of acts amended in the post-war period, the number of insured gradually rose, to reach almost the whole population in the early 1980s.

Stalinism 1949 - 1956: Kept in Suspense

"A worker has no support; the higher instances are separated from the masses and hear nothing what people say."[14] Similar opinions, illustrating the social atmosphere in the first half of the 1950s, perfectly demonstrate the effects of the new direction in social policy at that time. After the period dominated by interwar traditions, in the late 1940s Poland adopted the Soviet model assuming that economic progress will automatically give rise to a quick social progress. Words like 'unemployment', 'housing problems', 'poverty' and 'alcoholism' were deleted from the official language of the Stalinism because it was deemed as a unnecessary and harmful remnant of the capitalist period.

Poland, similar to other countries of the Soviet block in the early 1950s, started to introduce plans of strenuous industrialisation as a part of a Six-Year-Plan, which resulted in a mass migration of rural population to the cities. In these days migration probably involved almost two million people,

---

[13] Gortat 1972, p. 167-171
[14] cf. Brzostek 2002, p. 49

mostly leaving villages and becoming unskilled workers. At the same time the system of obligatory work for prisoners and work order systems were launched.

Promises made by the authorities at the beginning of the Six-Year-Plan included the increase of salaries by 40% and consumption by 50-60%. The state socialism promised to bring full satisfaction of human needs. However, the increased international tension caused the industrial development to focus on military production. This reduced the already small resources for the agriculture, the light industry, the food industry and the housing construction.

According to recommendations of the Cominform of 1948, which obliged all Soviet block countries to collectivisation in the same year, a resolution regarding the establishment of producer's cooperatives (*Polish kolkhozes*) was adopted. Collectivisation was forced, but it included only a small portion of land in comparison with the other countries of the block: around 10% of the land (without state-owned farms that covered another 10%).

The political priorities caused that the promises of improved living conditions could not be kept at any rate. Growing salaries never caught up with galloping prices, while provision-related difficulties resulted in food rationing applicable until 1953.

In this dramatic social and political situation, the structure of the social policy administration was changed towards full nationalisation, which produced mainly the dispersion of competences and administrative chaos. According to assumptions regarding the comprehensive action of the state as the subject of social policy, independent social organisations were liquidated and social care units were nationalised. Dozens of institutions vanished, including Orphan Nest Society (*Towarzystwo Gniazd Sierocych*) or Dormitory and Scholarship Society (*Towarzystwo Burs i Stypendiów*), but also the Central Social Care Committee. The honorable catholic charity organization 'Caritas' and Congregation institutions were taken over; sometimes buildings of orphanages or care centres were given to state institutions to be converted into offices and apartments.[15]

The responsibilities of the Ministry of Labour and Social Care were limited. In 1949, financial and educational support for children and youth were transferred to the Ministry of Education, a year later the smallest children, pregnant and breast-feeding women were taken under the care of the Ministry of Heath, which also supervised employees' medical care as a part of social security. Problems of salaries were in the hands of the State Economic Planning Commission (*Państwowa Komisja Planowania Gospodarczego).*

---

[15] Jarosz 2000, p. 187-188

The determining position in the social administration system was taken over by the trade unions. Institutions not prepared for this task were burdened with labour protection and inspection since 1954. On top of that, the Social Security Office was liquidated in 1955; its duties were taken over by the trade unions, the Ministry and national boards, an equivalent of the liquidated territorial government.[16]

Employment enterprises, supervised by the party, union and administrative machinery, started to play – so far only theoretically – the role of the 'patrons of local communities', and their social activities started to be a tool of direct impact on employees and their families. The tasks – guaranteed by the 1952 Constitution – to support in case of sickness, to take care of mothers with children etc. fell into the responsibility of the employment enterprises, which often generated conflicts with the interests of a growing production.

Resources to finance social activities in employment enterprises (health care equipment, nurseries, sanatoriums, holiday, cultural and educational activity) came from Warsaw and depended on the volume of the payroll fund (the more significant the enterprise and the higher the salaries, the higher the social fund). A special Employee Holiday Fund *(Fundusz Wczasów Pracowniczych)* was established under the management of the trade unions who quickly became a monopolist in the field of mass recreation. From that point on, organisation of collective subsidised holiday became the main drive for tourism development, as opposed to western countries where the development resulted naturally from the increase of citizens' income. Holiday care, treated by many potential beneficiaries as an unwanted passenger, was recognised as an important part of a modernising impact on the society.

This specific hierarchy of objectives resulted from the fact that work was, throughout the Stalinism, the main reference point for all actions. Work determined the place of an individual in a community and its usefulness for it.[17]

Despite the official negation of the need of a special shape of social policy, state authorities consequently followed the programme of transforming the Polish society into an industrial and urban society following the spirit of Stalinism. The ambitious assumptions of the system – expressed in numerous articles of the 1952 Constitution – were quickly eroded in contact with everyday life.

---

[16] Rosner 1973, p. 65-66
[17] Klich-Kluczewska 2005, p.129

Socialistic Social Policy 1956 - 1970: Reactivation

The year 1956 was a milestone in the history of Polish 'real socialism'. The new First Secretary, Władysław Gomułka, who had a good reputation, started to disperse Poland from the Stalinism system. An enormous number of producer's cooperatives was dissolved. Poland opened, to some extent, to the West and Gomułka promised to improve living conditions and ensure a certain pluralism in social life. Despite the fact that the social and political reforms following the spirit of liberalisation were quickly hindered, the emphasis was maintained to satisfy the 'small' everyday consumer needs. The years 1956 - 1970 are thus referred to in historiography as a period of only 'small stabilisation'. This term, taken from Tadeusz Różewicz's drama, was used in a press campaign as an accusation towards "some fractions of the society" that abandoned the great ideas in favour of 'small' consumer needs: An own flat, a washing machine, and holiday in an employee holiday centre became the emblems of social life in times when the main principle was egalitarianism. The family, as the primary social unit, was again in the centre of attention among politicians - together with education treated as a system of ideological and practical preparation of the young Polish generation to live in a 'socialist homeland'.

Egalitarianism and modernisation also influenced the new – more relaxed – policy, referred to as 'socialistic', but it did not result in changes in the field of state administration in this respect. Nevertheless, the combination of 'egalitarianism' and 'family needs' produced increasing investments in building construction – with minimised private spaces for as much people as possible. Groups of scientists developed appropriate spatial solutions based on minimum sizes of furnishings and 'anthropological parameters of the statistical Pole.' The result of these activities was the so-called 'optimum minimum' – creating a "living space of 42 sqm with blind kitchen and cabin bedrooms, making the functioning of the family difficult and encouraging them to stay outside of it and to use cafeterias or restaurants."[18]

Noticing the citizens' needs resulted in the restoration of the due social support that had been considered as unnecessary during the Stalinism period. The liberalisation enabled also the revival of social initiatives in the form of laicist and religious associations. Charitable actions reappeared in parishes after years of stagnation. However, the authorities still maintained closed control over personnel and financial policy of the social organisations. More-

---

[18] ibid., p. 201

over, nobody knew how decisions were distributed within the scope of social administration. It was still difficult to analyse any leading concept in proposed central solutions.

In 1960, the already insignificant Ministry of Labour and Social Care and its duties in respect of employment policy were taken over by the Labour and Payroll Committee (*Komitet Pracy i Płac*). The Ministry of Health and Social Care was established, taking over duties of the former ministry in respect of social care and rehabilitation of the disabled. The additionally realized restoration of the Social Security Office was most important and very positive from the social viewpoint.[19]

The actual milestone, however, was, according to the most researchers, the comeback to the position of the welfare assistants in 1959.[20] The tasks of the (in fact, unpaid) welfare assistants included financial help for their wards, protection for families, fight against prostitution, alcoholism and educational negligence. They organised and provided care in respect of elderly, handicapped and disabled people. The professionalisation of these activities started in 1966 when the welfare assistants were replaced by professional social workers.

What made these fundamental changes of welfare parameters necessary? In the 1960 the number of school children increased radically and unemployment reappeared on the labour market, flooded by young people of the so-called post-war population boom. The authorities were forced to consider the relevance of demography. Analyses of the situation resulted in system-related decisions to prevent unemployment at all costs. Working hours were reduced; the shift system was introduced; some of the young people were held in schools extending their formation process; some vacancies were made available owing to elderly employees through the lowering of the retirement age. Permanent and temporary migrations to large urban areas were reduced. Women were the main victims of the chaos on the labour market; they had to face the whole range of incentives to abandon professional careers, at least for some time.[21] Even if most women were not convinced that employment was the best way of self-fulfilment, the salary was necessary to keep the level of living standards.

An antinatalistic atmosphere was intensified at that time, not only in respect of the population boom, but also owing to the repatriation after 1956.[22]

---

[19] cf. Rosner 1973, p. 66-67
[20] Leś 2001, p. 105- 106
[21] Auleytner 2004, p. 120-128
[22] In this year many Polish people came back from Sowjet Union.

The public was scared that an excessive demographic development would produce difficulties of economic and social development in Poland. These apprehensions generated the right of abortion for social reasons (1956) and the increase of the age of marriage. Not before the late 1960s, the authorities suddenly noticed that demographic development did not need to be an obstacle, but a drive for progress.[23]

1970 - 1989: From Welfare State on Credit to Polish Poverty

After another political crisis in Poland in 1970, the position of the First Secretary was taken over by Edward Gierek who did not found the popular acceptance Gomułka had; therefore, he promised significant improvement of the population's living standards. In his speeches, he emphasised that the happiness of Polish families belonged to his priorities: "I want you to know that welfare of the country, happiness of every Polish family is the ultimate goal of our party; the everyday problems of the working class are close to the Polit-Bureau, the government and me, personally."[24]

He destroyed the current reserved policy of Gomułka completely. Great investments were realised regardless of their costs, financed by foreign credits. Coca-Cola and Fiat 126 polski, the most popular passenger car of the post-ware era, became available in Poland.[25] The increasing living standard came along with increasing prices. The salaries polarised; it turned out that some parts of the population were in fact more important for (oder as?) the others. The privileged industrial working class in selected economical sections (miners, steelworkers, metalworkers. etc.) earned incomparably more than the masses of people working for the average workers' rate, white-collar workers or old-age and disability pensioners receiving subsistence wages. However, all of them were entitled to various benefits.

The 1970s brought about an important evolution in social policy: from majority of immediate intervention and corrective actions in respect of individual social problems, to attempts of active prevention and execution of specific social goals. In this way, social policy played a more important inspirational role towards the general policy than before. The concentration on

---

[23] Latuch 1980, p. 57-66
[24] Głowiński 1993, p. 35
[25] Landau/Roszkowski 1995, p. 249-250

the situation of the most disabled groups was to be abandoned, while the inclusion of the whole population became the main scope.[26]

Gierek put the issues of social policy management into a new order: In 1972, the Ministry of Labour, Payroll and Social Issues was established and received its reports from the Social Security Office. Unfortunately, there was still no new act on social support, disability and rehabilitation – the act from 1923 was still valid.[27] In public opinion a social worker was generally associated with the nurses of the Polish Red Cross. The frustration resulting from the low social prestige of the profession was intensified by the difficult working conditions or the obedient relation to incompetent superiors.

The optimism of the authorities in the first half of the 1970s was based on another change of opinions in respect of the demographic stratification. While in the late 1960s authorities counted on positive effects of population movements from agriculture into extra-agricultural sections,[28] in the 1970s it was believed that a reasonable (meaning slow) population growth could support the society's progress. The importance of the problem can be confirmed by the fact that a governmental commission for 'coordination of interdepartmental actions in respect of population policy' was established in 1974.[29]

The population policy was closely combined with the migration policy, accepting the public assumption that a 'moderate concentration policy' would enforce the migrant families to abstain from more than one or two children.[30]

To ensure job vacancies for young people, almost one million employees were withdrawn from the labour market; mainly women, disabled and war veterans could optionally retire earlier. The domestication of women advanced by extending the offer of maternity and post-maternity leaves. New incentives in the field of agricultural policy promoted the restoration of cooperatives through a system of disability pensions and cash payments for farmers who were willing to transfer their property to the state. As a result, 200,000 farmers started to receive state-funded pensions in the years between 1974 and 1976.

---

[26] Danecki, p. 54-55
[27] Rosner 1980, p.28
[28] Latuch 1980, p. 57-66
[29] ibid., p. 67, 70-72
[30] Dziewoński 1980, p.103-106

Conclusion

The chance of modernizations of the state was wasted as a result of clumsy planning and the low qualifications of the decision-making authorities. The great crash started in 1976. Aroused expectations of millions of people run into a permanent economic crisis. The economy of shortage affected everyone: "Earlier, the social minimum was known only by insiders, experts and scientists; now millions of people learned, often to their astonishment, that there are lots of people and families in Poland living in poverty, whose monthly income is hardly sufficient to ensure modest needs. (...). Therefore, the word 'poverty' found its proper place in the colloquial and official language." [31]

Social disappointment in contrast to the promised prosperity and social justice led gradually to the formation of the so-called alternative society. Economic and social insufficiency of the state produced a kind of moral opposition to the authoritarian state, whose role in the field of social care was taken over by the voluntary civil initiatives. Economic crisis and growing poverty forced the authorities to tolerate the activity of these independent organizations and the support from the West.[32]

The post-war social system, defined as 'etatistic' model (dominated by the central and local authorities) occurred practically as a monopolistic one.[33] As the result of governmental incompetence the family remained the most important entity of social care while the individuals had to survive under minimal benefits and scarce goods offered by an unofficial, non-governmental system of the mutual aid.

References

Adam, John (Ed.): *Economic Reforms and Welfare Systems in the USSR, Poland and Hungary. Social Contract in Transformation.* New York 1991
Auleytner, Julian: *Polish Social Policy. The Forging of Social Order,* Warszawa 2006.

---

[31] Kolano 1981, in: Góralska 1986, p. 11
[32] Leś 2001, p.107-108
[33] Księżopolski 2006, p. 107-110

Danecki, Jan: *Kilka uwag o polityce społecznej* (Remarks on Social Policy). In: Mikołaj Latuch/Maria Namysłowska (Eds.): *Polityka społeczna. Uwarunkowania demograficzne, zadania, potrzeby.* Warszawa 1980

Dziewoński, Kazimierz: *Problemy ludnościowe w polskim planowaniu regionalnym* (Demographic Problems and Polish Regional Planning). In: Mikołaj Latuch, Maria Namysłowska (Eds.): *Polityka społeczna. Uwarunkowania demograficzne, zadania, potrzeby.* Warszawa 1980

Głowiński, Michał, *Peereliada: komentarze do słów 1976-1981* (*Peereliada.* Commentaries on words 1976-1981), Warszawa 1993

Gortat, Tadeusz: *Ubezpieczenia społeczne* (Social Security). In: Jan Rosner (Ed.): *Polityka społeczna i służby społeczne.* Warszawa 1972

Góralska, Helena: *Minimum socjalne. Metody obliczeń i interpretacja* (The Social Minimum). Warszawa 1986

Graniewska, Danuta: *Formy i metody pomocy rodzinie pracowniczej* (Forms and Methods of the Worker Family's Assistance). Warszawa 1980

Jarosz, Dariusz: *Polska bieda 1944-1956* (Polish Poverty 1944-1956). In: E. Tarkowska (Ed.): *Przeciw biedzie. Programy, pomysły, inicjatywy.* Warszawa 2002

Jarosz, Dariusz: *Polacy a stalinizm 1948-1956* (Poles and Stalinism 1948 - 1956). Warszawa 2000

Kersten, Krystyna/Szarota, Tomasz (Eds.): *Wieś polska 1939-1948* (Polish Countryside 1939-1948), vol.II, Warszawa 1968

Klich- Kluczewska, Barbara: *Przez dziurkę od klucza. Życie prywatne w Krakowie 1945-1989* (Through the keyhole. The private life in Krakow 1945-1989), Warszawa 2005.

Kolano, E: *Wyjść z dołka* (The uprising out of the low land). In: Nowiny, 10-12 VIII 1981

Krzeszowski, Konstanty: *Polityka społeczna. Wybór pism* (Social Policy). Łódź 1947

Krzyszkowski, Jerzy: *Między państwem opiekuńczym a opiekuńczym społeczeństwem* (Between the Welfare State and the Protective Society. The Local Environment of Social Care). Łódź 2005

Landau, Zbigniew/Roszkowski, Wojciech: *Polityka gospodarcza w II RP o PRL* (Economic Policy in Interwar Poland and People's Republic of Poland). Warszawa 1995

Latuch, Mikołaj: *Wpływ przeobrażeń demograficzno- społecznych na politykę ludnościową w Polsce Ludowej* (The Impact of Demographic Transformation on Demogaphic Policy in People's Republic of Poland). In: Leś, Ewa (Ed.): *Zarys historii dobroczynności i filantropii w Polsce* (Outline of the history of charity and philanthropy in Poland). Warszawa 2001

Mikołaj Latuch/Maria Namysłowska (Eds.): *Polityka społeczna. Uwarunkowania demograficzne, zadania, potrzeby* (Social Policy. Demographic Factors, Tasks and Needs). Warszawa 1980

Miernik, Iwona: *Derywacja potrzeb materialnych Polaków a działalność Centralnego Komitetu Opieki Społecznej* (The Derivation of Material Needs of Poles and the activity of the Central Committee of the Social Care). In: Elżbieta Kościk/ Tomasz Głowiński (Eds.): *Gospodarka i społeczeństwo w czasach PRL-u (1944- 1989)*. Wrocław 2007

Jan, Rosner (Ed.): *Polityka społeczna i służby społeczne w PRL* (Social Policy and Social Services in People's Republic of Poland). Warszawa 1972

Rosner, Jan: *Podmioty polityki społecznej (The Subjects of Social Policy). In:* Antoni Rajkiewicz (Ed.): Polityka społeczna. Warszawa 1975

Rosner, Jan: *Trzy koncepcje polityki społecznej. Tradycje Instytutu Gospodarstwa Społecznego i współczesność* (Three Conceptions of Social Policy. Traditions of the National Institute of Social Economy). In: Mikołaj Latuch/Maria Namysłowska (Eds.): *Polityka społeczna. Uwarunkowania demograficzne, zadania, potrzeby.* Warszawa 1980

Rusinek, Kazimierz: *Zagadnienia pracy i pomocy społecznej w działalności rad narodowych* (The Issue of Labor and Social Care). In: Praca i Opieka Społeczna, 1950, Nr. 1/2

Stawarza, Ludwika: *Dlaczego tak jest?* (Why is it that way?) In: Kazimiera Piechocińska/Zenon Piechociński (Eds.): *Pamiętniki serca* (The Memories of the Heart). Łomża 1996

Ustawa o opiece społecznej, 16 sierpnia 1923 r., Dziennik Ustaw 1923, nr 92, poz.726

Wódz Kazimiera, Służby społeczne w Polsce. Geneza, kierunki rozwoju, metody pracy, Katowice: Uniwersytet Śląski (The Social Services in Poland, Genesis, development, methods of work). , 1982.

Dobrochna Kałwa
Between Emancipation and Traditionalism – The Situation of Women and the Gender Order in Poland after 1945

The Emancipation Announced

The situation of women, like a number of other aspects of life in post-war Poland, reflects the characteristic dilemma arising from contradictions between the ideological project to build a modern socialist society and social reality. Contrary to historical facts, the communist authorities were trying to convince Polish citizens that women's equal political and social rights were a donation of the new system – and that full equality between men and women was only possible in socialism.[1] But in reality the emancipation of women was only a deceitful strategy to hide the traditional pattern of gender hierarchy and discrimination against women.

The attitude of the communist authorities to the issue of women's rights after 1945 was also ambivalent and contradictory to a large extent. In addition to the regulation on equal political rights of women and men, already declared in the interwar period, the constitution of 1952 (Article 66) referred only to women's issues:

"1. Women in the Polish People's Republic shall have equal rights with men in all fields of public, political, economic, social and cultural life.
2. The equality of the rights of women shall be guaranteed by:
    a) Equal rights with men to work and to be paid according to the principle 'equal pay for equal work', the right to rest and leisure, to social insurance, to education, to honours and decorations, and to hold public offices.
    b) Mother-and-child care, protection of expectant mothers, paid leave before and after confinement, the development of a network of maternity

---

[1] Indeed, a number of postulates of the pre-war feminist movement (the right to divorce, the property right, and later the right to have abortion) were fulfilled only after 1945. However, despite the propaganda messages women already enjoyed full political rights and equal rights with men in terms of education and labour in the interwar period (cf. Kałwa 2001).

clinics, crèches and nursery schools, the extension of a network of service establishments and canteens."[2]

In the Constitution of 1976, the female provisions laid down in Article 66[3] were supplemented by an additional but significant regulation that "the Polish People's Republic shall strengthen the position of women in society, especially of gainfully employed mothers and women." Consequently the regulations regarding the protection of families were extended.

These constitutional regulations reflected the official interpretation of the gender order, in which women had equal rights with men in the public sphere – and at the same time, included additional rights with regard to their maternity functions. This was not a revolutionary concept; apart from enumerating the privileges of women – a novelty in socialism – it reproduced the pre-war emancipation system: A compromise to combine equal rights for women and men with the idea of special treatment for women. In the interwar Poland the contradiction between the demand for full equality of the sexes and the requirement to provide special protection for women had been discussed also in feminist circles. The majority of them subscribed the concept that women were innately different from men, and determined biologically by the function of maternity. Therefore they did not refuse special treatment for women.

To realise that, the 'indirect emancipation model' was used, the 'egalitarian-protectionist' one – a system of emancipation that in communist Poland did not arouse any doubts, because it was considered as complementary and optimal: "The meaning of these regulations is defined by the biological function of women and their roles in the family, which narrows down the opportunities for women to participate in the social and political life.

Thus the constitutional regulations, based on the assumption that the maternity function is socially significant, tried to provide equal opportunities by emphasizing the development of material premises granted to women."[4]

The concept of the biologically determined nature of gender also affected the fields of women's activities in the public sphere, thus defining the issues of morality, welfare, education, health care and the protection of family interests as the principal ones. In addition to its positive characteristics, 'femininity' was also linked to categories which represented unwanted behaviour in a socialist society including such 'innate' traits as passivity, reli-

---

[2] The Constitution of the Polish People's Republic was enacted by the Legislative Sejm on July 1952.
[3] In the new constitution this was Article 78.
[4] Wieruszewski 1975, p. 37

gious and moral conservatism, subordination and attachment to the private sphere. The 'feminine (anti)values' defined in this way formed a contrast to the features perceived as 'masculine values', i.e. activity, public sphere, ideological commitment, struggle and progress.[5]

These two aspects – the slogan of equal rights and the essential 'nature of sexes' – were the determining factors of the framework for state policy throughout the period of the People's Republic of Poland. Depending on the political priorities which altered from one decade to another, the official policy struggled for a balance between the emancipation slogan meaning that women were encouraged to play an active role in the public sphere in the 1950s and the discriminating view of women who were primarily perceived from the perspective of the private sphere (i.e. that of the home and the family), which characterized the situation of women in the 1970s and 1980s.

A significant example of such ambivalence is provided by the history of the 'League of Women', a mass organization representing women's circles which remained active throughout the time of the People's Republic of Poland. The women's movement which revived immediately after the war shared the same fate as other socio-political organizations. Within the broader context of ideological unification and the centralization of social organizations women's associations were either banned or co-opted into the licensed 'League of Women', which gained control over the legal movement of the 'Circles of Rural Housewives' and 'Women's Cooperatives' The League soon transformed into a centralized, hierarchical and bureaucratic structure, strictly subordinated to the authorities of the Communist Party. Until 1953 the organization was supervised by the Women's Section of the 'Polish United Workers' Party' (PUWP), and later by the Party's 'Department of Organization and Propaganda', both of which determined the League's general policy and the developments in its activities.[6]

In the early years after the war the League's main aim was the struggle for equal rights of women and men and, above all, welfare for women, the basic objective of a number of social organizations at the time. In the 1950s the League was assigned the additional tasks of agitating among women for the Party's policy and encouraging women to take an active role in the political sphere and in the labour market. Despite its tasks concerning the public and the national spheres, the League's activities concentrated also on the private sphere, as evidenced by the fact that the most prominent organization

---

[5] Kenney 2001, p. 340
[6] Nowak 2004, p. 35

within the League was the 'Committee for Home Economic Affairs', which was established in 1957 and concerned with training female household instructors, holding courses, testing new appliances and publishing information. These initiatives gradually became the League's basic field of activity.

The League's women activists played the roles of representatives of the women's world in the local and central bodies of the state; so they were rather regarded as the living proof of the emancipation process than as actual actors in the decision-making processes (as in fact the decisions were made elsewhere – in the Political Office of the Central Committee of the PUWP and the local committees, both dominated by men).

'Productivisation'

The period of the People's Republic of Poland is a history of abandoning emancipation, a seemingly fixed and unquestionable element of the order of a socialist state even in the 1950s. Although the gender order was not questioned at that time, its redefinition with the assignment of new tasks for women was important indeed. Directly after the war women's main tasks included the reconstruction of moral order and their involvement in the welfare system,[7] but the scope of women's tasks was expanded in the 1950s. Now, an ideal socialist woman in Poland, as in other people's democracies, was to fulfil the following three significant roles: that of a worker, that of a mother taking care of her family and home, and that of a social and political activist.[8]

The state's social policy during the Stalinist period was based on two principles: 'a) everyone has the right to work; b) who does not work, neither shall eat'.[9] The most important aims within the process of a radical reconstruction of Polish society and modernization after the second World War were the elimination of unemployment, full access to the labour market and improvement of the standards of living. At the same time the economic objectives of the 1950s, namely rapid rebuilding of the country after the ravages of war and accelerated industrialization, required a maximum of occupational activities. The reasons for the involvement of communist au-

---

7   Fidelis 2006, p. 434
8   Nowak 2004, p. 113
9   Rusinek 2005, p. 54

thorities in vocational training for women and their access to the labour market in the 1950s are to be sought in this sphere.[10]

It was therefore logical that the propaganda promoted the new model of gainfully employed women who were engaged 'on equal terms with men' in the process of building socialism and economic development of the country. The names of female party-activists, female heroes of socialist labour or women engaged in 'male-dominated' professions appeared repeatedly in the press, on newsreels, in literature and in films – as the examples of socialist equal rights and political commitment of the 'new woman'.[11] The propaganda messages and agitation were accompanied by amendments to legal regulations. The ban on women to enter certain professions which posed risk to their health, enacted before the war, was abolished at the time. Consequently, the number of women increased who were employed in heavy industry or mining. The icons of the period – as in other communist countries – were female tractor drivers and brigades of women bricklayers.

The central authorities also strove to increase the employment of women in administration. State institutions and industrial plants were obliged to employ more women as office workers. Yet equal rights for women and men appeared illusive, since, as pointed out aptly by Barbara Nowak, "authorities did not promote equal rights because of an ethical concern for gender equality, but only to exert more control over women's labour potential".[12] Moreover, the concept of equal rights was not well received even among the supporters of the new system, not to mention some of its political worthies. Decision-makers on the central level, i.e. in ministries, industrial federations and state institutions, disregarded the Party's directives to increase the employment of women.[13] Furthermore in factories a hostile attitude towards women was practiced.

This misogynist attitude arose not only from mental conservatism, but also from pragmatism. As the regulations on the protection of women's labour included the ban to work overnight and under health-threatening

---

[10] Holzer/Wasilewska-Trenkner 1985, p. 131
[11] Incidentally, it is worth to mention that, paradoxically enough, the frequent use of female supporters of the new political order in the propaganda messages resulted from the perception of women as being conservative, attached to religion, and guards of traditional values. In this context the message about women supporters of the new system was to evidence the value of the communist ideology as acceptable even to women who were 'by nature' reluctant to novelties. (cf. Szpak 2007, p. 413-430).
[12] Nowak 2004, p.148
[13] Jarosz 2001, p. 220-221

conditions, the employment of women was avoided, or the law was disobeyed. It did not happen infrequently (It happened frequently) that women worked under hazardous conditions, on night shifts or overtime. Yet it should also be pointed out that the fact that some employers observed the protective regulations did not necessarily satisfy the female workers. All the more women earned less than men anyway, so their displeasure had economic reasons: their bare wages without extra money for better-paid overnight and overtime work were not at all sufficient to maintain a family.[14]

The welfare system was reorganized in the 1950s and became strictly connected with the workplaces. Only in this way people got access to benefits and financial support, health care, flats, a place in a canteen, a holiday or a summer camp for children. Only childcare facilities were organized and managed by the state. This system of central management proved to be ineffective, since the crèches and kindergartens did not satisfy the continuously growing demands. Childcare facilities in the 1950s were few, poorly equipped and far away from dwellings and workplaces. In practice the right to use childcare facilities was available only to working mothers, mainly due to the few places in such institutions.[15] But there were also other reasons for this fact. It was generally believed that unemployed women had no right to shift their maternal duties to the state. The institutional system – once intended to relieve women of parts of their duties – became an instrument of exercising pressure and a source of additional strain and frustration.

Despite the inefficiency of childcare facilities the number of women at work increased, a development that was strongly influenced by the system and of course also by economic motives. The number of working wives was growing consistently, so that they were in the majority in the early 1970s. Although the Stalinist social model suffered a defeat, women continued to be active on the labour market.[16]

---

[14] According to Fidelis women employed in the heavy industry, often categorized as unskilled workers, were most often given lowest-paid jobs and passed over in case of bonuses or awards.

[15] In 1951 there were 1.8 places in crèches and 14.5 places in kindergartens available to every one hundred women.

[16] Between 1950 and 1989 the number of employed women was rising from 1,475.000 to 5,499.000. In the beginning, 13% of the employed women were married, at the end 74% (Holzer/Wasilewsk-Trenkner, p. 193).

Diversification

Due to sudden political changes the Stalinism in Poland came to an end in 1956. During the so-called 'small stabilization' period, which lasted fifteen years, the communist authorities abandoned the concept of total control over the whole social life and only held the control over the public sphere.[17] In this wake of 'thaw', a period of political relaxation, the attitude towards women, their social roles and the gender order changed as well. The model of the gainfully employed woman was put in a new context of traditional values related to the private sphere.[18]

Above all, it turned out that the slogans of equal rights for men and women and the emancipation of women (promoted in the previous period) had altered the social understanding of the gender order: Maternity and running a household were much more than before defined as basic functions of women in society. In the media published in the years before 1953 there were very few statements suggesting that gainful employment of women (and in particular of mothers) was perceived as a source of troubles for women and the members of their families.[19] But now it appeared that women's employment was considered to be a problem. Having analyzed readers' comments in the press in the 1960s,[20] Szpakowska observed that not only men, but also some women regarded women's professional work only as a necessary evil.[21]

The female point of view seems not to be surprising, considering the fact that their decision to work usually resulted from their poor financial standing. Therefore women saw employment as a necessity, not a privilege. But obviously there were also women to whom professional work was a source of satisfaction, as it provided an opportunity for self-fulfilment, making their lives more interesting, or at least offering them financial independence. Yet even these women acknowledged the problem that it was actually impossible to combine professional work with housework and family duties.

---

[17] The exception here was a group of Party officials whose private life was subject to control and interference by Party authorities (cf. Dąbek 2006, p. 103).
[18] More on the private sphere in post-war Poland in: Klich-Kluczewska 2005.
[19] Jaworska 2006, p. 183
[20] Szpakowska analyzed readers' letters which were published in the press in response to contests and surveys announced in the newspapers and magazines (cf. Szpakowska 2003).
[21] Ibid, p. 57-58.

The term 'having two full-time jobs', which referred to the 'doubled burden' of women engaged in household and labour at the same time, was an important topic in the discussion on emancipation in the 1960s. A parallel phenomenon occurring in this period was something I would call the 'privatization' of the woman's question. Changes in the media and in social life indicated that there was more interest again in topics related to fashion, beauty care, married life and the upbringing of children. Fashion contests (including the Miss Poland competition organized since 1956) promoted the ideal type of a beautiful, neat and fashionably dressed woman. More serious subjects began to appear occasionally in the press as well, such as family life pathologies, alcoholism and domestic violence against women.

Examples showing the results of the 'privatization' of the woman's question at that time can be found in press articles published for instance on Women's Day, when the situation of women, always supplemented with the ritual expressions of admiration and respect, had to be described.

Another topic in the 1960s was that of a wife providing food supplies for her family (difficult enough in the times of crisis) and bringing up children. These articles, mainly published on March 8th, were mocking at those traditional husbands who were not prepared to carry out their part of the daily duties. But in reality the traditional model of partnership was not in doubt, while women's workload still was a marginalized issue with little significance for society.[22]

The process of 'privatization' of the 'women's question' also had an effect on the position of women in public life. An important, though not isolated, case of political exclusion in Poland is the gender-biased attitude of the communist authorities towards the strikes and protests in the winter of 1970/71. The riots triggered by workers of the shipyard in Gdansk, who protested against the planned price increase in December 1970, were treated as rebelliousness which threatened the political system. The army troops sent to Gdansk attacked the workers and provoked a deadly street fighting. Soon afterwards, in February 1971, approximately ninety thousand workers from the textile factories in Łódź, mainly women, went on strike. This time, the 'female' strike was treated by the authorities as a social protest, not a political one, and the strikers' demands were accepted.

According to Padraic Kenney, who analyzed both protests from the gender perspective, the decisive reason for treating the strike in Łódź in a different way was the scenario of women going on strike, which did not fall under the pattern of resistance-pacification used by the authorities in

---

[22] Kurz 2001, p. 499-500

Gdansk: "It was precisely the 'unstructured' nature of the strike that forced the regime's reversal, as the party had difficulty both talking with the strikers and understanding their motives. The violence on the coast had been easier to understand; in Łódź, the avoidance of violent tragedy was perceived to be one source of the strike's success".[23]

Another reason for this example of gender differentiation can be found in the attitude of the strikers themselves. Instead of negotiating with a strike committee, the government deputation, led by Prime Minister Jaroszewicz, had to talk to some three thousand people, mainly women, gathered in the Great Theatre of Łódź. What is more, the women on strike imposed their own language and understanding on the delegates, leaving no room for ideological phrases. The Prime Minister's explanations were interrupted by one of the striking women who screamed: 'Your wife loads ham on her sandwiches, while my children eat dry bread!' The language of the authorities became ineffective when confronted with the arguments of a mother with hungry children.[24] In this case women's 'privatisation' turned out to be salutary, but in the long run it increased their marginalization and excluded them from the sphere of politics.[25]

Domestication

Towards the end of the 1960s state authorities decided to introduce changes in social policy. One of the new priorities was to improve the protection of motherhood and to reduce the share of women in the labour market. The Sixth PUWP Congress in December 1971 approved a programme to protect motherhood more effectively and develop a system of support for large families. These decisions were made in response to the alarming data about a falling rate of birth in the decade before. The reasons for the drop in population was sought in the occupational activities of women, in the ineffective system of welfare as well as in the patriarchal models of partnership.[26]

Another issue which influenced the decisions was the problem of 'hidden unemployment' by maintaining economically useless jobs. The major

---

[23] Kenney 1999, p. 411
[24] Ibid, p. 410
[25] This attitude referred not only to the authorities, but also to opposition circles (cf. Penn, 2005; Kenney 2001, p. 238-251).
[26] Graniewska 1975, p. 5

objectives of the new social policy included the temporary withdrawal of young mothers from professional work, measures to stabilize the professional situation of unskilled female workers and "the development of forms of gainful employment for women that could be combined with family duties".[27] Professional activation of women was, apparently, no longer a priority.

Further changes in social policy were introduced by unpaid annual post-maternity leave for young mothers in 1968. The successive legal acts were concerned with two issues: extending the time of mother-child-relation in the earliest period of a childhood, and financial support for young mothers and their children. In 1972 fully paid maternity leave was extended from 12 to 16 weeks and unpaid post-maternity leave from one to three years.[28] The period of unpaid post-maternity leave was added to the number of years of employment, providing the amount of pension in later years. In consequence over 60% of employed mothers decided to take unpaid post-maternity leave. In the following years the scope of the state's financial support for mothers and children was further extended. In 1974 special benefits for disabled children were introduced. One year later a maintenance fund was established for single mothers, and the rates of family benefits were increased as well. In 1978 maternity grants paid for each child were introduced[29] to provide assistance especially for large families. The pro-natal and pro-maternity policy was rounded off by the government's resolution to introduce benefits for mothers on post-maternity leave fully compensating the lost wages. From that time on the decision whether to use post-maternity leave or not was no longer based on economic reasons.

The new social policy brought about amazing results. Some 280,000 mothers per year exercised their right to maternity leave; post-maternity leaves were very popular especially among blue-collar and unskilled female workers. In 1973, one year after introducing post-maternity leaves, 115,000 women used the opportunity.[30] In 1982 as many as 90% of the young mothers decided to take post-maternity leaves.[31] The contradictory character of the female 'doubled burden' was eliminated to a number of women who decided to withdraw to the private sphere.[32]

---

[27] Durajowa 1979, p. 45
[28] If another child was born, the leave was 18 weeks.
[29] Holzer/Wasilewska-Trenkner 1985, p. 132-133
[30] Graniewska 1975, p. 34
[31] Kurzynowski 2000, p. 197
[32] cf. Wedel 2007

Conclusion

The history of the relations between socialism and women's issues in Poland is ambiguous, as women were torn by the contradictory patterns among labour and public activities on one side and motherhood and housewifery on the other. Apparently, the gender order was stable and permanent, which is hardly surprising, because none of the significant social actors – neither the state authorities nor the dissident option-forming institutions of the Catholic Church and the Solidarity – was interested in changing women's roles. Still it is generally believed that it was the communist regime which made women equal and disturbed the 'traditional' gender order. As a consequence the anti-feminist backlash and reinforcement of the 'traditional' gender order, which took place soon after 1989, has been perceived as a policy of dissociation from the past, despite the fact that the 'socialist emancipation of women' was only announced, but hardly achieved.

References

Dąbek, Krzysztof: *PZPR - retrospektywny portret własny* (Polish United Workers' Party – a retrospective self-portrait). Warszawa 2006

Durajowa, Danuta: *Sytuacja społeczno-zawodowa kobiet w ocenie włókniarek* (Social and professional situation of women in opinions of female textile workers). In: Acta Universitatis Lodziensis: *Zeszyty Naukowe Uniwersytetu Łódzkiego. Nauki Ekonomiczne i Socjologiczne.* 44/1979, p. 43-64.

Fidelis, Małgorzata: *Czy 'nowy matriarchat'? Kobiety bez mężczyzn w Polsce po II wojnie światowej* (A new matriarchy? Women without men in post-war Poland). In: Żarnowska A./Szwarc A. (Eds.): *Kobieta i rewolucja obyczajowa: społeczno-kulturowe aspekty seksualności* (Woman and sexual revolution: Sociocultural aspects of sexuality). Warszawa 2006, p. 421-436

Graniewska, Danuta: *Aktywność zawodowa kobiet a potrzeby socjalne rodzin pracowniczych* (Labour activity of women and social needs of workers' families). In: Studia i Materiały Instytutu Pracy i Spraw Socjalnych, 12/1975. Warszawa

Holzer, Jerzy Z./ Wasilewska-Trenkner, Halina: *Poland.* In: Bodrova/Anker (Eds.): *Working Women in Socialist Countries: the Fertility Connection.* Geneva 1985, p. 129-165

Jarosz, Dariusz: *Kobieta a praca zawodowa w latach 1944-1956* (Woman and labour activity in 1944-1956). In: Żarnowska/Szwarc (Eds.): *Kobieta i praca* (Woman and work). Warszawa 2000, p. 217-241

Jaworska, Justyna: *Lucyna i Paulinka radzą sobie same* (Lucyna i Paulinka manage by their own). In: Żarnowska/Szwarc (Eds.): *Kobieta i rewolucja obyczajowa: społeczno-kulturowe aspekty seksualności* (Woman and sexual revolution: Socio-cultural aspects of sexuality). Warszawa 2006, p. 175-187

Kenney, Padraic: *The Gender of Resistance in Communist Poland.* In: American Historical Review, 104/1999, p. 399-425

Kenney, Padraic: *Pojęcie 'Matki-Polki' w języku opozycji i władzy* (A „Mother-Pole" concept in the language of the authority and the opposition). In: Szarota T. (Ed.): *Komunizm. Ideologia, system, ludzie* (Communism: Ideology, system, people). Warszawa 2001, p. 238-251

Klich-Kluczewska, Barbara: *Przez dziurkę od klucza. Życie prywatne w Krakowie (1945-1989)* (Through a keyhole. A private life in Kraków 1945-1989). Warszawa 2005

Krzyszkowki, Jerzy: *Między państwem opiekuńczym a opiekuńczym społeczeństwem. Determinanty funkcjonowania środowiska pomocy społecznej na poziomie lokalnym* (Between a welfare state and a welfare society: Determinans of social workers' activity on the local level). Łódź 2005

Kurz, Iwona: *Czas wolny na ekranie. Bohaterki filmu popularnego w PRL a 'budżet czasu wolnego'* (Leisure-time on the screen: Heroines of popular films in Polish People Republic and 'a leisure-time budget'). In: Żarnowska/Szwarc (Eds.): *Kobieta i kultura czasu wolnego. Zbiór studiów* (Woman and a leisure-time culture). Warszawa 2001, p. 495-507

Kurzynowski, Adam: *Przemiany wzorów karier zawodowych kobiet w latach 1950-1989* (Changes of women's professional careers patterns in 1950-1989). In: Żarnowska/Szwarc (Eds.): Kobieta i praca (Woman and work). Warszawa 2000, p. 187-215

Leszczyński, Adam: *Anatomia protestu. Strajki robotnicze w Olsztynie, Sosnowcu i Żyrardowie. Sierpień-listopada 1981* (An anatomy of protest. Workers' strikes in Olsztyn, Sosnowiec, and Żyrardów. August-November, 1981). Warszawa 2006

Nowak, Barbara: *Gender Discrimination in the Workforce as a Challenge to the Polish Feminist Movement.* In: Gorczyńska/Kraszyńska/Zakidalska (Eds.): *Płeć - kobieta - feminizm.* (Gender - woman - feminism). Gdańsk 1997, p. 147-156

Nowak, Barbara: *Serving Women and the State: The League of Women In Communist Poland.* Ohio State University 2004

Penn Shana: *Solidarity's Secret. The Women who Defeated Communism in Poland.* Ann Arbor 2005

Szpak, Ewelina: *Female Tractor Driver, Labour Heroine and Activist: Images of New Socialist Rural Women in the Polish Communist Press (1950-1975)*. In: Klusáková (Ed.): *Imagining Frontiers – Contesting Identities*. Pisa 2007, p. 413-430

Szpakowsk, Małgorzata: *Chcieć i mieć. Samowiedza obyczajowa w Polsce czasu przemian* (To want and to have. Self-knowledge on customs in Poland during transition). Warszawa 2003

Wedel, Janine R.: *Prywatna Polska* (Private Poland). Warszawa 2007

Wieruszewski, Roman: *Równość kobiet i mężczyzn w Polsce Ludowej* (Equality of women and men in Poland). Poznań 1975

Maria Roth, Raluca Crisan, Livia Popescu, Luminita Dumanescu

The Romanian Social System between 1945 and 1989

The framework of a New Period in Romania

In August 1944, when the government of general Ion Antonescu was dismissed and Romania accepted the armistice, the Red Army advanced rapidly into the country. Already in the first year after the war a procommunist government had been installed in Bucharest, but the political transition process lasted till the end of 1947, when the king was forced to abdicate and went into exile. Afterwards, all political decisions were directed towards the transformation of Romania into the Soviet model.

In the immediate period after the Second World War, the traditional laws and structures of the social system were partly maintained (or reconstructed), and efforts were made to build up a modern social infrastructure. Political debates were going on at all levels concerning mainly poverty, tuberculosis and the high mortality rates that had to be handled by the municipal administrations. Social Assistance Centers were placed in the greater Romanian cities including homes for children and youngsters, special units for problem children, settlements for the blind, folk canteens, prevention centers for persons with tuberculosis, orphanages and cradles for children. Until 1948 some of the social care institutions were still church related.[1] There was also a large range of secular and non-secular charity organizations, still regulated by the law of 1923 for the management of non-profit organizations.[2]

The only civil organization that continued during the whole period of communism was the National Red Cross. Though it was actively involved in organizing after war relief for people communities in need, like during the famine in Moldova in 1946-1947, in health education and in training of health personnel, Red Cross lost its autonomy after 1947. Till 1989 it was considered more an auxiliary of the Ministry of Health. In spite of its few resources, it continued to train volunteers.

---

[1] Catholic, Othodox, Reformed and several other churches continued their charity activities till the Law in 1948 has forbidden this.
[2] cf. Manoiu/Epurean, 1996

Changing Ministerial Responsibilities

The communist government inherited a social system which continued to function until 1948, when a new social law was promulgated. In 1947 the Ministry of Health, Labour and Social Care were divided into two entities: Ministry of Health on one side and Ministry of Labour, Social Care and Social Insurance on the other side. According to the decree number 149 from July 1948, the Ministry of Labour and Social Care became responsible for the organization, the guidance and the control of the social political activities. In 1951, certain tasks were transferred to other ministries. Children's homes, together with the primary schools for deficient children, went to the Ministry of Education while the units for children with behavioral disorders were assigned to the Internal Affairs Ministry. The National Institute of Medical Assessment of Work Capacity was founded in 1951, continued with the Institute of Gerontology and Geriatrics.

The area of social care faced both institutional instability and lack of long term concepts. The departments of Vocational Special Education and Social Care, which were separated in 1955, merged again in 1956. By 1957, the Ministry of Social Care ceased to exist, and a new Ministry of Health and Social Care was created. Responsibility for social care issues changed again in 1968 when it was transferred from the Health Ministry to the Ministry of Labour. As a result of these continuously changing arrangements the social care network was significantly damaged.[3]

Romanian Socialism After Stalin's Death

After Stalin's death some positive changes in social care became possible, although the crushing of the Hungarian revolt of 1956 conveyed the strong message that no kind of resistance in any countries of the Soviet bloc would be tolerated. Therefore the Romanian Workers Party (*RWP*) remained true to the Stalinist principles even when the political ideas in Moscow changed. However, since Romania professed neutrality in some foreign policy matters, the Western countries acknowledged an economic and technological support to the country. In 1964, a more liberal political course was ushered by the *RWP* and briefly continued under Ceaușescu, the new communist leader. The

---

[3] cf. Mănoiu /Epureanu 1996

ideological discourses became less dogmatic and there was a partial restoration of professional criteria in several social areas.[4]

Ceauşescu's regime (1965-1989) gained in its beginning the trust of the Romanian population as well as the confidence of the Western countries. His critical comments of the soviet intervention in Prague 1968 were highly appreciated. But Ceausescu's visits in China and North Korea inspired him to provoke a 'complete transformation' of the whole country and a pronounced glorification of his own personality. During his regime 'wayward' and 'incorrigible' people were put into psychiatric facilities and many were sentenced to imprisonment. The number of individuals murdered under those circumstances is not known.[5]

Social Problems and the De-Professionalization of Social Help

There were a lot of social problems that belonged to the heritage of Romania when the communist system began. For instance, the literacy rate of precommunist Romania was 57 %. The percent was lower among rural population and particularly among women.[6] In 1948, some reforms were started to educate the children of hitherto underprivileged classes such as workers and peasants. Another major task was to build a new reliable intellectual communist cadre. The members of the old professional and social elites were persecuted and their children banned from access to higher education.[7] Teachers and other intellectuals were determined to organize schools for adults, going out of the cities into remote areas. But despite all efforts to combat illiteracy the phenomenon could not be eliminated completely.[8]

In 1960, the Ministry for Social Care was authorized to coordinate the existing social networks and to develop new laws in fields of pensions, public health, hygiene, rehabilitation and gerontology, realizing the specific universalistic perspective on social policy that was, at that time, typical for the socialist state: Education in schools and kindergartens was free, and declared to be available for all those who wanted to learn; cultural institutions (such as libraries, museums, theatres or movies) were made available for all

---

[4] Popescu 2006, p. 433-434
[5] Tismăneanu (coord), 2006
[6] cf. Manuila/Georgescu 1937
[7] cf. Popescu 2006
[8] Illiteracy was officially denied during communism.

income categories. The health-care services were free since 1958. In order to get this free medical care in case of illness, people had to be employed, retired, or to be a family member of an employed or a retired person, a child (up to 16 years) or a student, a pregnant women or a mother, a sportsman, a war refugee or a person declared unable to work. The legislation for the protection of elderly was based on a Ministries' Council Decision from 1957, which guaranteed all seniors the possibility to move into a facility, to use the advantages of public care. Furthermore, there existed pensions for invalids, orphans and widows of war – and some kinds of occasional social aid.

All the services mentioned were included in the category of 'social provisions' because their purpose was not to obtain profit. The transition from socialism to communism was supposed to increase the quality of life and to minimize individualized forms of social risks through general measures.

Beside the regulated forms of social protection, the communist state considered that there existed no social problems, because life in communism was supposed to be so wonderful that people did not need further social protection.

Therefore, in 1952, the Superior School of Social Work called 'Princess Ileana' was transformed into an Institute for Social Assistance. The last graduation of social workers was in 1952, when the institute closed its doors.[9] This school had never been a part of the academic system, but several teachers were highly appreciated academics, and "students often continued an academic career in higher academic degrees, including doctoral studies."[10] After closing 'Princess Ileana' there existed only two 'Schools of Social Provisions' until 1952.[11] Later on, between 1959 and 1969, the cutback went on: The training on social work methods and social benefits was reduced to six departments for the vocational training of Medical Social Assistants. Another result of these de-professionalization processes was the reduction of qualified social-care nurses unto the number of less than 200 all over the country. Since 1969, the medical social-care education was completely eliminated, because the communist ideology considered it as useless.[12]

The contradiction between the claim of well developed social services on one side, and the reduction of professional social work on the other, became especially visible concerning the fact, that – more or less – only state em-

---

[9] cf. Rachieru, 2005
[10] Mănoiu/Epureanu 1996, p.152
[11] The Romanian names were "Şcoli Medii Tehnice de Prevederi Sociale" (Mănoiu/Epureanu 1996)
[12] cf. Buzducea 2005

ployed people were beneficiaries of the social protection measures. This means that social services were not available for those people with deregulated working conditions, like some peasants who escaped collectivization, or for small producers. Also unemployed people were not acknowledged, because unemployment did officially not exist. Needless to say, that there also was no social support for unemployed people.

Only those who found themselves in a temporary inability to work got social provisions by the state until 1962. The amount of money granted was related to the recipient's former salary. These people had also the allowance for health recovery and illness prevention.[13]

State Allowance for Children and the Family Law of 1965

The main social provision in Romania was the state allowance for children, laid down in a Ministry's Council Decision in 1960. It was paid to employed parents on their payroll; the amount of money increased beginning with the second child. If parents were entitled to more than one benefit, they had the right to choose the more convenient one. Other allowances were destined to mothers of 10 children, if at least eight of them were alive. Wives of soldiers got financial help if they were unable to work, pregnant or had young children.[14]

The state allowance for children was the most important social provision, but the legislation since 1965 made a difference between the previous 'bourgeois' legislation of Family Law (representing 'paternal power') and the new 'parental rights and duties', imposing an increased state control on family life. The law stipulated that in case the physical or moral wellbeing of the child was endangered, the child should be cared for by an institution for child protection or by another person. Any person, who knew about a child without according parental care, was obliged to announce the case to the local authority (*autoritatea tutelara*).[15]

---

[13] Stahl/Matei 1962
[14] ibid.
[15] Concerning the problems in the field of residential care, see the article of Roth in this book.

The Main Mass Organizations

In 1945, the amount of participants of the Communist Party in Romania was rather small (about 10,000 persons), but the campaign to recruit new members was rather successful, because political engagement and membership brought a lot of advantages. The main mass organization was the Trade Union, created in 1944, being very close to the purposes of the Romanian Communist Party.

Further on, the formation of the Young Workers Union was established in 1949. In the following years the organization tried to identify those who were 'enemies' of the system. A lot of exclusions followed – about 19,000 only between August 1952 and June 1953. One of the Young Workers Union ideas was to activate the children of peasant families in order to convince their relatives to hand their own land into common use. In the beginning, about 30% of the members were students, but the number of academic youth dropped to less than 10% in 1959, although it was almost impossible to attend college without membership.

The women's associations in Romania were also concentrated in one general organization with a strong ideological mission, especially in the field of family politics and bio-political purposes.

All children in Romania were generally organized in the Pioneer organization: They became members of the Pioneers when they were about nine years old – and they were supposed to exchange the membership for that of the Young Communists Union at the age of 14-15. Between 1949 and 1966 the Pioneers were coordinated by the Young Communists Union. In 1966, the Central Committee of the Romanian Communist Party decided, in order to obtain a better functioning of this organization, to entrust them its own leadership.[16]

In 1976, the party created a further organization for the younger children to activate them already in the pre-school period. The membership at the 'Country hawks' at the age of four years and included – besides sports and games – mainly activities in mass cultural performances and the official praising of Romania and their 'pater familias', personally the secretary general of the Romanian party: Ceaușescu.

---

[16] Concerning the structures of the Pioneer Organisation cf. the article of Popova in this book.

Reproduction Policy

The center of the communist state ideology in Romnaia was the pro-natalist policy to increase the population from 23 to 30 millions. Abortion was outlawed, birth control methods were banned and sexual education ignored. For women younger than 45 it was a patriotic duty to have four children.

Marriage and family life were territories under the strict control of the Communist Party: "In our socialist society the maintenance of marriage ceased to be a personal problem of the spouses. The society cannot be indifferent to the fate of marriage and family life."[17] The main role of the family was considered to be giving birth to children and to raise them in the new socialist spirit - making them worthy citizens of the communist society. The politics of Ceausescu aimed at fighting against the Western urban family type, and for the preservation of traditional Romanian values. This included an ideological strengthening of rural-patriarchal values, which was only partially successful, because, on the other hand, the influence of the state was inconsistent to the paternal rights.

In reality, urban nuclear families diminished their social functions during the communist regime. Especially the educational roles were transferred to society. Women had to return to their employment soon after birth, because they were entitled to a maximum of 117 paid days off from work. To make this possible, nurseries and kindergartens were offered to families. However, nurseries were notorious for being over crowded and for providing low quality childcare. Women were working equally like men, which was a progress compared to the pre-war dominant female role. However, this also meant more duties in a still patriarchal family decision-making model. Women knew that they had to work and contribute to the family income, because one (the husband's) wage was not sufficient for the family's living expenses. As the traditional roles of the women continued to be performed, women's duties were reduplicated.[18]

At the beginning of the 20th Century, the live birth rate (per 1000 citizens) was around 40. In 1930, it was around 30, and in the period 1940 until 1955 the birth rate dropped to about 25%.[19] A valuable study on the Romanian women's idea of sexuality and reproductive behavior was realized. They interviewed a representative sample of woman living in Cluj City, married

---

[17] Ionescu et al. 1975, p. 67
[18] Petre 1997
[19] Băban/David 1995

before 1990, with children, with high school studies, with rural origin, and having an orthodox religion. The authors concluded that sexuality was perceived as a personal stress factor. The initial shame and shyness of the couple's sexual life was followed by the fear of unintentional pregnancy. Lack of access to modern contraceptive methods and the inability and fear to use them, amplified this stress. These conditions removed the female control over their own sexual behavior.

Due to the restrictive reproductive health policies between 1966 and 1989, fertility rates increased up to 47,5% in just two years and maternal mortality reached heights unknown in Europe:[20] from 85 deaths per 100,000 live births in 1965, to 170 deaths in 1983. The reason for this dramatic account was the number of illegal and unsafe abortions. An average Romanian woman had at least five illegal abortions by the age of 40, and it has been estimated that approximately 20 % of them became infertile afterwards.

On the other hand, Romanian bio-politics were combined with a lot of provisions for children and their families. The social background of the Romanian child protection system was characterized by generally low incomes, which made it necessary to offer a large scale of subventions (for food, clothing, school materials). Because communism stated the equality of women and men, and encouraged women's participation in work force, nurseries and kindergartens for children under school age were necessary.

The most important regulations were:

- Paid maternity leaves for an approximately four-month period.
- Specialized health-care services for mother and child.
- Free health care system for all the citizens.
- A health-care system for pregnant women.
- Unpaid long-term leaves for mothers with children under the age of 7, and the possibility of maintaining the previous job.
- Paid leave to parents for the care of their children less than 3 years, in cases of illness.
- Reduction of work-time for breast-feeding mothers with infants.
- Creation of child-care services (crèches and kindergartens).
- Mothers having more than three children, who did not work because of taking care of them got a monthly allowance and pension for old age.

All these advantages were added to the general subsidies for electricity, heating and fuel costs, health and education expenditures. They were supposed to cover

---

[20] cf. Greenwell 2003; Kligman 1998

and compensate the social consequences of generally increasing poverty and lack of food, medicine and high quality health-care services, which were more and more evident at the end of the 1980s.

Compared to the needs and expenses of the family life, the state allowances proved to be insufficient. They roughly covered 20 % of the direct costs of child rearing [21] and made it necessary for women to maintain a high participation in economical life.

Gender Equality and the Division of Labor

Political equality, including gender, was stated by law 56 in 1946 and encoded in the Constitution in 1948.[22] The possibility for women to obtain political power and to receive better places in the professional hierarchy was goals for only a limited category of people, mostly high-level intellectuals. The former compulsory quotas of women (along with quotas for special minority groups) on all the levels of the communist organizations were not efficient to promote the female interests.

Since 1952, equal payment for equal work of women and men was laid down in the legislation, so women became equal work partners and reached the amount of 44% of all employees. But: Equality at the work place did not mean the same arrangements in the division of labor at home. Research on the organization of spare time revealed an average of almost six hours of total housework per day, per family. This was ordinarily composed by four hours and 24 minutes for women and one hour and 28 minutes for men.[23]

In 1973, the Communist Party declared the emancipation of women as one of the most important goals and a particular segment of the fight against exploitation of person against person. Nevertheless, women did not appreciate the rights the Party dedicated to them, because they realized the ambiguous character of such ideological commitments.

Instead, they allied with men against the common enemy: the oppression through the Party and the control especially enforced through the security. Measures were taken to ensure that outsiders would not find out what the

---

[21] Kligman 2000
[22] Buzatu 1978
[23] The real percentage depended on the age of the respondent: at the age of 16-25 women worked 150 minutes a day at housework, at the age of 56-65 453 minutes.

members of a family really felt, thought, and how they succeeded to obtain the means of their subsistence. Family as the main source of relative joy and freedom had to be defended.

Neamțu (1999) describes the following relation of citizens to the socialist state, that summarize the advantages, but do not mention disadvantages:

- „The main resources for citizens are their salaries; income based on private activity or property is insignificant for the majority.
- Economical equalization of citizens is given by the low rate of minimum and maximum salary.
- No official unemployment (only a hidden unemployment), which did not require unemployment benefits.
- Generalized pension and allowance system.
- Free education and health care for every citizen." (p. 64)

Conclusion

While in the Western countries social welfare comprised a large scale of models, from the reparatory medical model of case work to the group and community work models, towards social inclusion and social intervention models, in the Communist countries social welfare was blocked on the administrative level, with low or no individual need assessment.

Even though the literature on Romanian communism is yet rather poor we can extract some main ideas on how the communist Romanian state related to social care issues. First, there was a legal base to offer social protection for special needs: for abandoned children and children of families in need, people with disabilities, elderly and some other categories of dependent individuals. The lack of resources and of professionals imposed the absence of other services then residential homes. The Communist Party did not 'recognize' the existence of poverty, the discrimination of Roma (named gypsies), unemployment, alcoholism, HIV/AIDS, and the social correlates of numerous chronic diseases.

A large number of residential institutions that were supposed to be care facilities – like children's homes or psychiatric facilities – became places of deprivation, famine, abuse, and sometimes even cruelty and high death rates. Like the main mass organizations they served the communist party's purposes. So people, whatever they needed, were sacrificed for the glory of communism.

References

Băban, Adriana/David, Henry P.: *Voci ale femeilor din România. Aspecte ale sexualității, comportamentului de reproducere și ale relațiilor de cuplu în epoca Ceaușescu* (Women's voices in Romania: Aspects of sexuality, reproductive behavior and couple relations in the Ceaușescu's period). București 1995

Buzatu, Stana: *Condiția femeii - dimensiune a progresului contemporan* (Condition of women - Dimensions of contemporary progress). București 1979

Buzducea, Doru: *Aspecte contemporane în asistența socială.* (Aspects of contemporary Social Work). Iași 2005

Gal, Susan/ Kligman, Gail: *The Politics of Gender After Socialism: A Comparative-Historical Essay.* Princeton 2000

Georgescu, Vlad: *Istoria românilor* (History of Romania). București 1995

Gluvacov, Ana: *Afirmarea femeii în viața socială* (Achievement of women in the life of the society). București 1975

Greenwell, Karen Fern: *The Effects of Child Welfare Reform on the Level of Child Abandonment and Deinstitutionalization in Romania, 1987-2000.* Unpublished doctoral dissertation. University of Texas/Austin 2003

Ionescu, Adrian et.al.: *Familia și rolul ei în societatea socialistă* (Family and its role in the socialist society). Cluj-Napoca 1975

Kligman, Gail: *Politics of Duplicity: Controlling Reproduction in Ceausescu's Romania.* Berkeley 1998

Mănoiu, Florica/Epureanu, Viorica: *Asistența Socială în România* (Social Work in Romania). București 1996

Manuila, Sabin/Georgescu, Dumitru C.: *Populația României* (The Population in Romania). București 1937

Neamtu, George: *Asistența socială. Studii și aplicații* (Social Work. Studies and Practices). Iasi 2005

Petre, Zoe: *Tranzitia: un substantiv feminin* (Transition: A feminine noun). In: Social Dialogue Review 59, p. III 1997

Popescu, Livia: Romania: A Maverick or a Conformist? In: Rakowska-Harmstone/ Dutkiewicz (Eds.): *New Europe. The impact of the first decade.* Vol 2, Warsaw 2006, pp. 429-486

Roth, Maria/Popescu Livia/Rat Cristina: Children and Social Policies in Romania, In: Studia Universitatis Babes Bolyai - Sociologia. Cluj LI (2) 2006, pp. 69-94

Stahl H. Henri/Matei I. Ioan: *Manual de prevederi și asistență socială. Teoria si tehnica prevederilor sociale* (Handbook of Prevention in Social Work). București 1962

Tismaneanu, Vladimir (coordinator): *Final Report of the Presidential Commission for the analysis of the Communist Dictatorship* (Raportul final al Comisiei Prezidențiale pentru Analiza Dictaturii Comuniste din România). Bucuresti 2006

Maria Roth

Child Protection in Communist Romania (1944 - 1989)

This paper pinpoints some key elements during the history of child welfare in communist Romania.[1] By looking into the different stages of the communist regime the paper describes their effects on childhood and child protection. It includes fragments of interviews and testimonies which provide evidence on hardships children had to endure because their parents were accused of being anticommunist. It also shows the gradual disappearance of the helping professions, first of all the social work profession. Although the quality of life and welfare structures was shrinking, the number of families and children in need of care was increasing. As the strategies of the communist social policy could only partially diminish the number of children in residential care, the politicians struggled to control all the elements of the child welfare system, determined to prevent its 'glorious image' from being spoilt.

Child Protection in the New Political Regime

In the aftermath of the Second World War, Romania, like most European countries made efforts to protect children against the consequences of war, including lack of food, need of shelter and loss of family. The pre-war social legislation was continued for a few years, allowing both public and private institutions to extend protection and assistance to children. Under the Romanian Law of Social Care and Protection (March 1943) the county services were organized including cradles (orphanages for babies and toddlers), day-care homes, centres for child-care and educational institutions.[2] In addition, Roman Catholic and Orthodox nuns, along with religiously affiliated charities, organized shelters and children's homes. The royal family of Romania also lent its continuing support to such charities. Secular organizations such as the Red Cross (*Crucea Rosie*) were also active on behalf of children during this period.

---

[1] The author is very grateful to Daniel Lowy, PhD (Washington DC) and Kathryn Conley Wehrmann, PhD, LSW (Illinois State University) for critically reading the manuscript, for their insightful comments and their valuable contribution to make the contents understandable outside Romania.
[2] Manoiu/Epuran 1996

Children as 'Enemies of the People'

Pro-communist political pressure increased after 1947 as a result of King Michael's forced abdication from his throne. The social service activities of churches and civic organizations were interrupted by the communist government as soon as the soviet model was introduced and ignited the fight against religion and pluralism. The new Romanian government abolished a treaty with the Vatican and nationalized all religious educational facilities in August 1948. By 1949 all teaching, nursing, and other charitable activities (that had previously been performed by the churches) were banned, including orphanages, shelters, daycares, and free canteens.

With the adoption of the Stalinist model, the people of Romania became the target group of politically motivated investigations about their attitude during the Second World War, their political and/or religious opinions, their ethnic or social origins, work-related issues, or personal property. Some people were accused and found guilty of "crimes against the socialist regime and against the working people" and sentenced to political detention.[3] Families of those who were detained were stigmatized, and suffered significant consequences. Students whose families were categorized as 'bourgeois', 'landowner' or 'chiaburi'[4] were not accepted at universities and high-schools. Those already attending were expelled. Elementary schoolchildren were sometimes labeled as 'enemies of the people', and expelled from their school. Family members of people considered to be politically at risk were advised to improve their situations by engaging in hard physical work in factories or in construction.[5] In her autobiography Stoenescu (2007) described how devastated she felt when her school principal entered her classroom, and announced in front of her classmates that she was to be expelled, because she belonged to an 'enemy family'.[6] Most of the expelled children were sent back to their politically ostracized family members. In some cases, entire villages of ethnic Germans were deported to remote areas in the South-Eastern part of Romania. There they had to live with few conveniences and no access to health services, and were ordered to build up the region's infrastructure (roads, railway tracks, bridges, and canals). Other families of politi-

---

3 Stoenescu 2007; Majuru 2006
4 'Chiaburi' were the families, who owned more land then they could work themselves, and, therefore, had to hire agricultural worker.
5 Majuru 2006
6 Her father was sentenced to prison because he served as a clerk in the administration during the previous regime.

cally convicted people were sent to poor areas in Moldova, where they were required to contribute to the industrialization of that region. These forced moves produced the loss of homes, friends and educational opportunities for the children, who were deprived of the opportunity to receive their school certificates and academic formation.

The Moldova Catastrophe

In spring of 1946,[7] Moldova, located in the eastern region of Romania which was already impoverished by the war, was devastated by a terrible drought which produced a famine that lasted unto 1947. The Spark (Scînteia), the official daily newspaper of the Communist Party, launched a humanitarian appeal for assistance from other parts of the country to help the people affected by the drought and the famine that followed.

As children were the first victims of starvation the government sent out a call for Romanian citizens to help children in Moldova, in winter 1946. A committee headed by the famous novelist Mihail Sadoveanu,[8] was formed to control the rescue of children from the consequences of famine. Parents who had no food for their children gave them up for rescue transports that would take starving children to more affluent Romanian regions to be fostered until the famine ended. Disregarding possible political reactions in the Soviet Union, some international help was also accepted on behalf of the children. For example, 'Red Cross Switzerland', the Swedish government, and 'Save the Children' donated medicines, food and clothes. Queen Mother Elena and women from the elite society were also engaged in fundraising to support these children. Also trade unions were involved in the relief effort.[9]

The Communist Party leaders did not allow people from Moldova to seek help for themselves in other parts of Romania by traveling and purchasing grains and goods, because any case of self-help would have nourished the doubts concerning their care management. Those who tried to buy food in other parts of the country risked to be arrested. The regime wanted to maintain the impression that it was handling the crisis in Moldova, and having individuals going around the country seeking help would not have served that purpose. Thus, the crisis opened the opportunity for propagandistic ac-

---

[7] Tiu 2006
[8] CARS: Committee for Assistance for Regions affected by drought
[9] Tiu 2006

tions: One of the activities was the 'Transports of Souls', which sometimes included as many as 500 children, being officially welcomed at railway stops from Moldova to Bucharest, where they were screened for diseases and placed in shelters.

Adoption as a 'Patriotic Duty'

All these activities produced a break-up of many families, which was further complicated by the fact that contact information were not carefully collected in case the parents died. Instead of reuniting the children with living relatives, a call went out from the Communist Party to adopt children in need. It was considered a communist duty and a mark of solidarity to foster and adopt children for reasons of compassion; therefore, communist leaders were among the first to respond to the appeal for adoption - even after the end of the famine period.[10]

Although communist ideology had encouraged adoption as compassionnate behavior, there was no specific support by counseling or other services to families who adopted children. From a contemporary perspective, adoption might have given children a better chance for social inclusion compared to residential care preferred in centralized national states. The outcome of the adoptions, however, depended on children's physical and psychological health, the adoptive parents' motivation and their readiness to respond to the children's needs. But whatever the needs of the adoptive parents and children were, the archive documents demonstrate that adoptive families were left on their own to cope with their difficulties without the aid of social support services in any form.

Childcare Institutions

Following the implementation of the communist constitution of 1948, the socialist leadership was obligated to report on how social problems were

---

[10] Ceausescu, the former Secretary General, as well as Iliescu, the post revolution social democrat (and ex-communist) leader, Chivu Stoica, Iosif Chisinevschi, Pantelimon Bodnarenko, Alexandru Moghioros, Paul Niculescu-Mizil, are adoptive parents, cf. Tiu 2006

solved in the country, especially those related to children with special needs. Children who could not remain with their families (as orphans or in cases of neglect) were placed in 'appropriate' institutions, as defined by the Ministries' Council Decision 1954. The child care institutions constituted a complex system that was not regularly coordinated and evaluated, because the responsibility for the administration of these institutions was shifted between 1947 and 1968 among the Ministries of Labor, Health, Education, and even Internal Affairs. There were institutions for children under the age of three, children's homes for preschool and school-aged children, special schools, school homes and hospital homes.

With the increasing power of the communist regime, expropriation came into law in 1948, and collectivism extended in the 1950s. Private residences were regularly confiscated and became schools, child care institutions and hospitals. Among many others throughout the country, also castles formerly owned by Transylvanian nobility were expropriated and became institutions for children with disabilities. These large, well-built residences, in most cases surrounded by gardens, were often located far away from the cities, in rather remote places, where maintenance and heating costs were significant. Their remote locations contributed to the exclusion and institutional neglect. In 1989, when the world discovered the misery of the Romanian children's homes, particularly of the asylums for severely disabled children, the responsible administration had to admit that many of these institutions had no running water, no heating system – and no qualified professional staff.

The Makarenko Pedagogy

Makarenko was one of the founders of the Soviet pedagogy, elaborating the upbringing of children in collectives and introducing productive labor into the educational system. His theories emphasized the importance of physical labour, discipline, and the role of collectivism in education - individual needs had to be subordinate to the collective needs.[11] The success of his approach led to its use in residential institutions, homes for children as well as reeducation centers. The 'pedagogy of cooperation' and the principles of 'team

---

[11] Anton Semyonovich Makarenko (1888-1939) was a Ukrainian born Soviet educator and writer. In the aftermath of the Russian Revolution he established self-supporting orphanages for abandoned children. In the 1920s, Makarenko organized the Gorky Colony, a home for homeless children.

work' were part of the attempt to propose a 'new individual' It aimed at suppressing the positive affirmation of the individual self. Education was performed in the collectivity, through the collectivity, and for the collectivity, because any form of individual education was rejected.[12] This model probably had negative effects in case of adolescents, but it had disastrous effects on children under the age of three years. Ignoring the children's emotional needs it created an over-restrictive environment, giving place to effects of hospitalism and all kinds of psychological defects.

Training and Research in Child Protection

In the 1950s social work in Romania became more and more integrated into the medical system. From 1957 to 1968 the responsibility for providing social assistance was primarily controlled by the Ministry of Health, which contributed to the medicalization of social care for many categories of dependent people, and especially for small children and those with disabilities.[13]

Although the number of trained social assistants (social workers) who practiced in the field of child welfare was continuously reduced, and the 'Princess Ileana' Superior School of Social Work, located in Bucharest, was closed in 1952,[14] the communist regime prohibited any way of criticism about the state of child protection in Romania. The few social assistants who were trained between 1959 and 1969, visiting schools for nurses, were only partially able to address the staffing needs of pediatric hospitals and homes for children under the age of three.

These training courses began in 1959 – the year of the Declaration of Children's Rights by the United Nations. The UN Declaration contained several key principles including: non-discrimination, special protection, the right to a name and a national identity, social security, the right to medical treatment, education and special care, the right to love and understanding from parents and caregivers. The Declaration was debated in workshops and conferences throughout Romania. Plans were prepared for implementing the

---

[12] Cojocaru 2005
[13] After 1968 only the institutions for children under the age of three continued to be maintained under the control of the Health Ministry.
[14] Rachieru 2005

principles in schools, hospitals and child-care institutions, but their application was never monitored.[15]

The problems in the field of child care corresponded to the lack of research in this area. There were only a few doctoral dissertations written by physicians in Bucharest, for example in 1949 by Dr. Vlad, who analyzed physical and moral cruelties inflicted on children in the interwar period. Dr. Geica-Danet studied the phenomenon of mothers killing their babies.[16] In the same year Dr. Ionescu-Balenty defended a dissertation comparing children's living circumstances in the newly established crèches with their living conditions at home.[17] The research concluded that conditions of life at home were unhealthy, because their uneducated parents did not care properly for their children: their clothing was not appropriate for the season, and food was deficient in both calories and vitamins. Compared to these, the conditions in the crèches were healthier, food was provided to cover children's needs, and the caregivers were organizing educational activities.[18]

When, after 1968, the residential child care was located under the direction of the Ministry of Labor, the change contributed to even less poorer quality of care, insufficient food and medication, fewer staff and an extremely high mortality rate.

The Increase of the Birth Rate

After, in 1966, the regime had decided to ban abortions to create 'a big Romanian nation' and produce more workers for the industry, the birth rate increased significantly. The baby boom resulting from this anti-abortion-law led to a large number of unwanted babies born mainly by young single mothers, who only could solve their social problems by leaving their children in child care institutions.

Thus, one of the consequences of the the anti-abortion law was a dramatic increase of children in need. As, in principle, the government preferred public child care institutions in comparison to adoption or foster care, 32 new

---

[15] Macavei 1989
[16] Majaru 2006
[17] Crèches are day-care centers for babies and toddlers. They were state institutions, where working mothers left their children in the morning, and took them home in the afternoon.
[18] cf. Majaru 2006

cradles (*leagans*) were built between 1965 and 1988. The official rhetoric stated that the purpose of these new homes – playing a 'humanitarian role' in assisting orphans and abandoned children – was a significant part of 'building up the socialism'.[19] The reality of the 'humanitarian strategies' included the penalty of imprisonment for women who practiced abortion and the professionals who performed them.

The Example Cluj

Also in Cluj the anti-abortion law led to a increasing number of children in the Cradle. On January 1967, a record number of 351 children were Registered. Although the numbers decreased in the next two years, they remained higher than reported averages prior to the passage of the abortion law.

The decreasing number of children in the Cradle of Cluj resulted from the fact that more cradles were opened in neighboring counties, and a law was passed which mandated strict placement of children in the county of their mother's residence. In addition, the smaller number of cradle children in Cluj was related to the method of contraception of young couples who did not accept the prevention of birth control: 'Anti-baby-pills' were smuggled in from neighboring communist countries.

In response to this kind of resistance the regime on one hand intensified the legal punishment measures related to contraception. On the other hand the financial allowances for children and for mothers with several children increased to make birth more attractive.

But, as a consequence of the criminalization of abortion, desperate women turned to unsafe procedures for terminating unwanted pregnancy, which resulted in a greater number of children born with disabilities. These children were at greater risk of being abandoned, and were less likely to be adopted or reintegrated in their families. They made the residential staff's work much more difficult – and the quality of their life was extremely reduced.[20]

Life for children in the Cradle of Cluj at the end of the 1970s and especially the 1980s was characterized by a decrease in human and material resources. Groups of 30 babies were staffed by only one nurse and just a few care aides. It was often the case that no qualified nurses were present. Stimulation, play, physical contact with adults, and emotional communication were

---

[19] Greenwell 2001, p. 5
[20] Macavei 1989; Dobrin 1990

extremely limited for the majority of children. The most physically developed children received more care than the others, as they were more engaging. Food was generally sufficient, though poor in fruits, and not well matched to age or stage of development. The activities were monotonous, and children under the age of two spent most of their time in bed, or in empty play rooms. Only on extremely rare occasions the children were allowed to leave the building. Organized forms of education like participating in the daily educational drills (including language acquisition, poems and songs) were limited to a small percentage of children between two and three. Most of the children suffered from severe forms of hospitalism and subsequent developmental delays.

Proportion of children with disabilities in the Cradle of Cluj 1985-1989

	1985	1986	1987	1988	1989
Total number of children	220	205	213	256	202
Within normality	15%	12%	7%	5%	7%
Borderline	30%	27%	20%	20%	16%
Moderate retardation	30%	34%	40%	40%	33%
Severe learning disability	25%	27%	33%	35%	44%

(Registers of the 'Cradle' of Cluj)

Data on the psychological development of institutionalized children in the period from 1985 to 1989 help to illustrate the characteristics of the residents and the possible effects of a restrictive and unstimulating environment at the Cradle of Cluj. As can be seen the number of children with normal developmental trajectories is extremely low. The large proportion of children in the categories "borderline, moderate developmental retardation" and "severe learning disability" received the least stimulation and rehabilitation, despite the fact that the children had been institutionalized to compensate for the lack of parental capacity to raise them. Each year the severely retarded children over the age of three were sent to homes for handicapped children where their survival rate dropped year by year.

Quality of Life in Residential Homes

The regime ignored everything that it could not point out with pride. This included the fact that approximately 100,000 or more abandoned children lived in Romania's state asylums and homes for children – about 50,000 of them in institutions for handicapped persons. This was the main reason why the state protection system reduced the communication between these institutions and the outside world to a minimum.[21] There was a clear contradiction between official statements about child care and the reality of daily life in these institutions. Declared purposes, often stated at professional and political meetings, sounded good, but there were no material means and no interest, at any level, in carrying out the intention of providing qualified child care. The budget for children's homes was not officially published, but it was extremely low, especially over the last years of the dictatorship, when Ceausescu neglected the social services in order to pay off Romania's foreign debts and to implement expensive projects, such as the huge palace called 'the nation's house'.[22]

Conclusion

While this paper did not discuss all aspects of child protection, nor all the risks and the quality of care provided to them between 1944 and 1990, it described the effects of political pressure in the Stalinist period on children and families, including the problem of adoptions resulting from ideological pressure. It also examined the reasons for the increasing number of children in residential care institutions and its detrimental effects on them. In the last years of the dictatorship it was clear to everybody living in the country that Ceausescu's economic policy and his pro-nativity policy were failures with tragic consequences. Briefly stated, the child-care system was severely underfunded in all its components; children's needs and their rights were neglected, because there existed no professional service in the system.

---

[21] Zamfir 2000; Roth 1999
[22] 'Casa poporului', now the House of Parliament, considered to be the largest palace in the world.

References

Bocancea, Cristian/Neamtu, George: *Elemente de asistență socială* (Social Work elements). Iași 1999

Dobrin, Brindusa: Studiu arhivistic in leagănul de copii din Cluj *(Archive Study of the 'Craddle' of Cluj)- unpublished manuscript. Cluj 2000*

Cojocaru, Stefan: Metode apreciative in asistenta sociala. Ancheta, supervizarea si managementul de caz *(Appreciative methods in Social Work]).Polirom Iasi 2005*

Greenwell, K. Fern: *Child Welfare Reform in Romania: Abandonment and Deinstitutionalization, 1987-2000.* Bucharest: US Agency for International Development; and Washington DC: US Department of Health and Human Services 2001

Kun, Bela/Marschalkó Janos/Rottenbiller Ferenc: *A fiatalkorúak támogatására hivatott jótékonycélú intézmények Magyarországon* (Philantropic Institutions helping youth in Hungary). Budapest 1911

Macavei, Elena: Familia și casa de copii (The Family and The Children's home]). București 1989

Majaru, A. Adrian: Copilăria la români (Childhood in România). București 2006

Manoiu, Florica/Epuran, Viorica: *Asistența Socială in România* (Social Assistance in Romania). București 1996

Popovoci, Gheorghe: *Protecțiunea copiilor in Ardeal* (Child Protection in Transylvania). Cluj 1925

Rachieru, Silvana: *The human being able to practice human compassion. The challenge of training professional social workers in inter-war Romania.* In: Schilde/Schulte (Eds.): *Need and Care.* Opladen 2005, p. 221-235

Roth, Maria: *Az állami gondozás Romániában* (Residential child protection in Romania). In: *Család, Gyermek, Ifjúság,* 1/1995, pp. 31-35

Roth, Maria: *Activarea cognitivă in copilăria mică.* Cluj 1998

Roth, Maria: *Protecția copilului. Concepte, metode și dileme.* (Child Protection. Concepts, Methods, Dilemmas). Cluj 1999

Sellick, Clive: Developing Professional Social Work Practice in Romania. In: Social Work in Europe, 4/1998, p. 49-52

Stahl Henri H./Matei Ioan I.: *Manual de prevederi si asistenta sociala. Teoria si tehnica prevederilor sociale.* București 1962

Stoenescu, Lacramioara: *Copii - Dușmani ai poporului.* (Children – Enemies of the People). București 2007

Tiu, Ilarion: *Comunism – Liderii comuniști, părinți adoptivi prin excelență* (Communist leaders, adoptive parents). In: Jurnalul Național, 9/2006

Zamfir, Elena: *Politica de protecție a copilului în România* (Romanian Child Protection Policy) In: C. Zamfir/E. Zamfir (Eds.): *Politici sociale. România în context european,* (Social policies. Romania in European context). București 1995

Elena Iarskaia-Smirnova, Pavel Romanov

Multiplicity and Discontinuity in the Soviet Welfare History (1940 - 1980)

The Soviet history corresponds in many respects to the global modernization processes,[1] but it has the unique features of the Soviet society and ideology, that in a special way determined Soviet social policy. It is characterized by the increasing state intervention into private sphere, the official control and family support, as well as the constant extension of incentives, the rising number of welfare recipients and the tendency towards a prevalence of social guarantees.

It should be noted that there is a terminological problem in the discussion about Soviet social policy: as it seems, the term 'social policy' was not used in Soviet historiography (as well as in other social sciences) until the 1960s. On the one hand, it is linked to the precepts of Soviet ideology, specifically reflected in Stalin's work "Economic problems of socialism in the USSR", which actually removed the item of social problems from the agenda since "the satisfaction of constantly growing material and cultural needs" was geared to "the constant growth and perfection of industry".[2]

Thus, the discussion about social problems was automatically moved to the question of 'single difficulties'. Analyzing their evolution and dynamics as well as the ways of their solution became possible only within the context of criticism of western lifestyle and capitalist state policy. Among the most frequent notions close to the examined discursive field are care (*zabota*), work organization *(organizaciya raboty)*, experience in work with delinquents, orphans, women and invalids (*opyt raboty*), state control (*gosudarstvennij kontro*) and popular control (*narodnij control*). Occasional publications using the term 'social policy' appeared since the end of 1970s, but only from the 1980's on, the level of interest in those issues became extremely high. The term became more and more frequent within the context of description (quite often the laudatory one) and within the official announcements in respect of the improvement of well-being, the rapprochement of villages and towns and development of socialist living.

---

1   Sokolov/Tiahelnikova 1999; Scott 2005
2   Stalin 1952

The research on Soviet welfare 1945 - 1989 leads us, on the one hand to continuities reaching backwards to the prewar period, and to changes in social policy during the periods of Stalinism, 'the thaw' and 'stagnation', on the other hand. At the same time, the analysis highlights not mainly the evidence of horrors, but numerous antagonisms, lacunas and mechanisms that helped people to achieve a kind of inner freedom, to adjust numerous rules and regulations and to gain a certain level of social integration. The research leads us to the drama of Soviet socialism's and its unavoidable auto-collapse.[3]

War and Late Stalinism 1940 - 1953

In autumn 1945, the human loss caused by war came to one sixth of the whole population, while the amount of real loss in economic potential was more than five times as much as the national income of the USSR in 1940. After the total destruction of national economy it was necessary to come back to peacetime conditions. The high mobility of the population was realized through the renewal of the working class, the influx of women into national economy, and – immediately after the end of war – through the labor turnover at factories. In 1946, some efforts were made to fasten workers to their workplaces by controlling their transfer from one factory to another. As prior to war, the work force was increased by migrants from rural areas who, however, had rather low qualifications and a bad labor discipline. The Stakhanov movement[4] was reinitiated, although it caused disorganization of production and an uncontrollable raise of output quotas. The living standard of 1928 was reached only by 1954.[5]

The political and economic context of the war and post-war periods defined the direction of social policy; its scale and focuses were strictly orientated on a subsequent economic recovery. The high demand for work force in industry called for an intense labor mobilization. A number of legislative measures were taken that determined the repressive nature of labor conditions for many years. The threat in the workplaces in order to force more discipline was growing, including criminal liability for being absent without

---

[3] Yurchak 2005
[4] Alexej Grigorjewitsch Stakhanov was a working class hero. His enormous raise of produced out put activated other workers to follow his example.
[5] Vert 2006

leave. Minor absence caused criminal prosecution even for a woman, who ran home to nurse her baby. The systematical construction of labor resources began: the youth was drafted into trade schools and technical schools. Child and adolescent labor, but also introduced in industry and farming quite frequently. Children and adolescents were attached to labor in families, schools, children's houses and colonies.

Among the reasons for the fast industrial development in 1950 was the employment of multi-million Gulag convicts and prisoners of war. The scale of coercive labor in the USSR and the meaning of this system for various aspects of life can not be overestimated: In the beginning of the 1950s, the population of the camps came to five million people, and whole industries (like industrial lumbering) developed on the basis of Gulag Corporation. Many categories of people (from 'alien class elements' to representatives of politically dangerous ethnicities) contributed to the development of the labor-markets - and thousands of people were engaged in it's proper functioning and reproduction: In the formation of work load standards, motivation, payment, evolution of methods in labor protection, housing, and the supply of popular consumption goods and culture. As, however, the attention was mainly focused on the reconstruction of heavy industry the restoration of housing as well as the provision of food and the development of light industry got ahead very slowly

Social Protection in the Post-War Period

At that time the costs for social protection were considerable, because there was an extension of material aid for war victims, disabled, widows and orphans. After the war also the system of general elementary education was restored and a compulsory seven-year education was introduced. The salaries of factory and office workers were gradually raised, while the prices for consumer goods were constantly lowered. There was the restoration of leaves, the introduction of an eight-hour working day, and the improvement of sanitary and medical service.

New systems of material and symbolical stimulation of birth rate (aimed at solving the demographic problems) were created - the relief for mothers of large families and the title of 'Mother-Heroine' were introduced. The particularly severe life conditions of single-mother families were recognized and fixed for the first time in the 'Decree of Presidium of the Supreme Soviet of the USSR of 8.7.1944' on direct material assistance for mothers of large families and single mothers. As the result of the war and the repressions after 1945 the increase of single mothers became especially apparent. The government responded by offering special benefits for them, for example certain advantages at work. Though it was difficult for women to prove fatherhood and therefore to force fathers to support their children, the monoparental households were under protection of the collectivist welfare system - typical of planned economy, owing to which the primary goods and services were cheap and the employment opportunities were relatively broad.

The government provided a system of social incentives, social guarantees (though the minimal ones), which included free medical service, education, provision of pensions and preferential sanitary and health resort treatment. But the support of monoparental households and other poor citizens was still insufficient. The system of social guarantees preserved the dependence of provision on the workplace and the resources of factories where people worked: it was actually the factory or *kolkhoz* which was mainly responsible for the welfare of its workers and their families. The ordinary people that fell out of industrial employment were out of well-being: for example, crippled war veterans, who filled the streets of big cities, were massively banished to remote districts or to forced labor camps for political prisoners.

Life conditions in the USSR sharply differed from western countries, which quickly improved living standards and provided democratic rights and freedom. In spite of the 'iron curtain' between two political systems, there was a growing discontent among the people that pushed the government to measures typical of universalistic social policy - measures in welfare, public health service and education.

The period of 'High Stalinism' was a time of economic, domestic and literary 'storms' and 'fronts'. The party called itself 'the fighting organization' and its members were the 'soldiers of party' – corresponding to these glorifying habits the cult of conspiracy and artificially propagated images of 'enemies' contaminated the public temper.

The Thaw: 1953 - 1964

The large scale of Khrushchev's reforms (1956 - 1964) targeted in its rhetoric and, partially, in its practice at dismantling Stalin's dictatorship and recovering Lenin's principle of 'democratic centralism' concerning special forms of management. The new economic situation demanded a diversification of production for consumers, more freedom for factories and higher productivity of labor. Some industries, producing goods of daily consumption, indulged in experiments. Profit became one of the major criteria of effectiveness in fulfilling the plan, benefits for workers were distributed by raising salaries. The rapid growth in the production of consumer goods and the liberalization of rural economy were the results of a policy that promoted more balance between economic development and individual life chances.

But these achievements coincided with a hasty policy in the area of economic reforms ('the corn rush', 'the meat campaign in Ryazan', 'the dairy records'), accompanied by a heavy strain on the whole administrative system at the end of the 1950s. The unreasonable and contradictory reforms produced an ecological and economic crisis in 1962 and 1963. Another campaign searching for enemies, embezzlers and speculators made both shady dealers and small craftsmen to victims of repression. Within two years death penalty for economic felonies mowed down the live of 160 defendants, thousands were victimized and deported, stigmatized and deprived of property.[6] The constant broadening of the category 'the parasites of society' turned into a real witch-hunt.[7]

The years of the thaw were the years of contradictions, when risky initiatives of the party and new repressions coincided with progressive measures to improve the lives of Soviet citizens: The work conditions were improved, while the mobility of workers was simplified and the prosecution for being was abolished. The taxes on low-income groups were reduced, the salaries were raised, the work schedules were reduced and the length of paid leave was extended. The maternity leave (reduced to 70 days by Stalin) turned into 112 days again; the secondary schools became free of charge and coeducational.

Traditional for Soviet history, the positive effects of those measures was primarily felt by city-dwellers, while collective farmers were still deprived: they had neither passports, nor the right of free mobility outside their residence. Until 1964 collective farmers had no state pensions and their statutory retirement age came five years later compared with other workers.[8]

Nevertheless, restoration of social justice and reduction of social inequality became the political priorities at that period. By 1956 more than 16.000 political prisoners were released, and after the XXth Congress of the CPSU several millions of falsely convicted people got a long-hoped-for freedom, after special commissions conducted mass rehabilitations in detention camps.

---

[6] Vert 2006
[7] cf. the article of Sven Korzilius in this publication.
[8] Vert 2006

The success was considerable in the sphere of human rights, especially when the term 'enemy of the people' was abolished, the criminal liability age was raised to 16 years and other norms according to a mature legal culture were introduced.

During that period the number of benefits and grant recipients was growing. In 1956 and 1964, the legislation modernized the welfare system, and made it one of the most accessible in the world. The level of benefits was raised, the connection with the employment status became less relevant, and even some guarantees for low-paid workers were introduced.

According to the act 'About state pensions' passed by the Supreme Soviet of the USSR on July 14, 1956, the government committed itself to pay pensions through the fees of factories, institutions and organizations without payroll deductions. Since that time the reform of the pension system began: it became free of discriminating features that characterized it during the Stalin period. The pensions were almost doubled and the pensionable age was lowered (to 60 for men and to 55 for women). The act about 'Pensionary Provision of Collective Farmers' (15.7.1964) expanded the welfare system and covered peasantry, reducing - finally – the differences between workers and collective farmers in the social insurance sphere. Besides egalitarian principles, the reasons for the extension of social security on collective farmers were related to the depopulation of rural areas.

But, the tendencies towards the universalization of social policy appeared differently in the special spheres of life. For example, the intelligentsia was very much dissatisfied with the policy of laborization (*orabochivanie*) in the field of higher education:

- the obligatory scheme of two-year work in factory or at the *kolkhoz* after finishing eight-year school,
- the restriction of entrance to higher education institutions right after leaving secondary school,
- the introduction of military service as the condition for entering certain categories of higher educational institutions
- and the expansion of the role of preparatory support for workers entering an institute of higher education (*rabfaks*).

Those measures were introduced in order to gain educated cadres in the industry and to "strengthen the bonds between school and life". They should finally lead to overcome the dislike for manual labor and to spread technical professions among city-dwellers.[9] But the results of the 'labourization-

---

[9] Vert 2006

process' showed that the 'intelligentsia' mostly found ways to overcome those restrictions, because the institutional measures were insufficient.[10] Nevertheless, since 1959, industrial enterprises got the right to assign their workers to institutes of higher education as a reward for excellent work.[11] It became possible to get full secondary education on the polytechnic basis – at school and at factory.[12]

With hindsight, it is easy to see that Khrushchev's assertion that the Soviet Union was marching towards communism was wrong. It would be, perhaps, a better characterization to say, that in the late 1950s and early 1960s the Soviet Union was already sidling into capitalism – 'parasites' in the vanguard.[13]

Stability and Stagnation: 1964 - 1985

With the collapse of Khrushchev's regime in 1964, the political and economic conditions of social policy changed. The vector of socio-political development, however, directed towards a better access to public goods, was not only preserved, but enhanced: During the first decade there was a rise of living standard and a remarkable increase of personal income. Under the conditions of a gradual economic growth industrial workers were allowed to move between employers more freely. Farm workers got the guaranteed stable minimum wage, social benefits for farm workers were considerably raised and became equal to benefits for the rest of the population.

The preparatory departments which replaced the '*rabfaks*' were requested to admit "workers, collective farmers, and reserve soldiers, citizens having directives from industrial enterprises (...) kolkhozes and military units."[14]

---

[10] cf. Konstantinovskiy 1999
[11] The Decree of Presidium of the Supreme Soviet of the USSR from September, 18, 1959 № 1099 "About the participation of industrial enterprises, sovkhozes and kolkhozes in the recruitment for institutes of higher education and technical schools and in training of specialists for their enterprises".
[12] Vert 2006
[13] cf. Fitzpatrick 2006
[14] Gusev et al. 1982, p. 63

On the other hand, the Brezhnev period produced a certain stagnation, because the society started to live beyond its means and to waste resources in an unprecedented manner by using irrational management methods and distorted price structures.[15]

The low effectiveness of economy was also undermined by expensive armament strategies with military bases in Europe and Asia, by economic and military support of 'progressive' regimes in developing countries and by a hopeless war in Afghanistan. The shortage of commodities forced the local governments in almost all regions to control the food distribution and to introduce food cards and consumption rates on a wide range of goods (from matches, tobacco goods and vodka to soap, butter and sugar).

The Municipalization of Social Services

In 1977, the new Constitution claimed the advancement of a developed socialist society. This included: guaranteed general secondary education, free education and medical service, the right to work, the right to rest, the right to receive pension benefits and lodgment, democratic rights and freedoms.

In the course of municipalization of social services (preschools, clubs, resort houses, sanatoriums and polyclinics) all 'social objects' went under the control of local administration. But, the economic crisis and insufficiency of local administration led, in many cases, to a severe reduction of social services. The withdrawal of the state and the enterprises out of the domain of social protection meant that the costs and the responsibility for welfare maintenance were increasingly passed on to private households and to kinship support networks. These facts were lowering the living standards of most monoparental families, many-children families and other population groups, including those which previously were considered as rather well supported ones.

Nevertheless, in a number of aspects the Soviet approach encouraged economic equality and independence of women by methods that constituted the so-called "model of weak bread-winner."[16] This implicated that not only the head of the family had to be engaged in paid jobs but all adult members. Therefore, the employment of women rose to 92% and their educational attainment level was higher than the men's level, although their salary dif-

---

[15] Tiusanen 1994
[16] Lewis 1992

fered in almost one third.[17] The high rates of women's employment were determined by the extension of a supporting infrastructure, by kindergartens and polyclinics in particular, and by a relatively liberal maternity leave combined with childcare benefits.

In spite of all successes in economic and social policy, the living standards of Soviet people in the Brezhnev period were rather low - first of all due to low wages and lack of housing. The demographic trends including the marriages and divorces dynamics as well as the population mobility aggravated the housing problem. While in the end of the 1950s only 48 % lived in cities, in 1970 60 % were city-dwellers. In comparison with other sectors of social policy – welfare, health service and education – the housing policies were not corresponding to the needs of population. Despite considerable investments during the whole Soviet period, the problem of normal habitation provision was far from solution.

As the result of the prevalent policy the overall moral climate was, at the end of the 1970s, on the way to total stagnation: the last sprouts of public free-thinking were suppressed (dissidents were exiled, expelled, put into correctional and psychiatric facilities), the process of rehabilitation of repression victims stopped, the cult of personality was no more criticized. The social morality got worse: the motivation to quality work and labor discipline faded, the overall disappointment occurred, the level of alcoholism and criminality came to a peak.

The Contradictions of Soviet Social Policy – Conclusion

Summarizing that brief review of the USSR social reforms in the decades between 1940 and 1985, it should be noted that the Soviet system of social protection was considered as an instrument to speed up the economic development and the consolidation of socialism – as inspired by the ideas of Marxist classics and founders of the Soviet political system. Some loyal foreign contemporaries thought that social protection in Soviet Union was the practical expression of class solidarity[18] and humanity: "Visit the lands of socialism. You will see a new kind of human being – shaped in conditions where deep concern for others is basic, where there is a sense of real togetherness,

---

[17] Aivazova 1998
[18] Rimlinger 1971, p. 255

joined with deep concern for the highest development of individual excellence and initiative."[19]

As an ideal model, social protection was considered as the essential right of politically loyal workers and their families. However, social guarantees should not be given to those who could support themselves by their income, but to those whose income was insufficient because of employment peculiarities or sickness – 'according to needs'. In practice, that ideal model was realized in rather different ways in the various periods of socialist state history.

In its golden age, relating to Khrushchev's and early Brezhnev's period, the Soviet government built one of the most advanced systems of social assistance in the world, concerning the access equality as well as the volume and quality of services. In 1960, when social policy was the priority for the Soviet government, the progress in house-building, medical provision, welfare and education made the USSR the world leader concerning the growth rates and the volume of services. But since the end of 1970s, when the USSR entered the toughest stage of the cold war, the main weaknesses of the socialist social policy, its key points and institutional structure became more and more apparent. It was that period, long before perestroika, when negative tendencies in the quality of the Soviet citizen's life became obvious.

The system's justification was based on the dogmatic identification of social problems as inherent in 'alien elements' and, at the same time, on the rhetoric of struggle and sacrifice 'for a radiant future'. Since the 1920s, the social taxonomies 'friend or foe' were applied to political regimes, practices, social groups and individuals; in the situation of strict selection of the 'deserving' this distinction once again became the foundation for instable, changing self-definition.

The development of the incentives system extended the scope of social groups; it involved welfare, education, transport, housing, public health service and recreation, but the great social promises were not supported by their sufficient fulfillment. The consumers of social services were categorized as worthy and unworthy; the numerous types of transfers presupposed scanty payments and varied non-monetary benefits. The geographic disparity was also significant.

The resources of social policy were concentrated in big cities and capitals. The right and duty for labor determined the access to many social services directly from the workplace, while the segment of a universal welfare regime with typical disposition of domiciliary services available for all district residents extended as well. First of all, the transfer from an

---

[19] Paul Robson Speaks 1998, p. 64

industrial towards a territorial principle of medical care was realized in order to open the services not only for working class people but also for civilians not related to the production sphere.

The emphasis on collectivity and communality is a peculiar feature of Soviet social policy. Its first and foremost task was to care for the country, the motherland (*Rodina*), but friendship and love were also relevant elements of social services. Therefore, the welfare, educational and health care institutions were supplemented by social organizations of enterprises and schools, and by other civil associations. It was the private sphere through which social assistance and social control became the basic structure of Soviet society.

This kind of 'social work' was integrally connected to the governmental efforts in constructing anomalies and deviations, which were intensified in the 1950 and 1960s. The mass hunt for *stiliagi*,[20] black marketers and other 'parasites of society' dispelled the illusion about the liberalization of Khrushchev's domestic policy.

As a whole, there were four principles of social policy during the Soviet period, that fit into the reform processes in the late 1980s:

- Firstly, accessibility and equality were prevailing in the system of access to education, accommodation, health care and social protection - and common for the labour market as well.
- Secondly, unification, unity and strict hierarchy of the administration made the system clear, controllable and universal.
- Thirdly, there were stability and predictability in execution of certain guarantees provided by enacted laws and regulations.
- Fourthly, the pursuit to provide large number of clients meant the access to an according number of services.

The Soviet system, undoubtedly, had the developed system of social services in terms of organizing residential care for the elderly and people with disabilities, and care about the poor, orphans and students. That system was based on the principle of unification, which allowed the distribution of goods to every citizen according to his/her needs – a notion which formed the basis

---

[20] A Soviet youth subculture that emerged in the late 1940s and extended into the early 1960s. The term *stiliagi* (style) first appeared in the Soviet press in 1949 to provide a negative characterization of young men who pursued what they believed to be Western models of behavior, leisure, clothing, and dance styles; cf. Edele 2002.

of welfare ethics in many countries in the world. However, the so called 'developed system' of medical care and welfare meant in practice a standard of social services on a rather low level; and instead of equality there existed an unfair distribution of resources to separate elite centers – for capital dwellers and party nomenclature. In the social stratification of the USSR the monetary hierarchies were replaced by ideological ones.[21]

The character and the mechanisms of social service under state socialism are signified by some contradictions between state responsibility on the one hand, and individual and family responsibility on the other. In the whole course of Soviet history the configuration of 'private' and 'public' was in a state of constant redefinition and ambivalence. Under state socialism the need for social work could not be articulated since it was considered that all social problems could be solved automatically by the system. Therefore, the social, social-psychological, or social-medical services rather belonged to other domains of professional activities.

Consequently, many social problems were not recognized, or they were defined as medical or criminal issues. The recognition of such problems as problems generated by the system – would have meant the offence against the foundations of the dominating ideology.

References

Aivasova, Svetlana: Russkie zhenshchiny v labirinte ravnopraviya (Russian women in the labyrinth of equality). Moscow 1998, p. 82-83
Edele, Mark: Strange Young Men in Stalin's Moscow. The Birth and Life of the Stiliagi, 1945-1953. In: Jahrbücher für Geschichte Osteuropas 2002, p. 37-61
Fitzpatrick, Sheila: Social Parasites: How Tramps, Idle Youth, and Busy Entrepreneurs Impeded the Soviet March to Communism. In: Cahiers du monde russe et sovietique, 47/2006, p. 1-2
George Vic/Manning Nick: Socialism, Social Welfare and the Soviet Union. London 1980
Gusev, Ivan et al.: Professionalnaia orientatsiya molodezhi i organizatsiya priema v vysshie uchebnie zavedeniia. (The vocational guidance of youth and the organization of entrance to institutions of higher education). Moscow 1982
Klyamkin, Igor M.: Pod gipnozom velichiia. Novaya modernizatsiia Rossii nevozmozhna bez modernizatsii istoricheskogo soznaniia. (Hypnotized by greatness. The new modernization of Russia is impossible without modernization of historical consciousness). In: Nezavisimaia gazeta. 9/2007

---

[21] Shokhin 1987; Osipenko 1986

Konstantinovskij, David L.: Dinamika neravenstva. Rossijskaya molodezh v meniayushhemsia obshhestve: orientatsiia i puti v sfere obrazovaniia (Disparity dynamics. Russian youth in changing society: Navigation and ways in educational sphere). In: Editorial URSS, 1996

Korolev, Yuri A.: Brak i razvod: Sovremennie tendentsii. (Marriage and divorce: the modern trends). Moscow 1978.

Kruglova, Tatiana A.: Kul'turno-antropologicheskij podhod k analizu sovetskogo iskusstva. (The cultural anthropological approach to the analysis of Soviet art." Proceedings of the Ural state university), 29/2004, p. 75-86

Lewis, Jane: Gender and the development of welfare regimes. In: Journal of European Social Policy. 3/1992

Nobuaki, Shiokawa: The changes in the Russian and Soviet social security. In: Annales of the Institute of Social Science at the University of Tokyo, 27/1987

Osipenko, Oleg V. : Netrudovie dohody i formy ih proyavleniya. (Non-labour revenues and forms of its realization). In: Economic sciences, 29/1986, p. 63-70

Paul Robeson Speaks: Writings, Speeches, and Interviews - a Centennial Celebration (1998).

Ob organizacii podgotovitel'nyh otdelenij. (Decree of the Central Committee of the CPSU and the Council of Ministers of the USSR: About organization of preparatory training departments from 20 August 1969)

Ob ustanovlenii platnosti obucheniya v starshih klassah srednih shkol (Decree: About the introduction of chargeable education in upper grades of secondary schools and in higher school institutions of the USSR, and about changes in procedure of scholarships designation from 2.10.1940. № 1860. The collection of decrees of the Soviet government. 1940. № 27, p. 637)

Rimlinger, Gaston V.: Welfare Policy and Industrialization in Europe, America and Russia. New York 1971

Scott, James C.: Seeing Like a State. How Certain Schemes to Improve the Human Condition Have Failed. Yale 1999

Shokhin, Alexander N.: Bor'ba s netrudovymi dohodami: social'no-ekonomicheskij aspect. (The struggle against non-labour revenues: the socio-economic aspect), 1987

Sokolov, Andrey/ Tiazhelnikova, Victoria: Kurs sovetskoj istorii, 1941-1991. (The course of Soviet history, 1941-1991). Moscow 1999

Stalin, Iosif: Ekonomicheskie problemy socializma v SSSR. (Economic problems of socialism in the USSR). Moscow 1952

Tiusanen, Tauno: Linda J. Cook, The Soviet Social Contract and Why It Failed: Welfare Policy and Workers' Politics from Brezhnev to Yeltsin. - book reviews". Europe-Asia Studies 11/1994

Vert, Nicolas: Istoriya Sovetskogo gosudarstva (History of the Soviet State). Moscow 2006

Wiktorov, Aleksandra: Soviet Union. In: Dixon, J./Macarov, D. (Eds.): Social Welfare in Socialist Countries. London/ New York 1992, p. 184-207

Yurchak Alexei: Everything was forever - until it was no more: The Last Soviet Generation. Princeton 2005

Yulia Gradskova

Maternity Care under State Socialism (1945 - 1970)

The Main Developments Between 1917 and 1945

This article is dedicated to the Soviet social politics concerning mothers and children. After the Bolshevik revolution the lack of social support for mothers and children was declared by the new government as one of the most important deficiencies. Therefore, the Bolshevik government created 1918 a special unit as part of the 'Ministry of Health' named 'Department for Maternal and Infant Care'. Another important approach was the distribution of knowledge about childcare and hygienic habits amongst the wider population, including the appliance of pre-natal and post-natal maternity leave, and the organization of maternity clinics and nurseries.[1]

In the 1920s new Soviet women's organizations were taking active part in campaigns for maternity care, and maternity itself was seen as an important 'function' of Soviet women. Nevertheless, abortion could be legally performed in state clinics.

From the beginning of 1930s, Stalin declared maternity as one of the most important achievements of socialism – endorsed by large numbers of additional beds in maternity hospitals and places in nurseries. But the quality of the new institutions was rather low and special forms of care (like nurseries) were still inaccessible for most of the women.

In 1936 women's control over their bodies was restricted when abortion was prohibited by law.

The economic and human losses of the Soviet Union during the Second World War intensified this development by exalted glorification of motherhood, introduction of the decoration of 'mother heroine' and state allowance for single mothers in 1944.[2]

In the beginning of the post-war period the state care for mothers was restricted by the severe damages of the war. There was a growing number of

---

1 David Ransel 2000; Natalia Cherniaeva 2004; Olga Issoupova 2000, Yulia Gradskova 2007
2 Barbara Enge, 2004, p. 209-231

single mothers,³ a high level of women's occupation in the wage labour and a lack of child care facilities. Nevertheless, during this period serious changes happened. The ban of abortion ban was abolished in 1955, maternity leave was constantly growing – and 4,5 million children of pre-school age were visiting day care centres in the 1960s.

It is impossible to discuss all the changes in the further periods until 1989 in-depth, so I will focus on some aspects of Soviet maternity care between 1945 and 1970 – using mainly material of magazines and guidebooks. Furthermore, I will make some references to interview material collected for my research on everyday practices of maternity and hygiene.⁴

Post-War Motherhood and Growing Maternal Responsibility

While the discourse in the war period was overshadowed by appeals to women to defend the Motherland and to work for victory,⁵ post-war publications were dedicated to glorify maternity again: "No state in the world did as much as we did for our women."⁶ Other publications from the late 1940s showed pictures of the new maternity hospitals and day care centres – or stated that over 1,1 million children were attending day care centres.⁷ A book on maternity edited in 1953 mentioned the new benefits for mothers according to the law of 1944, and showed pictures of different mother's medals. The book also named maternity clinics, nurseries and milk kitchens at large, including the locations where mothers who had problems with breast feeding could get a substitute and special mother-child-rooms in big factories.⁸

At the same time, the consequences of the war, specially the huge number of orphans and the increase of homelessness and delinquency among

---

3   According to Therborn, in the late 1950s 14% of births in Russia were illegitimate (Therborn 2004, p. 167). According to Kurganov's data, the number of single mothers in the USSR were: 1950: 2 050 000; 1960: 3 135 000; 1965: 1 831 000 (Kurganov 1968, p. 198).
4   The results of this project were published 2007. I collected interviews with women born between 1919-1947 and living in three cities of the Russian Federation (Moscow, Saratov and Ufa).
5   Rabotnitsa, 1/1943, p. 6
6   Rabotnitsa, 5/1949, p.7
7   The collected interviews show that the number of parents who wanted to place their children into day care centres was much larger than the existing capacity.
8   Arkhangelskii/Speranskii, 1953, p. 9-13

adolescents,[9] led to a shift from maternity care to child care, escalating the demands on mothers' duties.

In the earlier discourses on motherhood, a rather low female level of involvement in children's education had been accepted. The notions of 'mother's duty' in the 1920s to the early 1940s was very limited, because the women's primary duty was their dedication to state and society: the duty to give birth – and to work in the industry. State and society were presented as mother's partners who shared the parental duties with her. The fact that all women were expected to work for the socialist economy provided the excuse for not paying much attention to the children, because they could be reared by public institutions. When the inability to care for children and to educate them was revealed, for instance through the bad behaviour of the children and the youth, schools, pioneer organisations, nursery schools and kindergartens were blamed – the parents were not considered to be the mainly responsible persons.[10]

The limited understanding of 'duty' was especially concentrated on women whose economic and living conditions proved to be very poor. But: as low living conditions were common at that time, almost every woman's excuse was accepted by the authorities, even if she handed her children into state institutions for extended periods of time or neglected her role as a mother.[11] Therefore the self-determination of women was limited, in respect of their own life as well as the life of their children: They were not allowed to have any abortion between 1936 and 1955, nor were they supposed to take full responsibility for their children's well being. The arguments that should – in spite of all obstacles – convince women to become a mother, focused not mainly on self-determination or loving motherhood, but on better social support: "All workers of our factory will help you"; "the factory will reserve a room for you and your child."[12]

But in the post-war period; dominated by a lack of resources and a need for a fast reconstruction of the society, which – according to Barbara Engel "had to begin at home"[13] – mothers were required to be increasingly more responsible for their children's upbringing. In 1946 the journal *'Rabotnitsa'* published an article with the title "Are you sure you know everything about

---

9   Zubkova 1998, p. 21
10 cf. Altgauzen et. al. 1929
11 Rabotnitsa, 16/1941, p. 18; Rabotnitsa, 15/1941, p. 11, Rabotnitsa, 6-7/1943, p. 10; Rabotnitsa, 2/1949, p. 8-9
12 Zhenshchiny (Mosfilm, dir. by P. Liubimov 1965).
13 Engel 2004, p. 225

your children?" – It criticized that mothers usually did not have the time to control what their children were doing and with whom they were spending their time. Although showing some sympathy for the plight of ordinary women after work, the author of the article insisted that mothers should speak with their children, ask them about their day at school and advise them to find their ways to the playgrounds, summer camps and study circles.[14]

Slowly and gradually the idea of moral responsibility of mothers for her children started to replace the previous significance of a mother's duty which was reduced to give birth, observe hygiene regulations and guarantee the children's basic needs. This change was associated with the beginning of a new public dialogue in the 1960s on the tasks combined with motherhood. Unlike the pre-Stalinist discourse it emphasized the importance of a well being mother-child relationship. This new discourse on responsible motherhood based on the idea that mothers as individual beings should take interest in the educational and moral progress of their children.

These arguments were similar to pre-revolutionary ideas about maternity and to certain ideas of motherhood described by Sharon Hays as the crucial 'Western' model of maternity.[15] This discourse on responsible motherhood was speeded up after the death of Stalin, when the authoritarian control over women's bodies was reduced. It was also supported by a new turn towards psychology and pedagogy, following the Western understanding of education.[16] For example Shimin suggested (referring to an international congress) "to teach girls the values of high humanity (maternal love, kindness, softness) regarding their successful fulfillment of female social functions: the function of maternity."[17] This ideological change suggests that the welfare for mothers in the 1960s was more and more constructing a moral personality than an effective child-producing body.

However, the everyday situation of Russian women during this period was very different from the situation in Russia before the revolution – or that of Western Europe. The Soviet women were working mothers (in 1950 47% of wage workers were women, in 1970 51%[18]). To a large extent they had accepted a positive view on working outside of home, although the gender relationship in the families and the consumption infrastructure continued to be very patriarchal. In interviews from Greta Bucher with women who were

---

14 Rabotnitsa, 6-7/1946, p. 13
15 Zhenskii zhurnal, 6/1927, p. 11; Sharon Hays, 1996, p. 12-14, 21
16 Ehrenreich/English 1979, p. 101
17 Shimin 1972, p. 169
18 Aivazova, Russkie zhenshchiny, p. 83

raising their children, a lot of negative psychological effects of this situation such as constant stress manifested and influenced women's everyday lives at that time.[19]

At the end of the Stalin's regime the advanced technology required a lower workforce and employees with higher qualifications. Therefore, the extension of pre-natal and maternity leave, as well as the industrial development, became an open contradiction to the idea of full employment of women. Many articles in *'Rabotnitsa'* from the 1960s are dedicated to the problems of nursery shortages as obstacles to women's ability to engage in wage work, as well as the discrimination of women who came back from maternity leave to their previous workplaces.[20] In one of the letters published in *'Rabotnitsa'* the head of a post office chastised a woman returning from maternity leave after giving birth to her second child: "What kind of worker and communist will become of you if you already have two children and later may have even more?"[21]

Even though maternity care still was declared as one of the main social political interests in the late 1960s, the internationally increased standards (like introduction of family allowances in several European countries) changed the context of the social motherhood discourse. Indeed, women's expectations towards the state were growing and led to a certain criticism of the state's capacity to care for its 'daughters' properly.

Medical Care for Mothers

Medicalization of pregnancy, childbirth and childcare was seen as one of the important parts of social policy in Soviet Union. After serious deterioration during the period of the Second World War, the variety and quality of the medical services was slowly improving in the 1950s. In addition to maternity clinics other forms of medical care existed, e.g. special holiday resorts and sanatoriums for pregnant women and mothers with young children. A housekeeping book for women called ‚To the Young Housewife' suggested: "It is very good to spend the last month before the delivery at a holiday resort for

---

19 Bucher 2000, p. 137-159
20 Rabotnitsa, 5/1958, p. 33; Rabotnitsa, 1/1964, p. 29; Rabotnitsa, 3/1966, p. 14
21 Rabotnitsa, 6/1964, p. 24

pregnant women, where you will be able to spend your holiday under the supervision of a doctor."[22]

The number of maternity hospitals and clinics was also growing.[23] Some publications show that the increased resources dedicated to maternity allowed most of the women (even in the countryside) to give birth in a hospital. It also contributed to a concept of hospitals as a place where a woman should stay – for her own safety – under professional supervision before the delivery and until the end of the birth process. For example, in 1960 *'Zdorovie'* complained that some women "absorbed by various domestic debts refused this reasonable measure [to go to hospital in advance]."[24] Even when women did not spend prolonged periods of time at hospital before the delivery, hardly any young woman in the late 1960s worked till the day of birth. They had to spend the period of maternity leave visiting maternity classes, spending time outside of home, eating well, sleeping well and trying to avoid too much 'hard' work, such as laundry or lifting any weight whilst cleaning.[25] It is beyond dispute that maternity leave before delivery was becoming similar to ordinary sick leave.

In the 1950s the 'medicalization' of birth began to encompass the concept of pain relief (however its interpretation was very limited) as a normal part of delivery, changing the previous notion that pain relief should only be used when there were serious medical complications. At the same time delivery and pain continued to be considered rather 'natural' for woman. The body of the normal woman who strongly desired a child was considered to be 'mobilized' during the delivery, and the birth was compared to a battle: "Sometimes, a woman who has a strong wish to have a child does not feel any pain during delivery, like a soldier who does nor feel his wounds in a plain battle when he aspires for victory."[26]

In the 1950 and 60s the use of pain relief mainly did not mean the insertion of medication, but rather that of special massages and respiration techniques.[27] The use of these techniques was usually presented in magazines and medical publications as a unique Soviet achievement. An article in *'Zdoro-*

---

22 Molodoi khoziaike, p. 42
23 In 1950 there were 143 000 beds in maternity hospitals, in 1960: 213 000 beds, in 1967: 223 000 beds. The number of maternity and children's clinics grew from 11,300 in 1950 to more than 20,000 in 1967 (SSSR v tsifrakh, p. 148).
24 Zdorovie 2/1960, p. 14-15
25 Zdorovie 6/1962, p. 9-10
26 Arkhangelskii/ Speranskii 1929, p. 34.
27 Zdorovie, 6/1962, p.10; Velvovskii 1963

vie' from 1955 mentions that before the revolution rich women used chloroform or ether during delivery. The article propagates the notion that a new method, known in the rest of the world as Lamaze's method, had actually been invented in the Soviet Union: According to the article, Lamaze was happy to learn more about pain relief from the Soviet doctors, when visiting Soviet Union in 1951.[28]

The proposed method was a technique of psycho-physiological preparation for childbirth and consisted of relaxation and controlled breathing. Even though this was not much help in relieving severe pain, it gave women some degree of control over their bodies and influence in the delivery process. On the other hand, the widespread propaganda promoting this method was aimed to reduce doctors' responsibility for the pain and could be used as a pretext for accusing the mother of poor pain management. A book about psychoprophylactic anesthetic methods, intended for hospital staff, stressed that some women need varying degrees of pedagogic effort in preparing them for childbirth and also pointed out that in order to get good results, sometimes an 'authoritative style' was important.[29]

In spite of the many difficulties experienced by medical institutions, I think that the medical model was seen as a guarantee for the survival of mother and child. The situation – lack of public discussions about maternity care and the absence of any alternatives to hospital birth - contributed to a higher level of acceptance of the state supported hospital births in spite of the drastic changes in all previous norms and regulations.

In the 1950s and 1960s women from Soviet cities – as well as a majority of women in Europe and the United States[30] – saw medicalized maternity as a common sense practice. In the 1970s, however, a growing women's movement in the countries of Northern Europe and in the USA was influential in developing a more mother-centered and sometimes even anti-medical discourse, which created alternative child welfare centers, and renewed midwifery.[31] While the Soviet women could not fully enjoy the positive side of medical assistance for maternity (for example possibility of choice of drug as pain relief), in the late 1960s the majority of them did not criticized the excessive medicalization of maternity. Even in the 1990s, the opposition was – according to the Russian ethnologist Tatiana Shchepanskaia – mostly unor-

---

28 Zdorovie, 11/1955, p. 29. See also Velvovskii, 1963, p. 263-269
29 Ibid., p. 95.
30 cf. Martin 1987
31 The Boston Women's Health Book Collective, 1984, p. 15-17

ganized and limited to slander and alienation of doctors and sabotage of some medical prescriptions.[32]

In the 1960s the hygienic medical discourse, stressing primarily the physiology of pregnancy and infant care, was slightly disturbed by the newly re-established psychological approach to maternity. New publications paid more attention to the emotions of becoming a mother and the relations between mother and child.[33] A picture published in *'Zdorovie'* in 1962 shows a mother and a baby in a relaxing home atmosphere, both of them looking very happy, due to the bond of communication between them.[34] In the same year an article in a different issue of *'Zdorovie'* mentioned the nervousness that accompanied mothers and children when coming home from the hospital and contacting the changed conditions of their family life.[35] Among many traditional elements of the medical discourse were the insistence on hygiene and a clean house, but the article contains many elements that previously had not been typical for this kind of text. For example, it mentions that the birth of the child requires redistribution of household chores, recommends not to offer the mother too many advices, because it could make her 'nervous' – and reminds that she needs time to rest and regain her strength after childbirth.

The practical information about the reproductive system, pregnancy and childbirth, that previously was published in a short, very physiological and impersonal form, begins to change from the 1960s. It returns to a friendly conversation with the mother[36] (as practiced in the 1920s) – on the other hand the new style constructed 'mothers' as well informed readers who want to deepen their knowledge.[37]

In 1960 an article in *'Zdorovie'* dealt with problems related to the final period of pregnancy, (explaining the need for hospitalization), in the same issue information about a special recreation centre for pregnant women near Moscow is given. The residents did not only receive good food and get a break from work, but also obtain information on childbirth: "Only the unknown is frightening. But when the young first-time mother becomes aware of her own capability to influence the delivery – all that is required is to

---

32 Shchepanskaia 1999, p. 389-423
33 Zdorovie, 6/1962, p. 10; Zdorovie, 10/1962, p. 31; Rabotnitsa, 12/1969, p. 27; Rabotnitsa, 8/1969, p. 28-29
34 Zdorovie, 6/1962, p. 8
35 Zdorovie, 10/1962, p. 31
36 Speranskii, 1929, p. 129
37 Granat/Medvedeva 1965

manage one's breathing and to keep some simple commands in mind – the fears that frequently made her feel bad, will disappear."[38] At the same period numerous articles about specifically female physiological processes and sexually transmittable diseases appeared.[39]

Articles in *'Zdorovie'* and *'Rabotnitsa'* as well as books about education published after 1955 payed more attention to the problem of communicating knowledge to adolescents about the female body, its physiology and reproductive capacities. These articles usually excluded any mention of sexual emotions or delight or contraception. For example, an article answering a question from a mother who wants to know how to prepare her young daughter for puberty, suggests to explain the process of ovulation and to be careful to "not awake the child's interest in sexual issues."[40]

The medicalization of maternity in the 1930 and 40s, was presented in the press as one of the major achievements of the Soviet regime. But, some of my respondents considered it to be to a larger extent a process of restrictions and control. In spite of this, the importance of medical knowledge in the form of supervision of pregnancy and hospital birth became a deeply internalised common value of Soviet women giving birth. In the 1960s the medical knowledge was presented as an absolute authority in maternity issues, while at the same time birthing women continued to suffer from the low quality and dehumanisation of public medicine. The medicalized maternity imposed by the state and the absence of alternative medical services obstructed the debates about it.

Conclusion

This brief overview on the maternal care from 1940 until 1970s shows that protection of motherhood continued to be a very important aim of the Soviet politics: The contradictions in the field of state care for mothers and children became a symbol for the socialist welfare system. This care was included in the collective imaginary – the whole society should pay special attention to mothers and children – and did not take into account the concerns and desires of individual mothers. Despite some educational publications starting in the

---

38 Zdorovie 2/1960, p.12
39 Zdorovie, 3/1958, p. 31; Zdorovie, 5/1958, p. 20-21; Zdorovie, 6/1968, p. 22-23; Zdorovie, 9/1963, p. 18-19
40 Zdorovie 9/1955, p. 14-15

1960s, which increasingly referred to 'parents', it was almost exclusively the 'mother' who appeared to be addressed by practical advices of childcare and children's education.

The care for mothers included three important elements – medical care, guarantees of the childcare facilities and protective work legislation. Only specific categories of mothers (single mothers or mothers of disabled children) could get state allowances until the beginning of the Perestroika time. Nevertheless, state care for mothers never was just a 'help', but was accompanied by growing demands of maternal responsibility for child's health, upbringing and education.

References

Aivazova, Svetlana: *Russkie zhenshchiny v labirinte ravnopravia. Ocherki politicheskoi teorii i istorii.* Moskva 1998

Altgauzen, Nikolai (Noson) et. al: *Besedy s devushkami o materinstve i mladenchestvee.* Moskva 1929

Arkhangelskii, Boris A./Speranskii Georgij N.: *Mat i ditia: shkola molodoi materi.* Moskva 1953

The Boston Women's Health Book Collective (Ed.): *Our Bodies, Ourselves for the New Century.* New York 1984

Bucher, Greta: *Struggling to Survive: Soviet Women in the Postwar Years.* In: Journal of Women's History, 12/2000, p. 137-159

Carlbäck, Helene: *Women – Wives or Workers? Discourses and Practices in Sweden and Soviet Russia in the 1960s,* in: Rebecca Kay (Ed.): *Gender, Equality and Difference: From State Socialism to the Post-socialist Era.* Glasgow and London 2007

Cherniaeva, Natalia: *Proizvodstvo materei v Sovetskoi Rossii. Uchebniki po ukhodu za detmi epokhi industrializatsii.* In: Gendernye issledovaniia, 12/2004

Engel, Barbara A.: *Women in Russia 1700-2000.* Cambridge 2004

Ehrenreich, Barbara/Deidre English: *For her Own Good. 150 Years of the Expert's Advice to women.* New York 1979

Gradskova, Yulia: *Soviet people with female bodies. Performing Beauty and Maternity in Soviet Russia in the mid 1930-1960s.* Stockholm 2007

Granat, Nikolai E.: *Gigiena beremennoi zhenshchiny.* Moskva (Ministerstvo zdravookhranenia SSSR) 1949

Granat, Nikolai E./ Medvedeva, Elena E.: *Devochka, devushka, zhenshchina.* Moskva 1965

Hays, Sharon: *The cultural contradictions of the motherhood.* New Haven and London 1996

Issoupova, Olga: *From Duty to Pleasure? Motherhood in Soviet and Post-Soviet Russia*, in: Sarah Ashwin (Ed.): *Gender, State and Society in Soviet and Post-Soviet Russia*. London and New York 2000, p. 30-55
Kurganov, Ivan A.: *Zhenshchiny i kommunism*. New York 1968
Lewis, Jane: *The Politics of Motherhood*. London 1980
Martin, Emily: *The Woman in the Body: A Cultural Analysis of Reproduction*. Boston 1987
Oakley, Ann: *The Captured Womb. The History of the Medical Care of Pregnant Women*. Oxford 1989
Ransel, David: *Village Mothers: Three Generations of Change in Russia and Tataria*. Bloomington 2000
Shimin, Nikolai D.: *Rol lichnosti zhenshchiny-materi v emotsionalno-nravstvennom razvitii detei v semie*, in: *Dinamika izmeneniia polozhenia zhenshchiny I senia*. Moskva 1972
Shchepanskaia, Tatiana: *Mifologiia sotsialnykh institutov: rodovspomozhenie*, in: *Mifologii I povsednevnost*, vol. 3, St. Petersburg 1999, p. 389-423
Speranskii, Georgij N.: *Azbuka materi*. Moskva 1924
Therborn, Göran: *Between Sex and Power. Family in the World 1900-2000*. London 2004
Velvovskii, Ilia Z.: *Sistema psikhoprofilakticheskogo obezbolivania rodov*. Moskva 1963
Zubkova, Elena: *Russia after the War – Hops, Illusions and Disappointments. 1945-1957*. New York 1998

Magazines:

Zdorovie: 1955-1968
Rabotnitsa: 1941-1970

Vesna Leskošek

Social Policy in Yugoslavia Between Socialism and Capitalism

Introduction

After the Second World War the emphasis of socialist politics was primarily on the equality of people.[1] The strategy to achieve equality[2] was the nationalisation of property and the abolition of private ownership, which led to the fact that the field of social policy was subordinated to general politics[3]. This model – known as 'egalitarian social policy'[4] – did not result in enhancing people's freedom, but in causing more uniformity concerning their social status.

Social rights, also laid down in the Constitution from 1974, were the right to be employed and to receive education, health care, a pension, social benefits and disability benefits. Women received more or less equal pay for equal work, child care was well-developed, and during the nine months of maternity leave mothers received a subsidy of 100% of their salary. Generally speaking social protection was dependent on employment. According to the Constitution from 1974, the welfare system was decentralised and the responsibility for social protection was a matter of the municipalities. Yugoslavia became a state characterized by a high level of social rights and a high level of women's employment[5].

Unlike many other Eastern European states[6] Yugoslavia established social services soon after 1945. But for all that the state only developed the

---

[1] Justice as the second important principle of social policy was not regarded as a significant issue of the socialist (egalitarian) social policy, cf. Rus 1990, p. 155
[2] Equality was mostly reduced to financial resources.
[3] Rus 1992
[4] Rus 1990, p.181; Connors 1979, p.340
[5] Novak 1999, p.170
[6] In the countries controlled by the Soviet Union, the welfare system was based on the belief that socialism itself, as a just system, would prevent social problems, cf. Milošević 1989. Yugoslavia was the first socialist state that professionalized social work.

public sector, while there were no non-governmental[7] or private social services. The public sector consisted mainly of a network of institutions. The first social services were established in the late 1950s, and till 1980 this network had been spread all over the country. The welfare system provided two types of services: the network of institutions for different target groups (for children and young people, for elderly, mentally handicapped and disabled people etc.) and the Centres of Social Work, which influenced the development of a specific type of social work practice and a specific type of intervention. Casework (in the traditional sense of changing an individual person and not his or her social situation) was the basic approach. Social work intervention involved a high level of social control. Helping professions, especially in the field of pedagogy,[8] psychology, social work and psychiatry, were primarily concerned with issues like pathology and deviancy. The consequence or result of this predominant attitude towards social problems was the fact that a lot of social problems were not recognised at all. Violence against women and children, sexual abuse, institutional rights, poverty, homelessness and similar problems were ignored and only dealt with for the first time at the end of the eighties when the first non-governmental organisations were established.

Social Work in Socialism

In Ljubljana, the social work education was established in 1955, beginning with a two-year high school program. The first curriculum was based on the recommendations issued in 1956 by the United Nations.[9] From the very beginning social work was conceptualised as an interdisciplinary profession aiming at investigating social problems as a combination of individual capabilities and the social situation of people in need. Although the school played a role in the development of social services, it did not influence social policy. The faculty of social sciences occupied the most important position in this field, i.e. they carried out most of the research and the surveys, and they also established a special department for social policy studies.

---

[7] There were some voluntary organisations, but they were not independent, because they were founded and financed by the state.
[8] Defectology is still one of the departments at the Faculty for Pedagogy.
[9] Milošević 1989, p. 79

In the period of socialism the social dimension was often talked about, but on the basis of the presumption that social policy was only a subordinate part of economic policy. This meant that due to the development of socialism the economy would prosper, and consequently (because of the abolition of exploitation) all social problems would automatically be abolished. In Yugoslavia's self-managing socialism the subordinate role of social policy to economic policy was explicitly declared exactly at the time when the country distanced itself further and also definitely from the residues of Stalinism and started to support liberal ideas[10]. This happened at the 7th Congress of the Yugoslavian Communist party in 1977. The Congress demanded the withdrawal of the state, because the role of public administration concerning the direct management and funding of cultural-educative activities, health care, social policy etc. was expected to diminish, due to the development of the socialist democratic system. The ideological demand for the state's withdrawal from these fields presupposed the theory of 'social automatism', which was based on the assumption that through a well-developed economy welfare would increase and the need for a special, autonomous social policy would gradually decrease. The demands for a special social policy were interpreted by the ideologists of socialism as an attack of anti-systemic forces opposing the development of self-management. The integrity of the two fields of social and economic policy was to grow along with the development of self-management, so that finally they would merge into each other completely. To strive for a separate social policy would mean that there was something wrong with socialism.

Although in 1948 Yugoslavia separated from the Soviet Union and developed a different type of socialism (not communism), which did not rest on the assumption that political equality would be sufficient to abolish social problems, the country nevertheless adopted this assumption in the 1970s. It started to carry out an intensive process of disbanding state social services, a strategy which was called the 'nationalisation' of the social care system. The strategy was presented in the document entitled 'Self-Governing Regime of Social Policy' (1984), which largely influenced social work. It should be pointed out again that during the period of socialism social work mainly operated within the state social services, because there were hardly any non-governmental organisations or private services[11].

---

[10] Dragoš 2005, p.178
[11] Leskošek in Hauss, Schulte, p. 41-43

The Deprofessionalisation of Social Work

The 'nationalisation' of social care was most remarkable at the end of the 1970s and in the first half of the 1980s. At the same time the first civil society groups began to emerge, which opposed the communist government because of suppressing freedom of speech. The more open the opposition criticized the authoritarian nature of the political regime, the stronger was the need to enforce the basic socialist ideas of the 'power to the people'.

Social policy was defined as "the widest active inclusion of working people and citizens, their self-managing bodies and communities, aiming at empowering all these people and institutions belonging to the political system of socialist self-management to build and create relationships in which the workers will be free enough in creation and decision-making to become real owners of their working results. This means that the workers will really be holders of rights, obligations and responsibilities in the whole system of social reproduction."[12] The workers would establish their position directly in relation to other people of the community and no longer through different services and institutions. Being included in the field of work and in the community, they would provide their own social security. Thus the provision of social security through work became increasingly a duty for workers instead of a right.

Nationalisation was the process of organising the citizens in such a way that they took over responsibilities and duties for the common good. The state's intrusion in these relationships had apparently negative effects and blocked the transfer of responsibilities to its citizens. In order to prevent this, the important role of state services needed to be reduced and activities had to be transferred to the community. The role of the state was merely to refer to ensuring the survival of the most endangered members of society[13]. As a result, social services were gradually losing their autonomy, and committees and commissions consisting of activists from the local communities were involved in making decisions on people's rights. In this way, their rights were no longer conceded on the basis of objective criteria, but were grounded on the estimates of these commissions, which determined who was a beneficiary of certain rights and who was to be excluded.

In addition to certificates about their income, the beneficiaries of social assistance also needed to submit an assessment of the "organisation of asso-

---

[12] Self Governing Regime of Social Policy in Slovenia. Officialle Gazette, 1984, p. 9
[13] Ibid, p. 13

ciated work" (their employers) for themselves and for their spouses, as well as an assessment of the local commission for social issues on their eligibility for social assistance. The local commission had to check whether the declared number of family members in the common household was correct and submit its opinion on the financial circumstances as well as the causes of the respective person's poor social conditions. Local commissions mainly made assessments on non-workers.[14] Activists were mostly functionaries who were considered to be 'trustworthy' and belonged to the Communist Party or another socio-political organisation. They fulfilled their duties by showing up unannounced at people's homes, checking the residents' material goods and lifestyle: what they had bought, whether they owned a car or not, how they were dressed and if they had a side income.[15]

Social workers in the social work centres, whose task it was to appraise the eligibility to get help, had to consider these assessments. And even if they came to the conclusion that a client was entitled to receive social assistance, they had to refuse his application if the assessment of the commission was negative. Commissions for social issues in the local communities also decided which social programmes would be implemented in their community and which would not be realized. Also in this case professionals from the social work centres were not allowed to make decisions on their own.

The idea of transferring power from public institutions to the community (from the state to the people) would be interesting and challenging, in case we could theoretically explain it within the framework of the concept of deinstitutionalisation or as a radical social work perspective. But such an approach cannot be applied to this communist regime that exercised a high level of control. What was actually transferred to the community was not the power, but the control over people who claimed their social rights. Mastnak defines this process as "totalitarianism from the bottom",[16] in which the civil society adopted the repressive role of the state. He claims that a repressive civil society like the one described above is even more dangerous, because it is a self-regulative body outside legal control, as the process of 'nationalisation' means that the withdrawal of the state weakens the legal system.

The basic question is why the regime decided to implement the important project of transferring 'power to the people' in the 1980s? To answer it we have to describe social processes during that period that were closely connected to the rise of social movements.

---

[14] Ibid, p. 144
[15] Ibid, p. 85
[16] Mastnak, 1987, p. 91-98

The Role of Social Movements in Political Changes

The late 1970s and early 1980s were the time when new social movements were created. The first sign of this development was the youth movement known as punk, which was very much defined by its music and the typical personal image. The different appearance and behaviour of young people and their politically critical music were indications of a new phase in Slovene political reality, which was supported by many of the critical intellectuals who started to raise the issue of human rights violations, especially with regard to the suppression of free speech.[17] Feminist, ecological and peace groups, gay and lesbian organisations and many others started to ask questions and make demands concerning the political agenda of the government.

The 1970s were also a very important period of time for the field of social work. Some social workers and future lecturers at the school of social work took part in these movements. Feminist groups started to raise the issue of violence against women; sexual abuse was the second important topic and women's NGOs started to create their own initiatives, such as establishing shelters and providing counselling services. They strongly criticised the state social services for misusing their power and ignoring the position of women, making them responsible for the difficult experiences they had. This was also the time when the anti-psychiatry movement started and was trying to adopt the Italian model of community mental health services. The first non-governmental organisations favouring alternative programmes based on a social and not a medical model were established in the mid-eighties. The main result achieved by these movements was a different perception of social problems, so that structural changes of society were demanded. At the same time it must be emphasized that civil society is not characterized by uniformity, but consists of many of different actors, groups or organisations that often oppose each other. Many of the social movements did not demand changes that would have lead to capitalism and conservativism. They were left-wing movements which believed socialism with 'a human face' was possible. Apart from these, others demanded the fall of socialism, a type of free market capitalism, a strong position of the Catholic Church etc.

This very brief description of this important period in Slovene history does not satisfy the more demanding reader, but can only contribute to prove our conclusion. The process of 'nationalisation' (replacing the state by 'private' activities) coincided with new social movements. Thus the intention of

---

[17] Hribar et. al. 2003

the regime was to build a self-sustained system of repression 'from the bottom' that would be capable to control and suppress demands for political and social changes. Considering social work as a profession it can be argued that the development beginning in the early seventies did not keep pace with the political wishes. The emphasis in the field of social work education was on community work, on projects focusing on the support and not on the change of the individual, on the demand for de-institutionalisation and similar issues. The socialisation of the welfare system was therefore also a way of preventing those changes from being implemented and becoming part of the practical work of social services. But it is also a fact well known to everybody that the regime failed and lost the battle.

Conclusion

As a result of the first phase, when the major focus was on establishing the legal foundations of the welfare system, and of the second phase, when the focus was primarily on all sorts of official documents, the current situation is characterized by a big gap between theory and everyday practice. The theory has adapted to the new concepts in social policy, the vocabulary has changed, and the contribution of civil society is appreciated and encouraged. But the practice is almost the same as ten years ago, especially with respect to the public social services, as it is rather the terminology employed in this field that has changed and not so much the actual attitude towards social problems and towards the user of the services. But on the other hand, there is a large number of newly established voluntary and nongovernmental organisations which are filling the gap between the needs and the services. Some of them have proved to be highly qualified, and through their advocacy work they are also contributing to social changes.[18]

But we still cannot answer the question what kind of welfare system we have or what is happening on the level of the relationship between providers and the users of the services? What we know is that the pluralist development of the welfare system should be regarded "as an irreversible process

---

[18] Women's organisations campaign for changing the legal framework for dealing with violence against women, for sexual harassment at working places, for equal rights of handicapped women etc. There is also a strong resistance to racism, nationalism, islamophobia and other kinds of discrimination prevailing official politics of the time.

which implies an increasing number of mixed solutions and innovations in the welfare area."[19] But this process can also endanger the welfare of certain social groups because of its complexity. It could undermine the principle of equality as well, and therefore it needs to be controlled carefully; its regulation cannot be reduced to exercising simple self-control. With regard to this aspect Svetlik points out: "If the agents responsible for the regulations in this field do not want to limit the productive and innovative potential of welfare pluralism considerably, they must supplement centralised by predominantly decentralised services and exercise their control indirectly in order not to prevent the perspective of solutions."[20] The regulative bodies must involve a diversity of providers, leaving room for a strong role for the people who use the services.

References

Connors, Walter: *Socialism, Politics and Equality.* New York 1979
Dragoš, Srečo: Socialni vidiki reform (Social aspects of the reforms). In: Toš, Niko (Ed.): *Pogledi na reforme* (Perspectives on the Reforms). Ljubljana 2005
Evers, Adalbert/ Svetlik, Ivan (Eds.): *Balancing Pluralism. New Welfare Mixes in Care for the Elderly.* Vienna 1993
Flaker, Vito: *Oblike bivanja za odrasle ljudi, ki potrebujejo organizirano skrb in podporo. Analiza in predlog ukrepov. Raziskovlano poročilo.* (Different Housing settings for people who need organised care and support. Research report). Ljubljana 1999
Hribar, Tine et a. (Ed.): *Punk je bil prej: 25 let punka pod Slovenci* (Punk was first: 25 years of punk in Slovenia). Ljubljana 2003
Leskošek, Vesna/Dragoš, Srečo: Community and Social Capital in Slovenia - the impact of the transition. In: *European Journal of Social Work,* 7/2004. p. 73-88
Leskošek Vesna: Power and Social Work under Socialism. In: Hauss, G./Schulte D. (Eds.): *Amid Social Contradictions. Towards a History of Social Work in Europe.* Opladen 2009. p. 35-46
Mastnak, Tomaž: *Totalitarizem od spodaj* (Totalitarianism from the bottom). In: *Družboslovne razprave,* 5/1987, p. 91-98
Miloševič, Vida: *Socialno delo* (Social Work). Ljubljana 1989
Novak, Mojca: *Razvoj slovenske države blaginje v evropski perspektivi* (Development of Slovenian Social Policy in European Perspective). In: Družboslovne razprave, 30,31/1999, p. 157-175

---

[19] Svetlik 1993, p.48
[20] Ibidem

Rus, Veljko: *Socialna država in družba blaginje* (Social state and welfare society). Ljubljana 1990

Rus, Veljko: *Social policy between Negative and Positive Equality: The Yugoslave case.* In: Ferge, Zsuzsa/Kolberg, Jon Eivint (Eds.): *Social Policy in a Changing Europe.* Vienna 1992

Svetlik, Ivan: Regulation of the Plural and Mixed Welfare System. In: Evers, A./Svetlik, I. (Eds.): *Balancing Pluralism. New Welfare Mixes in Care for the Elderly.* Vienna 1993

Zaviršek, Darja: *You will teach them some, socialism will do the rest.* In: Schilde, K./Schulte, D. (Eds.): *Need and care – Glimpses into the Beginnings of Eastern Europe's Professional Welfare.* Opladen 2005, p 237-274

Marina Ajduković, Vanja Branica

Some Reflections on Social Work in Croatia (1945 - 1989)

This paper may serve as a point of reference for further research on the history of social work in Croatia[1], rather than a detailed overview or a historical evaluation of the very dynamic socialist period that lasted 45 years. It is based on a number of sources such as official data, personal memories, recollections and analysis of the wider socio-economic context. The emphasis is on the rather neglected period from the late 1950s to the beginning of the 1970s. This period was marked by two important events for the development of the social work profession – the establishment of the first Centre for Social Work in 1959 and the beginning of publication of the journal 'Social Work' in 1960. The late years of this period were marked by the adoption of the Law on Social Welfare in 1969, the first law that regulated this field. Overview of the previous period from the end of the World War II until 1960 can be found in the report by Sandra Prlenda and colleagues (2006).[2]

The Socio-Economic Context

The analysts of the development of Croatia (within the former Socialist Federative Republic of Yugoslavia, after World War II until the breakdown of socialism and the Croatian war for independence in 1991), usually point out several phases. The first follows immediately after the end of the war in 1945 and ends in 1952.[3] It is the phase of administrative socialism characterized by strong state centralism. The reconstruction of the war-stricken country produced very difficult economical and political conditions.

---

[1] The Republic of Croatia was the constitutive part of the Socialist Federal Republic of Yugoslavia from 1945 to 1991. Throughout this period Croatia, as was the case with other federal republics, had certain level of administrative and legislative independence which enabled specific development of social work which is presented in this article.

[2] Final Report: History of Social Work in Croatia, 1900-1960. (Prlenda at al., 2006.) made within the scope of an international research project: History of Social Work in Eastern Europe 1900 - 1960 (www.sweep.uni-siegen.de)

[3] cf. Šućur 2003

249

The second phase covers the period from 1953 until 1965 and is marked by the introduction of the self-management system and the process of decentralization. In the field of social care the work, which had no administrative character, was transferred to the institutions outside the state bodies. The tasks of the social care services increased when the municipal authorities got the competence in guardianship issues. Also the changes in the criminal sentencing stressed the role of the social services in the domain of delinquency of the minors (giving case reports to the court with suggestions of educational measures). This period ended with the economic reform in the mid 1960s, which had the goal to introduce more market orientated elements into the existing economy, and increase the independence of economic subjects.

The third (1965 to 1974) and the fourth period (1974 to 1984) were marked by different economical reforms and legal changes intended to develop self-management as an alternative to democracy. The districts obtained significant political and economic independence, and the economic subjects became almost fully independent. The development was intensified, especially in the industrial area, and the rate of the national income was high. But the political situation in the country was tense. However, this was probably the most favorable period in the development of Yugoslavia, and especially in Croatia and Slovenia regarding the standard of living and the economic activities.

This period ended with the program of economical stabilization to cope with the increasing economical difficulties (huge inflation, export-import deficit, difficulties with production of basic goods and their rationalization on the market, significant decrease in living standard).

The last period from 1984 to 1989 was also marked by significant economical difficulties and a further decrease of the living standard. According to Šućur (2003) a significant number of workers could not meet the basic needs with their income. The social support system was facing huge demands, and a lack of funds was compensated by lowering the financial assistance under the legal minimum – striking first of all the needy.

Bilandžić (1985) gives us a similar division, but he selects the periods before and after 1971, when more progressive republic political elites (the so called 'Croatian Spring') were taken over by the mainstream. In the years following 1971, and especially after 1974, the processes of economic and then political crisis began. The basic characteristics were: failure of the political elite concerning the political situation in the country, domination of political criteria over economical ones, decreasing industrialization, inflation, foreign debts and the awakening of the national identity in the different parts of Yugoslavia.

"Forced modernization and high level of social rights have proved the socialist model in the first phase of development to be relatively successful in spite of all its shortcomings and repression it practiced. However, exhausted development possibilities in the economic and social sphere, especially lack of civil and political rights, in the second phase of development, greatly lowered its development potentialities and led to a break down."[4]

In order to describe the specific path in the former Yugoslavia in relation to the other socialist countries, it is necessary to return back to the period immediately after the World War II.

The Self-Management System

After the break with the Soviet Union in 1948, significant political changes began with the introduction of a worker's self-management system. This new orientation of the political structure influenced the constitution from 1953. The introduction of the self-management system was accompanied by the decentralization and improvement of the public services. In 1957, a resolution was passed by the Federal Parliament concerning the general consumption, providing an increase of expenditures to improve the living standard of people and, particularly, the non-economic goods as education, health care and social welfare.

By the 1960s, Yugoslavia had already adopted the most important social laws, which defined social security of the employees:

- Law on social security of workers and employees and their families (1950)
- Law on health insurance of workers and employees (1954)
- Law on pension insurance (1957)
- Disability insurance (1958)

From the beginning of the 1960s, the system of social security was decentralized, and independent Community Funds for Social Security were founded in municipalities. The introduction of the so-called community system in 1956 was important for the further development of the social welfare system.[5]

---

[4] Puljiz 2006, p. 24
[5] Šućur 2003; Matutinović 1962

Nearly all population was covered by the health insurance in the 1970s, and by introducing pension insurance for the farmers nearly all population categories were covered. Namely, the local government bodies were given significant authority and considerably more funds, so that they could provide a multitude of proactive strategies. For instance, they could introduce local voluntary taxes for the foundation of kindergartens, schools and other services. The municipalities, as "communities of life and work", were responsible to enable their inhabitants to realize all their needs. The best illustration of the importance of such services is an interview held by Daria Zaviršek with a social worker in a kindergarten: "There were not many kindergartens in Slovenia before 1961. Women often said, 'I've locked the child in the flat and went to work'. And I asked her: 'When will you get home?' – 'Around two or three pm.'; this meant that the child was on its own for four or five hours. I also locked up my children, when I had three weeks of maternity leave only."[6]

By the beginning of the 1960s Yugoslavia recorded its biggest economic growth. Not only the production increased, but also the import of goods and the mass consumption. For the first time in history the population of the country was not predominantly rural.

Dragomir Vojnić (2006) explains this phenomenon making a clear distinction between the dogmatic socialism of the Soviet Union and the socialism based on self-management in Yugoslavia. The dogmatic socialism – so Vojnić – denied the two basic institutions of the modern civilization – market and democracy. The population in the Soviet Union lived far below the standard which was objectively possible, and the agriculture, which had excellent export potentials could not produce enough food even for its own population.

In contrast, Yugoslavia started the development of the socialism based on self-management already in the 1950s – a reaction of the Yugoslav political elite to the general crisis of socialism in the Soviet Union. In 1962 systematic measures were undertaken towards the socio-economic reform, foreseen to begin in 1965. Its goal was to develop a market orientated self-managing economy, with greater orientation towards international markets.

"It took only 13 years, from 1956 to 1972, to increase the living standard for three and a half times (...) Joint consumption rose and exceeded the economic possibilities of the country. Its share in the gross national product increased from 7,2% in 1956 to 14,5% in 1972."[7]

---

[6] Zaviršek 2006, p. 68
[7] Bilandžić 1985, p. 387

The elements of the socio-economic reforms encouraged pluralism and democratic trends, but at the same time fears relating to national and confederation issues arose. This was the period when the importance of the national issue could be easily observed, and it manifested itself in two aspects – differences between the developed and underdeveloped regions in Yugoslavia and the distribution of earnings in foreign currency.

"The explosion of the Balkan nationalism prevented pluralism and democratisation of the self-managed socialism model. That was the first attempt to create a model of sustainable development (...) Although the self-managed socialism did not survive, its positive effects are unquestionable. These effects are of two kinds. First, they stimulated reforms in other, especially Central European, counties. Secondly, they accelerated the collapse of the Bolshevik option and even the overthrow of the Berlin wall."[8]

The further research of this period can provide internationally significant knowledge about the interaction of social work and social welfare development with the very specific socio-political and economical context of the "third way". The uniqueness of former Yugoslavia in comparison with other socialist countries is, for example, the fact that while in the other countries (Bulgaria or Hungary) already existing schools for social work were closed, the profession of social work was supported and schools for social work were opened in the 1950s.

Organisation of the Social Welfare – The Foundation of Social Work Centres

The decentralization process and the development of the community system led to significant changes in the organization of social services. The key event for the social work practice was the opening of the first social work centre in Pula in 1959 (it was called Centre for socio-medical work). The task of these centres was to register and solve social problems within the local community. Following the recommendation of the Federal Assembly of the Socialist Federal Parliament from 1961, the social work centres were founded throughout the whole country and became the fundamental social welfare institution. As Šućur (2003) stated, in 1962 there were ten, and in 1964 already 15 community social work centres located in the former Croa-

---

[8] Vojnić 2006, p. 419

tia: "By the beginning of 1961 and on recommendation of Irena Bijelić, Secretary of the Council for Social Welfare of the Socialist Republic of Croatia, I started to work in the just founded Office for Social Work of the City of Zagreb. They employed qualified associates – advisers established in the field of social welfare and social work … The basic task of the Office was to research, follow up and give proposals on measures for solving social problems within the limits of the City of Zagreb and outlaying communities. After the reorganization of the City Council the greater part of us was taken over by the joint Centre for Social Protection of the City of Zagreb."[9]

Centres for Social Work as institutions of social welfare proved themselves to be quite efficient and have contributed to more efficient and competent solving of social problems. For this reason they were recognized internationally as an institutional innovation in the social welfare field. Ksenija Bralić-Švarcer remembers about the work of social workers of that time: "I think that there is a big difference between the social work in the late fifties and nowadays. For us it was inadmissible and unthinkable to call people in. We were always in the field; we were present in the local communities. I spent, for example, from 14 to 16 PM in the local community premises or from 13 to 15 PM in the school premises and everybody knew that it was the time of the social worker. In our work we did not use much the word – consumer, maybe client, but even this reluctantly. I think that the work was done in a different way – I will not say it was better or worse, but simply different."[10]

However, as stated by Šućur (2003), it is necessary to emphasize that the period until the mid 1960s was characterized by the unbalanced development of social welfare and care in the developed and undeveloped communities, the lack of capacities in social institutions, and the adverse personnel situation in the greater part of the community social services (about half of the personnel in 1963 had only elementary school education (eight years).

Social Welfare Laws

The adoption of the Republic Law on Social Welfare in 1969 was important for the improvement of the Social Work Centres activities. The status and

---

[9] Interview with Ksenija Bralić-Švarcer, 2007
[10] ibid.

competences of the centres were regulated on the legislative level and they received a wide field of work in solving social problems. This law had foreseen that the Centres for Social Work on community level were responsible for all activities connected with 'social welfare'. In those communities in which the Centres had not been founded, the state administration bodies responsible for 'social welfare' were to perform those activities. Besides adoption of the law, the concepts of the organization and cooperation between social services on local level were also created. Case work was differentiated and classified, instead of installing a dichotomy between pecuniary aid and institutional placement. As Šućur (2003) stated, in spite of the achieved improvement the interventions into the social welfare and care could not effectively respond to the real needs as the Funds had no independence and secured revenues.

The Law on Social Welfare from 1974 had brought further changes. The most significant was the closing of previously mentioned Funds and the introduction of the Self-Managing Communities of Interest as a "basic and obligatory form of association" in the field of social welfare and care. The law made the difference between the general social needs (to be covered by the Republic and municipalities budgets) and collective needs (covered by taxes and contributions on wages and salaries) within the social welfare and care. The collective needs comprised: assistance to the enable-bodied population, protection of children without adequate parental care or whose parents were abroad, assistance to persons with physical and mental disorders, assistance to single working parents, assistance to ex convicts etc. The right for permanent pecuniary aid was granted only to permanently disabled persons, who had not enough means to support themselves and exceptionally to unemployed mothers and working single mothers.

Due to a number of difficulties in the implementation of the Law, for example the problem of protection of the senior rural households, a new Law on Social Welfare was passed in 1983. It represents a further step in the transfer of social welfare and care activities to the local municipality. The Republic kept only two liabilities: secure enforcement of correctional measures on minor criminal offenders whose number continually increased and provision of funds for construction and reconstruction/improvement of institutions in which these measures were to be enforced. A novelty was the possibility for the senior rural households, whose members were not longer able to perform their agricultural activities and could not obtain social security in any other way, to realize the right to permanent pecuniary aid under condition that they transferred their land or other property to public ownership. As

Šućur (2003) writes this law had foreseen quite a number of different forms of pecuniary aid (permanent, temporary, single and other pecuniary aid).

It is visible that the law solutions in the social care field were intended to follow decentralization, but also to balance economic difficulties and crises in the eighties with the needs for social security of citizens. Unfortunately, that was not successful because the decentralization in the conditions of economic difficulties brought even bigger differences between particular municipalities in respect to the level of social welfare and care and in this way contributed to the rise of horizontal inequality. Also, due to the increase of the number of single pecuniary aid to users outside the social welfare and care system as pensioners, unemployed or poorly paid employed, led to significant delays in payments and a decrease of the amount of permanent financial assistance below the granted minimum.

Social Care Institutions

The process of decentralization on the one hand was responsible for a quick development of the community services engaged in everyday implementation of activities relating social welfare and care, but on the other hand the founding of institutions, which were interesting for a wider number of communities, i.e. children or elderly homes, became more and more difficult. The interest of the communities for such institutions was low, and tendencies demanding their closure were present. The institutions were often placed in former mansions and isolated from main roads and urban areas, thus rehabilitation expenses were high and the integration of clients into normal life was even more difficult.

How the decentralization processes reflected on the functioning of the social welfare institutions can be learned from a book, issued at the 60th anniversary of the Correctional institution for girls in *Bedekovčina*.[11] It was an institution[12] that the Ministry of Social Care of the Peoples Republic of Croatia founded in July 1945 for the upbringing and education of girls aged between eight and 18. The reasons for placement in the institutions in the

---

[11] Hršak et.al. 2005
[12] The correctional facility was founded in the baroque mansions of the Vranyczany family built in the 18 century. The mansion was nationalized in 1945, namely became state ownership and was put at the disposal of the Ministry of Social Care of the Peoples Republic of Croatia.

period between 1953 and 1955 were vagabonding, theft and prostitution, and in the 1960s school drop out, educational neglecting, promiscuity and association with persons of asocial behaviour as well as psychical disturbances. In the period from 1970 to 1990, the reasons for placement were still school drop-out, vagabonding, aggression and association with persons of asocial behaviour, but there was an increase of young female clients that were identified as delinquent, alcohol and drug abusers.

The concept how to approach these girls was based on working in workshops – printing house and bookbinder's shop, hairdresser's shop, tailor's shop and farmland. The life conditions were hard: "The buildings of the institution reminded of privation and looked cold. The beds are weak and uncomfortable, and the bed linen warned out. The inmates' clothes are very modest. The institution has a lot of debts. At one time their account was blocked. The difficulties arose because many national community committees did not regularly pay sustenance fees."[13]

This quotation show that the work of the institutions was based on self-financing – sustenance fees that were paid for the girls by the National Community Committees and inmate work. Periodical financial 'injections' for the maintenance of the building or shops were allocated by the Social Institution Fund and the National Health and Social Politics Council, but financing was unsteady: "The year 1966 was important for the life of the Institution. What was expected and dreamed of for years finally begun to be realized. *Bedekovčina* was going to get water. The Republican Secretariat for Peoples Health and Social Welfare gave the Institution allocated funds for installation of water pipes."[14]

It turned out that the concept of work in workshops was a failure as the workshops were unprofitable, and work hours interfered with these young women's education. The number of qualified educators increased only after 1965: "The year 1965 was a turning point for education and personality improvement. The standard everyday regime can be described in this way: the inmates attended productive work in workshops in the morning, and attended classes in the afternoon, and learned with the assistance of tutors in the evenings. Work on our farmland was slowly abandoned. More and more attention was given to inmates leisure time. (…) Following the Conference on re-socialization of children and youth with behavioural difficulties held in 1967 (…) modern forms of case work become more and more a standard procedure, and were focused mostly on the personality and needs of every individ-

---

[13] Memorial 7 for 1958, in: Hršak et.al. 200, p.13
[14] Hršak et.al. 2005, p. 16

ual inmate, so that their integration into society could be as successful as possible and in accordance with their own possibilities."[15]

These short excerpts from the Memorial book of the Correctional Institution *'Bedekovčina'* show that the processes of social development and decentralization in the period of self-management socialism sometimes took their toll over the lives of the most vulnerable, and in this particular case, girls and young women with behavioural problems. The first 20 years of the work in the institution were marked by difficulties in financing (the idea of self-financing of institutions, which proved unsustainable, and continuous state monetary interventions from different funds, lack of educational work concept (work as the primary educational method), and lack of qualified personnel. In the period of the seventies and eighties the individualised and group treatment much improved, including psychotherapy for girls by qualified staff, but through this period the institution faced financial difficulties causing a slowdown in activities as well as in treatment improvements. As it is stated in the Memorial book: "The 1977 was generally difficult for the whole society, especially for community services (...) 1989 was also difficult for the financial management of institution. All sources of financing are poor. All aspects of work in the institution would require reorganization"

It would be interesting to continue research work with the clients from that period and obtain their view on their former life and learn more about the influence placement in a correctional institution had on their life in general. It would be also interesting to make a parallel analysis of the life in children's homes, institutions for male delinquents and compare it to the organization and conditions of life in the correctional institutions for girls in order to judge the hardness of living conditions of the girls from the gender point of view.

Development of the Social Work Profession – The Educational Program (1952 - 1971)

In spite of the communist believes that the „social problems„ will disappear in a short period of time, and in accordance with the trends towards international cooperation with the western countries, schools for social workers were founded in Yugoslavia. The first school was founded in Croatia in 1952

---

[15] ibid., p. 64-65

(Ajduković 2002), the second in Slovenia in 1955 and later, in 1958, schools were opened in Belgrade, Sarajevo and Skopje (Završek 2006).

It is interesting to look at the substantiation given by the Council for public health and social politics of the Government of the Peoples Republic of Croatia for founding the School for Social Workers in Zagreb: "On the territory of the Peoples Republic of Croatia live about 200,000 persons (children, juveniles, adults, invalids, old people, chronically ill) that are enabled to work and etc., who are entitled to some kind of social protection. Our Republic spends 15 billions dinars per year for these purposes. For different forms of social security five billions are spent, and for children's allowance about 10 billions per year (...). The expenditure of these considerate financial means is regulated by progressive socialist laws and regulations of our country. However, the implementation of these laws and regulations is managed by clerical staff not able to cope with this task, what leads to irregular implementation of laws and irregular use of the above mentioned considerate financial means. Such a situation has distinct negative consequences for our finances as well as for our endeavors to create better life for people. Therefore, it is indispensable to establish a Professional College for Social Work in Zagreb, and this way establishes the profession of social workers, who will be capable to implement into life the progressive socialist legislation and secure rational management of considerate financial means that our country allocates in the field of social welfare for better life of our people."[16]

Darija Završek gives a critical opinion of the role of the social workers and social work profession of that period: "...the establishment of social work training was marked with an interesting paradox. Social work was an unwanted profession as well as a needed one. This initial ambivalent position, gave social workers and social work profession an ambivalent status not only among communist leaders but also at the level of ordinary life among people themselves. Social workers were needed as they provided social benefits and 'protection'. At the same time they were rejected, as they were the instruments of the state, who control, punish and espionage over individual persons. The universal ambivalence inscribed in almost every social work practice, the one between help and control, could be found already in the early days of the professional social work in Slovenia; and in the period of political and social changes that followed after the communist power had been established."[17]

---

[1] Ajduković 2002, p.19-20
[17] Završek 2006, p. 71

Our preliminary investigations show that the social workers of that time did not see their role with such eyes. Ksenija Bralić-Švarcer, who was a 1956 graduate from the College for Social Workers in Zagreb was never a member of the Communist Party and had a reputation of the 'bourgeois child', recollects her memories of her student years as follows: "Everything I learned and experienced during studies influenced my work as social worker. Namely, I think that the methods of the professional social work, team and different approaches enable us to work and solve problems 'together with' the person in social need in order to train him/her with more of less success for the further life, and with full respect of the human dignity. And this, that a person should always be respected, I learned from Prof. Bresler (one of the founders of the College for Social Work in Zagreb), who was special, he felt no aversion, or repulsiveness. The message was 'Respect a person and his/hers way of living. You, as social worker, are the one who should improve it a bit, secure a better start' – I think that the quality in professional social work is to give the opportunity to a person to form himself by training. Surely, such approach to problems can not depend on social workers and social services only."[18] From this quotation we can learn something about the values taught students by the founders of the College for Social Work.

During the period of the 1950s and 1960s the education on the College for Social Work ran smoothly without any major changes or critical moments. Similar to the period prior to the foundation of the College for Social Work, and in the early years of its work, all contacts with the international professional community were kept and continued: "I got acquainted with Erna Sailer in Zagreb, where she held several meetings and lectures for the social welfare higher officers, but she also addressed the first students of the College for Social Work. I met her for the second time in 1964 at the Social Workers' World Congress, where I represented Yugoslavia. On that occasion the fellow of the Yugoslav Academy, Dr. Eugen Pusić, was chosen for the President of the International Council on Social Welfare. Together with Dr. Erna Sailer we held a focused discussion on social work in the community (about 200 persons)."[19]

---

[18] Interview with Ksenija Bralić-Švarcer 2007, p. 231
[19] Interview with Božo Skeledžija, 2006

Parallelism in the Education of Social Worker (1972 - 1981)

Following the world's trends to improve the academic level of social work, but also the need of the society for better educated profiles of social workers, the University of Zagreb on June 28, 1971 passed a decision establishing a study at the inter-faculty level for education of social workers performed by the Faculty of Law, Faculty of Humanities and Social Sciences, Faculty of Medicine, Faculty of Economics and High School of Special Education. The first generation of students was enrolled in the academic year 1972/1973.

In her comparative review of the development of the education of social workers in the world from 1950 to 1978 Kathrin Kendall (1978), doyen of social work and President of the International Association of Schools for Social Work for many years, marked this interdisciplinary program as one of the possible development paths of the social workers' university education. Also, she considers the introduction of this program as a significant step forward in relation to the previous two-year post-secondary education of social workers in our country, which, as she points out, had a 'technical' orientation.[20] Therefore, such a concept of study was a significant novelty and improvement not only for our country, but was also internationally relevant. Many of its aspects were innovative. The inter-faculty study encouraged active participation of students in research work and their social actions, like opening of the Juvenile Guidance Centre managed by students. Teachers published books that incorporated the best and most recent knowledge in the field of social work, for example the book of Nada Smolić-Krković 'Supervision in Social Work' (1977). But, did everything go so well?

Already the very fact that three organizational forms of the study management had been undertaken during nine enrolled student generations shows that students and teachers faced different organizational difficulties related to the coordination of the program. It was tried to be solved by introducing organizational and program changes, but the whole program would not have been possible without the enormous energy and enthusiasm of students and the social work core subjects teachers. Although it lasted for a relatively short period, such a form of interdisciplinary university program was essential for the further development of social work education at four year university level only. The College for Social Work continued to

---

[20] Kendall 1978, p. 157

function parallel during the whole above-mentioned period, and the conflicts between teachers and students of these two programs were not rare.

Conclusion

This paper briefly deals with the development of social work in Croatia during under socialism. Already in the 1950s the development of socialism in former Yugoslavia based on self-management begins which should be distinguished from dogmatic socialism. These political changes corresponded with the foundation of the first school for social work in Zagreb in 1952. It was opened as part of reformatory trends towards decentralization and opening toward international society. The decentralization process and the development of a community system led to significant changes in the organization of social services. The key event was the opening of the first social work centre in 1959.

The period from 1960 to 1969 was the time of significant development in the social care system concerning the legislative, institutional, organizational and programmatic level. The degree of professionalism of the employed performing duties of social assistance and care was gradually improved. However, the economic reform had given some undesirable social effects, too. In the first place, an increase of unemployment and emigration of citizens to West European countries in order to work. That caused problems for their families (especially children). Also, as Šućur (2003) wrote, there was no significant improvement of the state of social assistance and care after the implementation of the economic reform in the seventies and the eighties of the twentieth century.

Better understanding of the professional social work functioning and development would require further research work in the area of personal recollections and experiences of those who had been the social services' users, as well as those who acted as social workers during that period. The key issues of further research should be related to (1) the continuity of social activities and development of social work as a profession in the discontinuity of social-political situation, (2) the influence of the international processes on the development of social work during socialism, (3) the specific impact of socialistic system values on the social workers' identity and the social welfare system, (4) the proactive or reactive role of the social workers' profession during the political and societal changes and economic crises during the socialist period.

As it was stated earlier, the further research of that period can provide internationally significant knowledge about the interaction of social work and social welfare development with, in the case of former Yugoslavia, very specific socio-political and economical context envisioned through workers' self-management as the 'third' way of society development. It would be useful to learn more about the impact of the workers' self-management approach and the typical socialist values on the social work curriculum and practice in Croatia compared to the main stream social work education and practice in Western Europe and USA of that time.

References

Ajduković, Marina (Ed.): *The Fifties Anniversary of the Department of Social Work 1952-2002*. Zagreb 2002

Bilandžić, Dušan: *History of the Socialist Federal Republic of Yugoslavia – Main processes 1918-1985*. Zagreb 1985

Bralić-Švarcer, Ksenija: *My Working Path as a Social Worker*. In: Annual of Department of Social Work, 14/11 2007: p. 221-232

Hršak, Anica et.al.: *The Sixtieth Anniversary of the Correctional Institution Bedekovčina*. Memorial Book 2005

Kendall, Kathrin: *Reflections on Social Work Education*. New York 1978

Matutinović, Ante: *Some Current Questions Relating to New Organizations of Social Welfare Services*. In: Social Work Journal, 1/1962, p. 23-32

Prlenda, Sandra et. al.: *Final Report: History of Social Work in Croatia, 1900-1960*. Research project 2003-2005: *History of Social Work in Eastern Europe 1900 – 1960*. (www.sweep-uni-siegen.de)

Puljiz, Vlado: *Social Policy and Social Activities in Croatia in the Period from 1900 until 1960*. In: Annual of the Department of Social Work, 13/2006, p. 7-28

Skeledžija, Božo: *The Work of High School for Social Workers in Zagreb – A Personal Perspective*. In: Annual of Department of Social Work, 13/2006, p. 133-142

Smolić-Krković, Nada: *Supervision in Social Work*. Zagreb 1977

Šućur, Zoran: *Development of Social Assistance and Social Care in Croatia after World War II*. In: Social Policy Review, 10/2003, p. 1-22

Vojnić, Dragomir: *Reform and Transition. Critical Review of Events in the Crucial Time Periods*. In: Economic Review, 57/2006, p. 393-419

Zaviršek, Daria: *Gender, Social Welfare and Social Work Education under Socialism in Slovenia*. In: Annual of Department of Social Work, 13/2006, p. 63-74

Contributors

Marina Ajduković, Ph.D. psychologist and sociologist, professor; University of Zagreb, Faculty of Law, Department of Social Work; Head of the Chair for the social work; Head of the Doctoral program in social work; Introduced and teaches the elective course History in social work. Participated in the international research project "History of Social Work in Eastern Europe 1900 - 1960."

Marcel Boldorf, Dr., researcher at the Ruhr-University Bochum, PhD thesis on 'Social welfare in the GDR, 1945 - 1953', second book on 'The transition of proto-industrialised regions in the industrial period. A comparison of Silesia and Ireland, 1750 - 1850'. Other research interests: France under German Occupation (1940 - 1944) and the change of European economic elites after the Second World War.

Vanja Branica, social worker, research assistant, University of Zagreb, Faculty of Law, Department of Social Work, Ph.D. student, Participated in the international research project "History of Social Work in Eastern Europe 1900 - 1960"

Ulf Brunnbauer is Chair of History of Southeastern and Eastern European History at the University of Regensburg and director of the South-East Institute, Regensburg. He holds a PhD in history from the University of Graz. His research focuses on the social history of the Balkans in the 19th and 20th century. Among his books is 'Die sozialistische Lebensweise.' Ideologie, Politik und Alltag in Bulgarien, 1944 - 1989 (Vienna 2007).

Raluca Crisan is doctoral student in Sociology, Babes-Bolyai University in Cluj.

Luminita Dumanescu is Researcher in History at the Centre of Population Studies, Babes-Bolyai University in Cluj.

Yulia Gradskova, graduated from the Moscow State University, Department of History, 1990. In 2007 she defended her PhD dissertation at Stockholm University ('Soviet People with Female Bodies: Performing Beauty and Maternity in the Mid 1930-1960s') She works at in Sweden at Södertörns Highschool.

Sabine Hering, Prof. Dr. habil, born 1947 in Hamburg, studied sociology and literature. She was lecturer at the Universities of Tübingen, Kassel, Berlin (TU)and Frankfurt/Main. 1983 she founded the 'Archives of Feminist Movement' in Kassel. Since 1993 she is professor for 'Socialpedagogy, Gender and Welfare History' at the University of Siegen. Her main subjects in the fields of research, publication and teaching are: History of feminist movement in Germany, comparative aspects of international welfare history, jewish sources and traditions of social work, as well as theoretical and methodological research strategies in social work.

Elena Iarskaia-Smirnova, Dr. of Sociology, Professor at Saratov State Technical University and Higher School of Economics, Moscow, Advisor of the Center for Social Policy and Gender Studies, co-editor of the Journal for Social Policy Studies; research interests: social policy, gender, disability, social anthropology, visual studies.

Lenka Kalinová, studied at the Charles University in Prague and focuses her work on social history. She published numerous studies in the Czech Republic and abroad. Her last publications include: 'Social changes during the period of socialist experiment' (Prague 2007), contributions to Bohemica 42/2 2001 and the books of Hübner (2005), Klassemann (2005) and Gehrke/ Reiner (2007).

Dobrochna Kałwa, Dr., is assistant professor at the Jagiellonian University, Faculty of History, author of numerous publications on women's history of modern Poland and methodology of gender history; her recent research concerns memory of communism in context of oral history.

Anelia Kassabova is Associate Professor at the Ethnographic Institute and Museum at the Bulgarian Academy of Sciences, Sofia. She has a PhD in history from the Bulgarian Acadamy of Science and a PhD from the University of Vienna. Anelia Kassabova's main areas of research are history of ethnology, migration, history of social work, and family policies.

Barbara Klich-Kluczewska, historian, assistant professor at the Institute of History, Jagiellonian University, Cracow, author of the book *Przez dziurkę od klucza. Życie prywatne w Krakowie w latach 1945- 1989 Through the Keyhole: Private Life in Cracow, 1945 - 1989* Warsaw 2005. She specializes in social and urban history of Central Europe under communism and the methodology of private life. Her current projects include a comparative study on taboo topics in Polish and Czechoslovakian society during 1960s and 1970s.

Sven Korzilius, Dr., studied law and history (Saarbrücken, Lisbon); 1998-2001 he was post graduate in a project on criminal policy in the 20th century (VW Foundation). Lawyer (Berlin); since 2007 post-doc in the Post-Graduate-Programme Slavery – Serfdom – Forced Labour (DFG), University of Trier.

Vesna Leskošek, PhD in Sociology, lecturer at the University of Ljubljana, Faculty of Social Work. Her research topics are: social inequalities, gender, globalisation, welfare state, new social movements. Books: Rejected Tradition: Women and Femininity in Slovenia 1900-1940. Ljubljana 2002; Co-editor with Zaviršek Darja: History of Social Work. Between Social Movements and Political Systems, Ljubljana 2006.

Ingrid Miethe, Prof. Dr. habil, born 1962 in Plauen, studied education, political science and sociology at Technical University Berlin, PhD in political science at Free University Berlin, Since 2001 she is a professor for General Education at Protestant University of Applied Science, Department for Social Work, Her main subjects in the fields of research, publication and teaching are: Social movements, Gender Studies, History of Education, Education and social inequality and research methods.

Livia Popescu is Professor in the Social Work department of Babes-Bolyai University in Cluj.

Kristina Popova, Associate Professor at the Chair for Bulgarian History and Archival Studies, South-West University "Neofit Rilski" in Blagoevgrad. She is member of the editorial board of the journal "Balkanistic Forum" and organizes the International University Seminar for Balkan Studies and Specialization. She is author of: The National Child: the Educational and Charity Activity of the Union for Child Protection in Bulgaria 1924 - 1944.

Pavel Romanov, Dr. of Sociology, Professor at Higher School of Economics, Moscow, Director of the Center for Social Policy and Gender Studies, Editor-in-Chief of the Journal for Social Policy Studies; research interests: social policy, organizations, social anthropology, professions.

Maria Roth is Professor in the Social Work department of Babes-Bolyai University in Cluj.

Dorottya Szikra is an Associate Professor at Eötvös University in Budapest. Her main research interest includes the history of social policy, social work and family policies. Her recent publication is: Tradition Matters: Child Care and Primary School Education in Modern Hungary. In: Hagemann, Karen et. al. (Eds.): Child Care and Primary Education in Post-War Europe. New York and Oxford 2009.

Eszter Varsa is Ph.D. Candidate in Comparative Gender Studies at the Central European University in Budapest. Her main research interests include intersections of gender, ethnicity and class and the histories of social work and child welfare.

Dr. Heike Wolter, born in 1976, studied history, German language and literature at Dresden Technical University and received a doctorate on GDR tourism history at TU Dresden. Publications on tourism history and on ‚living space'. She is member of the Executive Committee of the International Association for the History of Traffic, Transport and Mobility (T2M) and alumna of the Studienstiftung des deutschen Volkes.

Social Work

Sabine Hering & Berteke Waaldijk
Guardians of the Poor—Custodians of the Public
Welfare History in Eastern Europe.
In cooperation with Kurt Schilde and Dagmar Schulte. Preface Walter Lorenz.
Helfer der Armen – Hüter der Öffentlichkeit
Eine Wohlfahrtsgeschichte Osteuropas. In Zusammenarbeit mit Kurt Schilde und Dagmar Schulte. Vorwort Walter Lorenz
2006. ISBN 3-938094-58-3

The bi-lingual book describes the results of case studies about the history of social work in Eastern Europe between 1900 and 1960 in eight countries: Bulgaria, Croatia, Hungary, Latvia, Poland, Romania, Russia and Slovenia.
The book reads one half in English, the other identical in German.

Walter Lorenz: Perspectives on European Social Work
From the Birth of the Nation State to the Impact of Globalisation
2006. ISBN 978-3-86649-008-6

The book offers explanations and clarifications for the bewildering variety of titles and job profiles in the social professions in Europe. It presents them both as a product of specific national welfare arrangements and as a sign of a special kind of professional autonomy that so far helped to correct national welfare trends.

Kurt Schilde & Dagmar Schulte (Eds.): Need and Care—Glimpses into the Beginnings of Eastern Europe's Professional Welfare
2005. ISBN 3-938094-49-4

The book gives a collection of case studies by national researchers from the project „History of Social Work in Eastern Europe 1900–1960 (SWEEP)". This collection is directed at teaching Social Work and History of Social Work in an international context since it focuses on Latvia, Russia, Poland, Hungary, Croatia, Slovenia, Romania and Bulgaria.

www.barbara-budrich.net

Social Work

Roland Brake & Ulrich Deller (eds.)
Community Development—A European Challenge
2008. ISBN 978-3-86649-205-9

International experts discuss community development in its historical trends, its present state and its theoretical concepts as well as its practical implementations in eight European countries (Belgium, Bulgaria, Germany, Hungary, Lithuania, Romania, Spain) and the USA.

Gisela Hauss & Dagmar Schulte (eds.)
Amid Social Contradictions: Towards a History of Social Work in Europe
Social Work Between Serving the State and Serving the Client
2008. ISBN 978-3-86649-150-2

How does social work keep its balance between the requirements of its clients and its role as agency of state and society? In the historical analyses from various countries international experts show, how social work has succeeded in keeping those conflicting demands at bay. The contributions look at the historical situations in Finland, Germany , Hungary, the Netherlands, Poland, the Republic of Ireland, Russia, the former Soviet Union, Switzerland, and former Yugoslavia.

Hans-Uwe Otto & Andreas Polutta & Holger Ziegler (eds.): Evidence-based Practice—Modernising the Knowledge Base of Social Work?
2008. ISBN 978-3-86649-121-2

The quest to create an evidence-based Social Work practice is emerging strongly in different fields of Social Work and social policy.
In this volume internationally renowned proponents and opponents of this approach deliver profound analyses of the meaning and implications of an evidence based perspective which clearly challenges the nature of the knowledge base of the established Social Work practice and apparently reevaluates and reshapes the character of welfare professionalism.

www.barbara-budrich.net

Focus on Social Work

STEFAN BORRMANN &
MICHAEL KLASSEN &
CHRISTIAN SPATSCHECK (EDS.)
International Social Work
Social Problems, Cultural Issues and Social Work Education
2007. 189 pp. Pb. 16,90 € (D)
ISBN 978-3-86649-087-1

SABINE HERING (ED.)
Social Care under State Socialism (1945-1989)
2009. 264 pp. Pb.
28,00 € (D)
ISBN 978-3-86649-168-7

WALTER LORENZ
Perspectives on European Social Work
From the Birth of the Nation State to the impact of Globalisation
2006. 208 pp. Pb. 16,90 € (D)
ISBN 978-3-86649-008-6

KURT SCHILDE &
DAGMAR SCHULTE (EDS.)
Need and Care –
Glimpses into the Beginnings of Eastern Europe's Professional Welfare.
2005. 296 pp. Pb. 33,00 € (D
ISBN 978-3-938094-49-5

Available at your local bookshop or directly through

Verlag Barbara Budrich •
Barbara Budrich Publishers
Stauffenbergstr. 7. D-51379 Leverkusen Opladen
Tel +49 (0)2171.344.594 • Fax +49 (0)2171.344.693 • info@budrich-verlag.de
US-office: Uschi Golden • 28347 Ridgebrook • Farmington Hills, MI 48334 • USA •
ph +1.248.488.9153 • info@barbara-budrich.net • www.barbara-budrich.net

Weitere Bücher und Zeitschriften unter www.budrich-verlag.de

Focus on Childhood and Youth

RENÉ BENDIT
MARINA HAHN-BLEIBTREU (EDS.)
Youth Transitions
Processes of social inclusion and patterns of vulnarability in a globalised world
2008. 379 pp. Pb. 36.00 €
ISBN 978-3-86649-144-1

MARY LINDNER
**Evaluation Study on
the Effects of the Child Mind Project**
2009. Ca. 220 pp. Pb. Ca. 22,00 €
ISBN 978-3-940755-30-8

PAMELA OBERHUEMER, INGE SCHREYER,
MICHELLE NEUMAN (EDS.)
**Professionals in Early Childhood
Education and Care Systems**
European profiles and perspectives
2009. Ca. 450 pp. Pb. Ca. 39.90 €
ISBN 978-3-86649-249-3

REINGARD SPANNRING, GÜNTHER OGRIS,
WOLFGANG GAISER (EDS.)
**Youth and Political Participation
in Europe**
Results of the Comparative Study
EUYOUPART. Preface by Lynne Chisholm
2008. 178 pp. Pb. 16.90 €
ISBN 978-3-86649-146-5

Verlag Barbara Budrich •
Barbara Budrich Publishers
Stauffenbergstr. 7. D-51379 Leverkusen Opladen
Tel +49 (0)2171.344.594 • Fax +49 (0)2171.344.693 • info@budrich-verlag.de
US-office: Uschi Golden • 28347 Ridgebrook • Farmington Hills, MI 48334 • USA •
ph +1.248.488.9153 • info@barbara-budrich.net • www.barbara-budrich.net
Weitere Bücher und Zeitschriften unter www.budrich-verlag.de